THE STORY OF

BRITAIN'S
BEST BUILDINGS

THE STORY OF

BRITAIN'S
BEST BUILDINGS

DAN CRUICKSHANK

WITH PHOTOGRAPHS BY JOHN PARKER

BBC

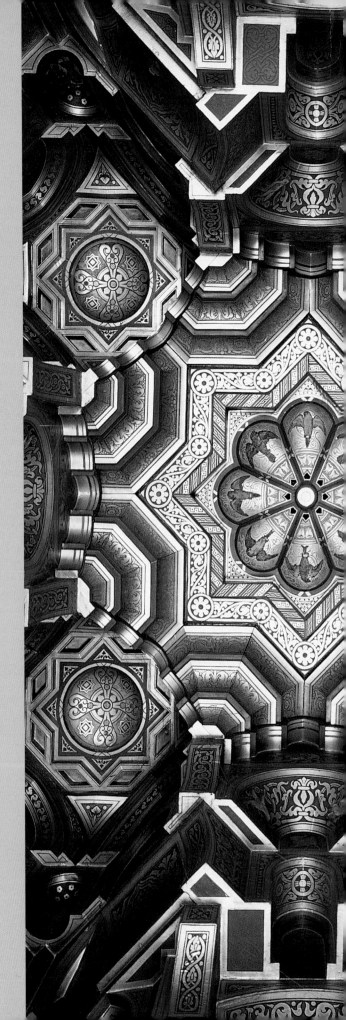

This book is published to accompany the television series
Britain's Best Buildings, first broadcast on BBC2 in 2002
Executive Producer: Basil Comely

First published 2002. Copyright © Dan Cruickshank 2002.
The moral right of the author has been asserted.

ISBN 0 563 48823 9

Published by BBC Worldwide Ltd,
Woodlands, 80 Wood Lane, London W12 0TT

Commissioning Editor: Emma Shackleton
Project Editor: Martin Redfern
Copy Editor: Patricia Burgess
Art Director: Linda Blakemore
Designer: Bobby Birchall, DW Design, London
Picture Researcher: Rachel Jordan
Production Controller: Christopher Tinker

Set in Simoncini Garamond and Akzidenz
Printed and bound in France by Imprimerie Pollina s.a.
Colour separations by Kestrel Digital Colour, Chelmsford

Previous page: The south front of the Upper Ward at Windsor
before (bottom) and after (top) being remodelled to the
designs of Sir Jeffrey Wyatville from the 1820s.
Right: Ceiling of the Arab Room in Cardiff Castle.

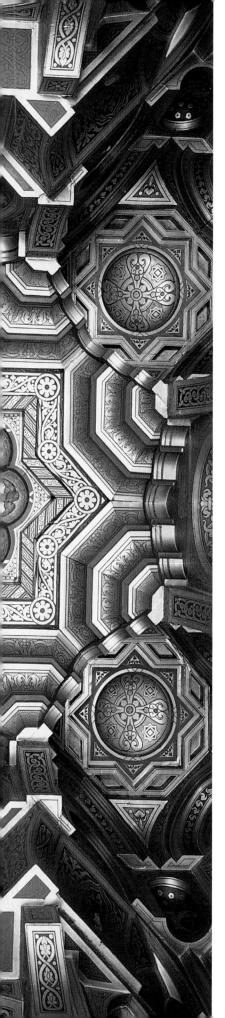

Contents

Introduction

The history of Britain is enshrined in its buildings. An exploration of the island's architecture offers dramatic insights into the often strange, even unlikely, juxtapositions that have given the nation its cultural identity. This book explores a thousand years of Britain's history through the story of eight buildings. These buildings represent different epochs and regions but they all express the creative fusion of ideas and ideals – artistic, spiritual, technical, social, political – that go into the making of great architecture. They also show that great buildings are corporate works of art, often conceived and constructed by many people over many years, and they reveal ways in which buildings can be enriched through generations of adaptation as they evolve to meet changing needs.

All eight buildings develop ideas about the nature of architecture, and their stories reveal a diverse range of inspiration. Durham Cathedral is a monument both to the creative power of foreign influence – in this case Norman ideas about Romanesque architecture – and to the way imported ideas can be fused creatively with local artistic tastes to create a distinct national and regional architecture. Furthermore, Durham is a spectacular example of the way archi-tectural and structural innovation can explode from within a well-established design and construction tradition. The realization, during the 1120s, of the pointed transverse

arches of the Durham nave is a key moment in Western architecture. The arches show how architectural thinking, ever evolving, can be launched in a new direction by a moment of revolutionary brilliance that re-evaluates the established way of doing things.

An exploration of Durham's architecture is also an exploration of architectural meaning. As a great cathedral, Durham was built to express the Christian religion through forms and symbols. To understand the cathedral and decode the secrets embedded in its stones, it has been necessary to attempt to enter the minds of medieval men and see the building and God's Creation – the world – through their eyes. A prime key to unlocking the mysteries and meaning of Durham has been an investigation of the geometry that underpins its design and construction. In the Middle Ages geometry was seen as a sacred science, a divine force latent in nature and an expression of God's creative power, which man could harness to form his own works in harmony with God's cosmos. Durham Cathedral is a powerful expression of this belief as is St George's Chapel in Windsor Castle.

As with Holyroodhouse in Edinburgh, Windsor Castle is a complex and ancient structure, more a village than a building, that tells the story of its nation. Both Windsor and Holyroodhouse have evolved to fulfil differing roles, ranging from defensive site and refuge to epicentre of royal pomp and power. Both have sought to give physical meaning to the changing institution of monarchy.

Blenheim Palace, in Oxfordshire, is an expression of both personal power and national glory. As a very explicit monument to military triumph, paid for by the government, it is hardly the typical English eighteenth-century country house. The architecture of the palace – massive, theatrical, portentous – was also exceptional. But the process through which the house and estate was created is a story of high drama that throws light on the way a great work of art is formed.

The three nineteenth-century buildings explored in this book each reflect aspects of the great developments and debates – scientific, technical, artistic and religious – that galvanized that tumultuous century. The Midland Grand Hotel at St Pancras Station, London, ushered a new building type into Britain – the grand railway hotel – and utilized the revolutionary and pioneering building technology of the railway age. Cardiff Castle is an extraordinary product of the great conflict between traditional, doctrinaire Christian religious thinking and the new and objective discoveries of science, which questioned the basic tenets of orthodox Christianity. Created during the 1860s and 1870s for one of the richest men in Britain, it offers a bizarre commentary on the shifting values and perceptions of the times. An extreme example of the mid-Victorian passion for the mock-medieval, it is also a shrine to the inspirational power of nature.

While Cardiff Castle represents the conflict between Victorian theology and science, Tower Bridge in London encapsulates the struggle between the artist-architect and the engineer, between a concern for history and for manifest technical progress. Tower Bridge is, in a very idiosyncratic way, a marriage of these conflicting principles. Its towers are built around a steel frame and the hydraulic machinery that operates its drawbridge roadway represents the high point of nineteenth-century steam-powered technology. Yet this engineering masterpiece is concealed within façades of history-conscious Gothic-detailed stonework. In this odd combination, Tower Bridge perfectly captures the topsy-turvy artistic values of late Victorian Britain. But, flawed and dishonest compromise or subtle and sophisticated fusion of history and modernity, Tower Bridge has captured the imagination and hearts of the public. Of all the structures discussed in this book it is the only one that, virtually upon completion, passed from the mundane world of function into that of myth. It has become a symbol – an image – of the capital itself.

Highpoint in London is in many ways the quintessence of twentieth-century British architecture. It carried an ideological message intended to bring about social and political change, and the physical form that message took was the radical and thorough use of new technology to create high-rise housing in an idyllic and healthy setting. Highpoint was a declaration of intent for the future and was meant to revolutionize the way people live in cities and the way cities themselves are planned and built.

These eight buildings have fascinating individual stories to tell but, collectively, they present a portrait of Britain, and identify and investigate some of the key issues that have possessed the nation over the last 1000 years.

Durham Cathedral

Perched high above the River Wear, Durham Cathedral represents one of the most powerful images in Britain. Entering the cathedral can be an overwhelming experience, evoking emotions that are initially strange and difficult to understand. The first thing that strikes the visitor is, perhaps, the bold simplicity of the architecture. The decoration is abstract, restrained, sophisticated. It has a rational beauty that transcends architectural style, time and place.

Although nearly 1000 years old, the interior of Durham Cathedral seems strikingly modern and sculptural, bold yet immensely rich, if now obscure, in meaning. Visual power comes from the sheer planes of wall and vault, from simple and elemental forms, notably the massive and drum-like nave columns, from the way the construction is expressed almost ruthlessly, and from the way in which interior volumes are revealed and defined by raking light. Those with even a rudimentary knowledge of the history of architecture will make

another observation. The cathedral is the supreme example in Britain of Romanesque architecture – the style that thrived throughout Europe in various regional and characteristic forms during the tenth and eleventh centuries, and which was based on a remote and inventive interpretation of Roman classical architecture. Romanesque architecture is characterized by massive walls, small, round-arched windows and doors, stout columns, barrel or semicircular groin vaults, and often outlandish decoration, combining naive classical forms with ancient

pagan imagery. All these elements are, in varying degrees, present in the late eleventh-century work at Durham, although the decorative details are unusually refined, simple and abstract. The nave, however, is quite different. Dating from the 1120s, it combines Romanesque architecture with the first stirrings of the immensely more sophisticated Gothic. Its pointed transverse arches and rudimentary flying buttresses concealed within its triforium make it a pioneering piece of engineered architecture, which anticipates many of the main elements of Gothic that was to blossom in northern France 20 years later. The nave of Durham is, arguably, Britain's first piece of modern architecture, displaying a new under-standing of the structural potential of certain forms and materials. It is quite simply one of the most significant and exciting constructions ever created in England. It is a breathtaking monument to innovation, experiment and sheer invention.

Whoever designed and built the nave vault realized – perhaps through observations of nature or through knowledge of the new ideas coming from eastern Islamic cultures – that material could be given added elegance and strength through design and by the use of certain naturally strong forms. This was a scientific approach to building that had languished in western Europe since the fall of the Roman Empire.

And if the visitor loiters in the south transept, he or she will perhaps be struck by yet another sensation – of an all-engulfing mystery surrounding

Previous page: Durham Cathedral from the south-west. The twin west towers were completed by 1128.

the building. It's as if the stones carry a message or meaning that it now seems impossible to decode. The six massive nave columns are divided into pairs, each pair embellished with a different, bold and abstract surface decoration. From west to east each pair of columns is, in turn, fluted, patterned with chevrons and covered with a net-like design of lozenge or diamond shapes. In such an important and sacred building nothing of so much visual significance can be just the subjective whim of some long-forgotten Norman mason. The decoration must have had great and significant meaning: someone with knowledge and a story to tell must have ordered its creation. But what does the decoration mean?

The slightly earlier columns in the choir and transepts are covered with two types of spiral decoration, while one at the south end of the south transept is unique. It has a surface decoration that appears to be an odd mix of spiral and chevron. For years cathedral guides have singled out this column as a happy example of the fact that even the creators of such great buildings as Durham Cathedral were only human and could make mistakes. The column is now regarded as a pleasant joke, an error, which of course it is not. If a mistake, the decoration could easily have been corrected. The column is saying something about its location in the cathedral, about man's inability to create perfection. It's a pointer – but to what. To a quest?

Even these few superficial observations are enough to make it clear that Durham is a most powerful sacred building, swathed in meaning and mystery, and of immense architectural and historic significance. The riddle of its stones offers an understanding of the aspirations, the beliefs and nature of the men who made it – men with a profound knowledge of construction and veneration for God.

But who were these men, what was their knowledge and where did it come from?

St Cuthbert, the Pagans and the Book of Revelation

In 793 the Antichrist appeared out of the mist of the cold North Sea. Without warning, pagan raiders from Denmark set upon the main religious establishment on the east coast of Britain: Lindisfarne. The monks ran for their lives, for it seemed as if the apocalyptic prophecy of the Book of Revelation (20:1–3 and 7) was being realized. 'And I saw an angel come down from heaven, having the key of the bottomless pit, and a great chain in his hand. And he laid hold on the dragon that old serpent, which is the devil and Satan, and bound him a thousand years. And cast him into the bottomless pit, and shut him up, and set a seal upon him, that he should deceive the nations no more till the thousand years had been fulfilled…and after that, he must be loosed a little season.'

It seemed that Satan – 'the dragon that old serpent' – was arriving in the dragon-prowed Viking warships, and that the long-dreaded 'season' had arrived when darkness and evil would possess the world.

But the end of the world did not come – not immediately at any rate. In fact, the monks at Lindisfarne held out for 80 years, resisting and rebuilding after raids, but then in 875 they decided they had finally had enough. The bishop and his monks packed their precious and sacred objects and left their monastery to the mercy of the elements and the Viking raiders.

The most precious thing the monks carried away with them was the body of a man long dead.

Cuthbert, born in 635, had lived an exemplary life as a holy man, hermit and, in his later days, as the abbot-bishop of Lindisfarne. He was venerated during his lifetime, and when he died in 687 was buried in state at the monastery within a stone sarcophagus. Stories started to circulate about his saintliness, and when the tomb was opened 11 years later his body was said to have been found 'incorrupt' – as sound as the day on which he was buried. This, by tradition, marked him out as a saint who could intercede on behalf of the living, who could answer prayers, work miracles and heal those who invoked his protection or who made a pilgrimage to his shrine. Amazingly, there are surviving fragments of the timber coffin in which St Cuthbert's body was replaced in 698. It looks hastily made, with its top and sides emblazoned by simply incised figures. On the sides of the coffin are images of the 12 Apostles, the five Archangels and the Virgin with Christ on her knee. But it is the lid that is most revealing. This shows the four beasts of the Apocalypse flanking the figure of Christ, confirming an early association between the removal of St Cuthbert's body and the prophesies contained in the Book of Revelation. These beasts, which were also the symbols of the Evangelists, are named: the angel and winged lion are Matthew and Mark, and the winged ox and eagle are Luke and John.[1]

Possessing the sacred relic of a recognized saint was a great honour for a monastery. It was also a valuable source of income since pilgrims inevitably spent money and gave gifts to the guardians of such a holy possession. Gradually, Cuthbert became the great saint of the north of Britain, but the cult that arose around him had distinctly odd characteristics. Following an unfortunate sexual encounter with a treacherous Scottish princess, Cuthbert was, it is said, instructed by God that henceforth 'no woman should resort unto him'. Consequently, women were not allowed to enter a church dedicated to him, nor could they, as pilgrims, approach his body.

In 875, when Cuthbert's body was removed from Lindisfarne to avoid destruction by Viking raiders, it started upon a lengthy journey that ended in 995, when the wandering monks arrived at the 'hill-island' of Dunholm. This was where one of the monks had been advised in a dream that Cuthbert was to be buried. Dunholm was Durham, and so the monks arrived at the saint's final resting place.

On a rock standing high above a loop in the river the community built a small cathedral to contain the body of St Cuthbert. This modest structure, known as the Whitechurch, was completed within the year, and for almost 100 years was to be the centre of ever-increasing pilgrimage. The congregation of St Cuthbert changed to reflect the more relaxed, affluent and seemingly less ascetic and spiritual atmosphere that now surrounded the saint. It became a mixed

Left: Late twelfth-century wall painting in the Lady Chapel, believed to represent St Cuthbert.

community, with celibate monks joined by secular and married clergy. But despite the introduction of women into the community, the traditional strictures against them approaching the saint were maintained. Cuthbert remained very much a man's man.

The Normans at Durham

In 1071 William the Conqueror made a Norman cleric, Walcher, bishop of Durham. But this was to be a bishopric like no other in the land. The exposed position and strategic importance of Durham in the continuing Norman conquest of England led to the bishop of Durham being given the powers of a head of state. He could raise his own troops, mint his own money, grant vassals the right to fortify their dwellings and held other prerogatives usually associated with an independent potentate. The Prince Bishop, as he was later to be known, was the ruler of a mini-state of which Durham formed the capital.

Walcher is, arguably, the unsung hero of Durham. Before his elevation to that bishopric he had been a canon at Liège, one of the chief places of learning in Europe during the mid-eleventh century. Here much knowledge from the Muslim world – particularly about mathematics, engineering and architecture – was gathered in the decades before the crusading movement established regular links between East and West. Walcher must have been a learned man when he arrived at Durham, but he wanted to learn more, this time about the people he was to govern. To this end he read the history of the Northumbrians and Anglo-Saxons, especially Bede's *Life of St*

Cuthbert (written in *c.* 730), and his history of the Church in England.

Walcher's masterstroke, no doubt hatched with William, was to found a monastery at Durham and to give the shrine of St Cuthbert the status it had once enjoyed in the monastic setting at Lindisfarne. As a consequence the lay monks and married canons who served the shrine could be replaced by new men – holy and celibate monks – of Walcher's (and no doubt William's) choosing. This move must have upset the local clergy who were suddenly ousted, but all had to agree that the Normans were treating the traditional saint of the north (and Bede, whose body had been moved into the Whitechurch in 1050) with great respect and reverence. It was a move of genius in the battle for the hearts and minds of the Northumbrians.

It seems likely that Walcher initiated the construction of the monastic buildings that were to house the monks, and that he decided the monks should come from the most ancient order, best versed in the mysteries and rituals of religion – the Benedictines. Certainly this is implied in a most remarkable early text about the church at Durham, started in about 1105 by a monk called Symeon and continued at various times during the twelfth century.[2]

But in 1080, just as this great project was getting under way, Walcher was murdered. Allegedly the victim of a feud between his steward and local Norman lordlings, he might also have been assassinated by Normans who distrusted his policy of appeasement.

If the start of the monastic buildings and the introduction of the Benedictines do date from

Walcher's time, then it must be assumed that a rebuilding of the old Whitechurch was not only being considered before 1080 but that a plan had perhaps already been sketched. This is crucial speculation for if that was the case, then at the very least the essential geometry underpinning the design of Durham Cathedral must have been resolved by 1080 and have been the work of erudite monks of the Benedictine Order.

The death of Bishop Walcher opened the way for the most famous figure in the making of Durham Cathedral. William St Calais, a French cleric from Normandy and a former abbot of St Vincent le Mans, was made bishop of Durham in 1081. He continued the construction of the monastic buildings and confirmed, or perhaps introduced, the Benedictine Order in Durham. What is certain is that in 1082 the Benedictine monastery was officially founded there. St Calais is recorded as bringing 24 Benedictine monks from nearby Jarrow and Monkswearmouth, one of whom was made prior.

The choice of 24 monks is significant and suggests that St Calais wanted to continue another of the traditions associated with St Cuthbert – the use of the Book of Revelation as a guiding sacred text for the creation of the religious community and buildings at Durham. Chapter 4 includes the passage: 'and I behold a throne was set in heaven, and one sat on the throne…and there was a rainbow round about the throne [and] four and twenty seats, and upon the seats I saw four and twenty elders sitting.'

The 24 Benedictine monks that St Calais installed at Durham replicated Revelation. They

were to oversee the creation of the monastery and cathedral in the image of the Bible.

But by 1088 St Calais was in trouble. He made the mistake of becoming involved in the dynastic power struggle that broke out between William I's two sons – Duke Robert of Normandy and William II – after the Conqueror's death in 1087. St Calais backed an English rebellion in favour of Duke Robert and was, for his trouble, forced to flee into exile in Normandy. He was away until 1092, and the intervening years were to be vital in the evolution of Durham Cathedral.

During his exile, St Calais would have seen the great new abbey churches of Normandy – St Etienne of *c.* 1060–81 and La Trinité of 1062–1130, both at Caen, and Jumièges Abbey of *c.* 1040–67. All of these were to have a clear influence on certain aspects of Durham Cathedral.

And while St Calais was away studying new buildings and talking to French master masons and monks, the Benedictines at Durham, perhaps with their own team of masons, must have been working up designs for the new cathedral.

As the Benedictine Order was founded before the schism that divided Eastern and Western Christian churches, it possessed much eastern or secret knowledge that was later frowned on, thought blasphemous or irrelevant to orthodox Christianity. These disciplines included an understanding of sacred geometry. The Benedictines also had particularly direct access to the Muslim world and its reservoirs of knowledge. Monte Cassino, the site of their principal monastery, is near the port of Amalfi, which had strong trade links with the Arab world, so many ideas found their way to the monks. They would have been aware of the recently rediscovered works of Pythagoras and in the 1120s Euclid's *Elements of Geometry* (obtained in Arab translations from Arab libraries). They would also have acquired knowledge of classical geometry, which Muslims had been applying to the construction of mosques. Monte Cassino itself displayed this new knowledge, for as early as 1066–71 mosque-inspired rib vaults and pointed arches were executed by Amalfi masons in the reconstruction of buildings within the monastery. The Benedictines had also became aware of Pythagoras's theory that musical tones can be measured in terms of space, with musical consonances expressed in ratios of whole numbers. This geometrical and mathematical link between music and architecture connects the Gregorian tones of the monk's chant (named after the Benedictine Pope Gregory the Great) with the stone-vaulted architecture of Benedictine churches, including Durham. Architecture and music were to work in harmony to produce higher states of consciousness. The stone-vaulted choir where the tones were chanted was seen as an instrument that would resonate, like a tuning fork, when sympathetic notes sounded within it.

In 1092 St Calais returned to Durham, where he seems to have rapidly combined his new knowledge of contemporary Norman church architecture and engineering with the works the monks had been pursuing. Perhaps masons were brought back from Normandy, or an English master appointed. We simply do not know, but to judge by the eastern portion of the cathedral as it rose during the following decade, the big ideas may have been French but the details and character were distinctly and uniquely English. It seems, therefore, that the influence of English monks or masons prevailed. In 1092 St Calais ordered the demolition of the old Whitechurch and, on 11 August 1093, he and Prior Turgot laid the foundation stone of the new cathedral.

Construction Begins

Building work started at the east end. This was traditional, for it was essential to complete the most sacred portion of the church first – the choir and altar – so that the building could be operational as quickly as possible. This must have been where the foundation stone, now lost or long destroyed, was laid.

But before a single stone could be positioned a certain ritual would have to have been followed, and the geometry of the entire cathedral and its related monastic buildings would have to have been settled.

Geometry, to the religious mind of the Middle Ages, was much more than a way of organizing coherent design and construction of a building. It was seen as a gift of God, the principle underpinning all of God's creation – animal, vegetable and mineral. It was the way in which meaning and spiritual power were given to a building. But sacred geometry was not just a way of giving a design symbolic meaning. It was also seen as a means of attracting certain heavenly forces, and as a way of achieving the physical framework in which Christian worship and the miracle of the Mass could take place. Geometry was seen as a vital force capable of making inanimate stones speak.

The first move in translating the sacred geometry of the cathedral design into stone and mortar would have been to divine the correct orientation of the building. Christian churches in western Europe had long been orientated towards the east so that worshippers, when they faced the altar, were looking in the direction of the holy city of Jerusalem, in the direction of new life and resurrection as represented by the daily rising of the sun. But merely orientating a cathedral east was not enough: its main east–west axis had to be aligned with the rising sun on a certain day of the year, usually with the feast day of its patron saint. At Durham this meant that the axis of the cathedral had to align with the sun as it rose on 20 March, the feast of St Cuthbert. Monks would have stuck a staff in the ground as the sun broke above the eastern horizon, then marked the long shadow cast across the top of the rocky peninsula on which the cathedral was to be built. By organizing the entire building around this axis, they tied the cathedral into the cosmos at a particularly propitious moment. Since the monastic cloister was in all probability started in the late 1070s, certainly by 1082, and given the fact that the cloister and cathedral are intimately integrated (they share a wall), it seems likely that this ritual of orientation would have taken place at least a decade before construction of the cathedral started.

The Choir

The choir is constructed in a typical Romanesque manner. In this 'wall' architecture the main structural role is played by the walls which, to carry the loads imposed on them, have to be thick in section and relatively unpierced, and therefore unweakened, by window openings. When, in this type of construction, columns or piers take the place of walls, they are also massive in section, and the round arches between them are narrow of span. All this suggests a lack of ability to calculate, or even to understand, the structural potential of different forms and materials, with

Left: The west towers of the cathedral seen from the cloister garth. The cloisters were rebuilt in the early fifteenth century.

the consequence that all is over-designed, with masons erring on the side of caution when confronted by any structural challenge.

The basic plan of the choir is also typical of the time. It is derived from the Roman basilica which, although of pagan origin, was adopted by the early Christian Church as it evolved into the state religion within the late Roman Empire. Consequently, in basilica fashion, the choir has a wide, tall nave divided by columns from two lower, narrower aisles. The general proportion of the choir is also classical. It is a double-square in plan, twice as long as wide, like many Greek and Roman temples. The east end of the choir, as was usual with both Roman basilicas and late Norman churches in England, was formed by a series of apses. The larger, at the east end of the nave, was to contain the shrine of St Cuthbert. Placed east of the high altar, this shrine was to occupy the most sacred site in the cathedral.

But despite the almost conventional late Romanesque manner of the choir, there are numerous startling details. First the Benedictines decided to cover both nave and aisles with stone vaults. This was a bold move because the spaces were tall and high – the choir nave is 30 feet (9 metres) wide and 74 feet 6 inches (22.5 metres) high. They clearly believed this Herculean task was well worth the effort, not simply because the result would look good and offer a sound and relatively fireproof home for St Cuthbert, but because it would improve the functional quality of the space created. The stone shell of the choir would, with the chanting of the monks, provide the cathedral with a suitably potent spiritual powerhouse.

As the vault over the choir nave rose from about 1100, it put Durham in the forefront of contemporary architectural achievement. Semicircular in form, it was a groin vault, which means that it was divided into a series of compartments, each of which was formed by two semicircular vaults intersecting at right angles to each other. The divisions between the compartments were marked by stone ribs – semicircular bands of stone projecting beyond the surface of the vault itself and spanning right across the nave. In addition, and this was new in England, the edges of the groin vaults were also stiffened by ribs. This structural innovation gave the vaults greater strength and made them lighter than earlier groin vaults since the role played by the ribs meant that the vaults themselves, and their supporting walls, could be less massive. Ribs allowed the outward thrust of the vaults to be gathered at fixed points on the wall, so it was necessary to reinforce only these points with stout, buttress-like pilasters.

This pioneering piece of construction set the pattern for Durham's later vaults and established the high rib vault as a standard element in cathedral construction.

But there were problems. Vaults of semicircular profile have major structural limitations caused by their own inflexible geometry. A semicircle has, by its nature, a fixed proportional ratio: its height must always be half its width. This is not necessarily a problem, but when the span is great the height must also become undesirably, and unnecessarily, excessive. So if, say, a width of 40 feet (12 metres) is to be spanned, the vault must rise a massive 20 feet (6 metres) above its springing point. But there is worse still. In a groin vault the semicircular ribs running at diagonals within a bay must almost certainly have a wider span than the semicircular transverse arches running at right angles across and dividing the bays. This would be the case if the bay were square in plan, but exaggerated if, as was usual, the bay were rectangular, with the long side running parallel with the wall between nave and aisles. So the semicircular diagonal ribs and the transverse ribs will always want to rise to different heights, but for structural and visual reasons this cannot be: they must rise to the same height. There has to be a compromise – a fudge. Usually the diagonal ribs are flattened and/or the transverse ribs 'stilted', that is raised on short, vertical bases. This solution can look odd and even introduce a flaw into the construction – a flaw that can lead to catastrophe since all vaults, whether semicircular or pointed, are potentially unstable, dynamic constructions. Due to their nature, and to the force of gravity, vaults want to spread and collapse. The weight of the material from which they are made forces the vaults down and, because of their curved form, also out.

There were several possible solutions to this problem. The traditional one, favoured by Romanesque builders, was simply to build the retaining walls on a massive scale so that they would act as abutments to contain, by weight and physical mass, the outward thrust of the curved vault. But if the wall should itself move, perhaps due to poor foundations, or if the vault should be too flat in parts or in other ways unsound, then eventual failure was inevitable. This happened

with the pioneering choir vault at Durham. When St Cuthbert's shrine was being installed in 1104, part of the timber supporting the vault collapsed. This was a bad sign. The vault, then nearing completion, was probably already on the move. Perhaps the lime mortar within which the vault stones were bedded was excessively thick and therefore shrank too much as it dried, opening cracks, or perhaps the engineering was wrong and caused a serious fault to develop. However the problem arose, the vault failed, was patched up, but stood for little over a hundred years before the monks were compelled to replace it – and its replacement is a startling story in itself. But the choir aisle vaults survive, and these smaller and slightly earlier (*c.* 1095–1100) versions of the nave vault still show the avant-garde beauty and the visual and structural limitations of this early vaulting system.

One of the problems faced by the designer of these vaults, but not really resolved, was how to reconcile the different heights of nave and aisle vaults. Both had to meet at the column dividing the nave from the aisle, but how was this column to support the springing of the ribs for both a high and a low vault? The solution hit upon was charming if extraordinarily clumsy. The ribs for the high nave vault spring logically from the abaci above the column capitals, but the ribs for the lower aisle vaults spring from shafts attached to the aisle faces of the columns. This, in fact, reduced the columns to a curious hybrid – part drum-column and part compound shafted pier.

Opposite: Vault in one of the nave aisles. These semicircular rib groin vaults date from around 1110–20.

This was an embarrassing solecism, not to be repeated in the later nave of the cathedral.

More visually startling now are the columns and column capitals within the choir. These come in two scales. Most obvious are the stone columns – over 23 feet (7 metres) high – that separate the nave from the aisles. But also curious are the columns and capitals that form a blank arcade along the outer walls of the aisles. This arcade, formed by round arches that overlap to form pointed arches, became a common late Norman detail in England but, like so much of the late Norman vocabulary in Britain, this detail seems to have been first introduced at Durham. But the detail was not new when it appeared there. It has an ancient origin: the motif showing round arches being transformed into pointed arches appears in Anglo-Saxon art and architecture, and in mosques, particularly in Muslim Spain.[3] Were the designers of Durham attempting to create an interior calculated to appeal to local sensibilities by giving it some traditional details, or were they declaring the influence of Islamic learning on the design and construction of the cathedral?

Easier to understand are the capitals that the columns support. These are simple, almost abstract, in form. They are called cushion capitals, for fairly obvious reasons, and are distinctly English rather than Norman French in origin. Despite their simplicity, they are geometrically sophisticated. They appear to express a belief in the power of primary, elemental, geometric forms. They are, perhaps, a basic exercise in the ancient problem of squaring the circle. That is, the problem of combining a square with a circle of the same surface area or of the same perimeter length and circumference – a symbolic unity thought to reconcile the material

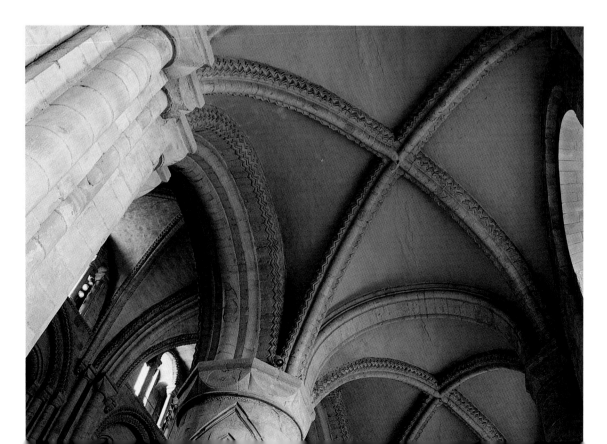

world (the square) with the spiritual (the circle). The cushion capital consists of an upturned dome supporting a square abacus, with portions of dome sliced away to present semicircular lunettes. Sometimes the dome is elongated to form an up-ended cone. On one or two occasions at Durham the paired cushion capitals on the wall arcade are replaced with a form of scallop capital in which two capitals share three lunettes, or scallops. The occasional appearance of these scallop capitals appears to be random but, no doubt, is not.

The four columns of the choir are all incised with a large-scale spiral decoration. The pair to the west has spiral decoration that is hollow, while the pair to the east has spiral decoration with cabling. On the columns the spirals twist up

Above: Arcade dating from 1100–5 in the north transept showing columns with incised spiral ornamentation.

from right to left, an auspicious direction when, traditionally, right is regarded as sacred and left as sinister. The two pairs of columns are separated by piers formed by attenuated round shafts. This arrangement – piers alternating with columns, with piers supporting the transverse ribs of the vault and the columns supporting the triforium gallery from which spring the diagonal ribs of the groin vault – was adopted from Jumièges. This constructional arrangement could well have been the contribution of St Calais.

Columns in Christian temples are always significant because they were key parts of one of the most exemplary sacred buildings described in the Bible – the Temple of Solomon.

Ultimately, biblical texts were the root of all Christian sacred buildings because it was believed that man is created in God's image and that a church represents the body of the Lord – as expressed in John 2:21, where Christ spoke of 'the temple of his body'. The designer of any cathedral would therefore have been acutely aware of the biblical analogy between a church and Christ's body, and could not have used columns without being aware of the association with Solomon.

When creating Durham, the Benedictines were taking the Bible as their design guide.

Solomon's temple is described in various books of the Old Testament. For example, in II Chronicles 3:15–17 it says that Solomon had made 'the house two pillars of thirty and five cubits high…and he made chains…and put them on the heads of the pillars, and made a hundred pomegranates and put them on the chains. And he reared up the pillars before the temple, one on the right hand, and the other on the left, and called the name of that on the right hand Jachin, and the name of that on the left Boaz.'

The interpretation of this biblical description of the columns greatly exercised the medieval mind. What form should they take?

One of the most common representations of the Solomonic columns is the spiral, serpentine or barley-twist form. It is hard to know precisely how this interpretation evolved, but it was perhaps inspired by the description in Kings of the pillars having 'two rows round about'.

So it seems the Benedictines at Durham, with their spiral-embellished choir columns, were trying to recreate the Temple of Solomon. But to what end? What was the spiritual significance of such an act of mimicry? In Hebraic myth the pillars were said to carry the discoveries made by the descendants of Adam and Eve; masonic legend states that they served as repositories for the secrets of the Ark of the Covenant.

Another, more curious, myth relates to Zoroaster, a king and founder of the Zoroastrian religion, who lived at Balkh in northern Afghanistan about 2750 years ago. He is said to have inscribed all seven liberal arts (grammar, rhetoric, logic, arithmetic, geometry, astronomy and music) on 14 columns to preserve knowledge against a vengeful God. This story relates, perhaps, to the spectacular remains of the cubic ninth-century Mosque of the Nine Domes at Balkh. Its long-lost domes were supported by massive round columns with proportions and capitals similar to those of columns eventually built in the nave of Durham Cathedral. Balkh stands near one of the great international trade

routes of the ancient world, the Silk Road, which connected China and India with the West. So it is possible that the wonders of this great mosque would have been known to the Benedictines, not least because Balkh was, in 1207, the birthplace of Rumi, the great Sufi mystic, poet and sheikh of the Dervish community, who regarded sacred music as 'food for the soul', bringing man closer to God.

Before starting construction work in 1093 St Calais must have discussed with his monks and master mason a wide range of relevant ancient and contemporary precedents, and prototypes for the new cathedral. An obvious reference was to the greatest church in Western Christendom – the basilica of old St Peter's in Rome. It has been pointed out that the basic dimensions of old St Peter's correspond very closely with some of those at Durham.[4] For example, the length of the east–west axis of both buildings is virtually identical, while the width of Durham's nave and two aisles is the same as that of the central aisle in old St Peter's. But, more significantly, the shrine of St Peter in the basilica was flanked by Solomonic spiral columns, and it is probable that these columns provided the most direct inspiration for the spiral columns at Durham. If this is the case, then St Calais, by taking the shrine of the Prince of Apostles as a model, was making his entire cathedral a shrine for a great English saint.

A memoir written in the mid-sixteenth century by a former Benedictine monk describes the appearance and rituals of the cathedral in the last years of the Catholic faith before the Reformation. His description of St Cuthbert's shrine embellished with a 'picture of our Saviour sitting on a rainbow to give judgement' is both vivid and revealing. It confirms that, right up to the Reformation, St Cuthbert and his cult remained closely associated with the Book of Revelation for the image on the shrine of Christ and a rainbow comes from chapter 4: '…and there was a rainbow round about the throne, in sight like unto an emerald.'

St Calais, the driving force behind the construction of the cathedral, did not live to see even the choir completed. He died in 1096, and for three years the monks and their mason worked on with no bishop. By the time a successor, Bishop Ranulph Flambard, was appointed in 1099, construction work had started on the transepts to the west of the choir and on the massive piers that were eventually to carry the great tower that was to rise above the centre of the cathedral.

These were uncertain and turbulent years, both at Durham and in the world at large, and the troubled but exciting times are reflected very dramatically in the fabric of the cathedral.

Islamic scholarship, its rational architecture and ways of worship – notably Sufi mysticism with its powerful and rhythmic chanting – had a gradual and profound influence on Western Christianity during the eleventh and twelfth centuries. And this was hardly surprising since they are both monotheistic religions derived from the same book (the Bible), sharing an almost equal veneration for a wide spectrum of divine and saintly figures, ranging from Abraham and Moses to the Virgin Mary and Jesus Christ.

But on 27 November 1095, just as the choir of Durham Cathedral was rising towards heaven, Pope Urban II launched the first Crusade. This was a fatal move that was to usher in over 300 years of intermittent warfare and divide the known world in a tragic and irreparable manner. On 15 July 1099 Jerusalem itself was taken. This was a great triumph for Christendom, but also a great tragedy. The battle-crazed Crusaders behaved disgracefully, massacring both Muslims and Jews, and causing a rift between Islam and Christianity that is felt to this day. The immediate response of Islam – truly shocked that religious warriors and followers of the peace-proclaiming Christ could behave so barbarously – was to identify Christians as fiendish enemies and a threat to God. A jihad (holy war) was proclaimed, and the Crusades assumed a fanatical quality.

Left: Detail of a column, capital and arch from the ninth-century Mosque of the Nine Domes in Balkh, Afghanistan.

Despite the increasing bitterness engendered by the Crusades, the prolonged contact they brought between East and West accelerated the pace at which Eastern knowledge, particularly in the fields of science, medicine, architecture and geometry, was acquired in the West. This knowledge came from Arab libraries, where texts, lost in Europe since the fall of Rome, were stored.

At Durham the death of St Calais and the resulting lack of coherent leadership and a well-connected fundraiser combined with the uncertainty of the times to compromise the design and construction of the transepts.

Just how the money to build this great cathedral was raised in a part of England devastated only 20 years earlier by William I is one of the great mysteries – indeed, miracles – of the enterprise. It would initially have been funded primarily from the revenues of the bishop's estates, which in 1130 (when in the hands of the king) yielded about £400 per annum in disposable income – that is after all overheads and rents had been paid. So all of this sum, which was probably about 40 per cent of the gross income of the estates, could in some years have been spent on the cathedral. This sum would have been supplemented by a certain amount of 'free' labour (the bishop's feudal tenants would have worked on the cathedral rather than on his estates), and – very important – by direct gifts and oblations from worshippers.

Perhaps the uncertain flow of funds explains why the north and south transepts, constructed during the first decade of the twelfth century, differ from the choir in detail and quality, and, indeed, differ from each other. The south transept

was constructed first and adjoins the cloister, which was already nearing completion. This transept, like that to the north, consists of a nave 72 feet 9 inches (28 metres) high and 30 feet (9 metres) wide, with an aisle to the east only. The nave and aisles are divided by a screen formed by a central pier flanked by two columns. The west wall of the south transept is most odd. At high level it is clear that there have been alterations. Above the triforium is a gallery, a walkway that was eventually to run right around the cathedral, cutting through piers or running as a narrow and vertiginous ledge below or in front of the high-level clerestory windows. Original openings in this gallery have clearly been blocked, as the straight edges of jambs are visible in what are now apparently solid walls, and at gallery level concealed and blocked arches that were once open are visible. Why this change of mind? It seems that the monks, after the difficulty and expense of constructing the choir nave vault, decided against repeating the experiment in the transept. After all, this space was not primarily intended to hold chanting monks, and the acoustic quality of a stone vault was not so important. Almost certainly the south transept originally had a cheap and simple timber roof.

While the south transept was being completed, the north transept was started. This is a very different affair. Perhaps the new bishop, Ranulph Flambard, was beginning to pull his weight, to raise building funds and make his presence felt. The gallery is well handled, with large and well-designed tripartite openings instead of the timid, simple gallery piers built in the south transept. These strong arched openings, along with the design of the walls below, make it clear that the north transept was, from the start, designed and constructed to support a stone vault. The rib vault that now covers the transept is a glorious piece of work completed by about 1110. In the absence of the original vault over the choir nave, it is the earliest high-level rib vault in Britain.

But the well-designed and built north transept, like the south transept, contains what appears to be an odd and apparently inexplicable fault in its composition. The spacing of the piers and columns dividing the naves of the transepts from their aisles are strangely irregular, with the outer bays painfully cramped to the north and south. The inner bays of both transepts look fine, their width reflecting that of the choir and nave aisles. But the subsequent bays, moving towards the outer walls of both transepts, are gradually compressed. The ultimate bays of each transept – those adjoining the outer walls – are so narrow that the central column in the triforium arcade has to be omitted. Clearly there was a boundary, physical or notional, to either the north or south of the cathedral that had to be honoured, or boundaries on both north and south. If on only one side, then one transept had, out of a respect for symmetry, to be compressed to match the other. Monastic buildings were being constructed to the south of the south transept, but the building that now adjoins the south wall of the south transept – the chapter house – was not completed until 1133–41, although, of course, its position could have been fixed earlier. This design oddity in the transepts is one of the major mysteries of the cathedral. Another of the

cathedral's great mysteries – the 'odd' column – lurks in the south transept.

Three of the four columns in the transepts are incised with a spiral pattern like that on the choir columns. One of these spiral columns (that at the north end of the north transept) contains cabling in its spiral, like the pair of columns at the east end of choir. The transept columns to the north and south of the crossing have incised, spiral-like columns at the west end of the choir.

However, the south column in the south transept is a hybrid. It has a chevron or zigzag pattern incised on its surface, which on both the north and south faces of the column suddenly becomes a spiral. But in this case the spiral rises partly from the sinister left. This column is unique in another respect: it has a cut detail inside its chevrons that does not appear on any other columns in the cathedral.

It is popular now to regard this column as a humorous mistake. This is clearly not the case. For one thing, the 'mistake' of mixing a chevron pattern with a spiral is repeated twice, on both sides of the column. But, more importantly, if this was a double mistake, then it could easily have been put right because the Durham columns are made in a very particular way. The decorated surfaces were not carved *in situ* after the columns were constructed, but were carved on the individual stones before the column was assembled. This curious system demanded great precision in sizing the individual stones, which have to be identical, and great accuracy in placing and carving the part-pattern on each stone. The advantage was that the stones could be mass-produced at speed in the controlled conditions of the mason's yard, and that mistakes were easier to accommodate here than when carving *in situ*. So, like Solomon's columns, these Durham columns are, in a sense, hollow. They are formed by a shell of cut stone, which is filled during the construction process with a core of rubble and lime mortar. This system of prefabrication, using a limited number of standard, mass-produced elements, must have made the columns relatively quick and cheap to make. But perhaps the Benedictines also wanted an acoustic resonance that could only be achieved from stone columns with a smooth, closely bonded outer skin and a soft centre.

One of the beauties of this structural system is that even apparently complicated patterns, such as chevrons, can be achieved with only a couple of types of deftly carved stones, each capable of being used in both up and down positions. In fact the 'mistake' on Durham's hybrid column – the point where the chevron becomes a spiral – had to be carved specially and is not created by one of the standard stones.

So much for this 'odd' column being a mistake. But what does it mean? Perhaps its surface

Below: East elevation of the north transept, showing how the bay spacing becomes more compressed to the north (left).

pattern gives a clue. Since the pattern was built into the column when it was being assembled in about 1099–1104, it is safe to say that it represents the first time the chevron pattern was used in Durham Cathedral. This is significant since the chevron was to become the standard, ubiquitous detail of the next phase of construction in the cathedral. Indeed, through the example of Durham, it was to enter the vocabulary of late Norman builders throughout Britain. Typical is the stone vault that was finally constructed in the south transept between 1110 and 1120. Its ribs are, for the first time in a Durham vault, emblazoned with a bold chevron pattern.

Above: Detail of the 'odd' column in the south transept.
Opposite: Looking east along the nave, showing the pointed transverse arches in the vault and the decorated nave columns.

The column, despite its apparently flawed surface design, is clearly very special, for it introduced a pattern that had a very important meaning and which was to characterize the architecture of the next phase of the cathedral.

Certain biblical references do, perhaps, throw light on the meaning of this column. In a parable recounted in Mark 12:10, Jesus indicated that God can be vengeful if His gifts are abused and His messenger spurned, and he suggested that righteousness and justice can come in an unlikely guise. Christ made this point using an architectural analogy: 'And have ye not read this scripture? The stone which the builders rejected is become the head of the corner.' So the rejected, faulty, stone could become the keystone – one of the most important parts of the building – the stone that holds other stones together. The analogy is to Christ himself – rejected and crucified by men, yet the 'keystone' to their salvation.[5] The scripture Christ referred to is Psalm 118:15–23, which concludes: 'The same stone which the builders refused is become the head stone in the corner. This is the Lord's doing and it is marvellous in our eyes.'

The Nave and the Birth of Gothic Architecture

The nave is, with the exception of its vault, broadly a continuation of the architecture of the choir, but there is one other notable amendment. The columns that alternate with the shafted piers are larger and formed fully in the round. So the problem of using the same column to support the high and low vaults of nave and aisle had been

simply and elegantly resolved. The column, with its capital and abacus, was now large enough to support all the ribs and shafts that spring from it.

The three pairs of mighty and majestic columns that frame the nave are among the most striking sights of Durham. They are elemental yet also elegant, quintessentially English but, with their bold surface decoration, strangely exotic and puzzlingly hermetic.

The nave, up to the springing of its vault and including most of the west towers, was completed by 1128. The route of approach – the path representing the initiate's progress through the sacred world of the cathedral from west to east, from baptism to the promise of resurrection, from the portal to the shrine of St Cuthbert – was achieved. The great columns, with their enigmatic patterns, must have been intended to play a key role in the journey pilgrims made through this great temple built, as the Bible said it should be, in semblance of the body of Christ. The connection would have been clear to all: the very plan was that of Christ on the cross, with the choir representing his head, the transepts his arms, the nave his legs, and the centre of the cathedral – the crossing below the tower – Christ's heart, the vital centre of the sacred body. In a spiritual world such as this, created through great thought and skill, the patterns on the nave columns could not be merely arbitrary or the playful decorative flourish of some mason. The patterns, like the columns, had an important part to play in the scheme of spiritual initiation planned by the

Benedictine monks, an initiation that marked the soul's journey through the world. But, as with so much of the cathedral, the meaning of these patterns has been forgotten or obscured. The columns, like most of the cathedral interior, were originally painted. Perhaps the colours, or their relative tones, would have made it easier to read the stones.

Since the progress through the cathedral was from west to east, it is wise to look at the west columns first. The dimensions and proportions are immediately apparent. Famously, these nave columns at Durham have an unusual characteristic – their height and circumference are the same: 22 feet 3 inches (6.75 metres). Why? There is no structural advantage in this symmetry, nor is the correlation visually apparent. As with the hybrid column in the south transept, this fact is now merely noted as a curiosity and ignored. But this relationship of girth to height reveals a very simple truth about the columns, and offers a clue to understanding the thinking and priorities of the men who made the cathedral.

The ratio between the height and circumference is 1:1, which is the ratio of a square. So the columns in the nave are, in very simple terms, formed by rolling squares into cylinders. The action of making a cylinder with the surface area of a square would have had great significance to the medieval mind. The exercise of 'squaring the circle' obsessed masons, mathematicians and theologians during the Middle Ages. The objective, which cannot be achieved through mathematics, was to come up with formulae that would reconcile a square and circle with the same surface area or same perimeter length.

Opposite: Looking east along the nave's north aisle, with a chevron column in the foreground and lozenge columns behind.

The meaning of this reconciliation was simple. In medieval symbolism and sacred geometry a square represented the material world, as seen, for example, in the four seasons, the four elements and the four humours. The circle represented the spiritual world, for, like God, it has no beginning or end, and its all-embracing primal shape contains the lesser forms of the square and the triangle. The designer of the nave columns was therefore attempting an exercise in squaring the circle, marrying the material and the spiritual, and, in his own terms, scored a great success.

But the meaning of the form of the nave columns is only part of their message. What of their surface patterns?

The most westerly pair of nave columns appears to be the most classical, with Doric-style fluting. Yet there is more to this design. It is formed by a wave of convex and concave curves, with both types of curves being a segment of a circle of equal diameter. The axis through the concave and convex curves is on different planes, with the axis through the concave curve being higher than that through the convex curve. Consequently, the concave curve rises higher than the convex curve so that the two types of curves are separated by a sharp arris.

What does all this mean? Is the pattern making a point about duality – concave and convex, the same within as without, the same above as below, the seen and the unseen? This concern with duality is inherent in Christian, Muslim and Judaic theology and sacred philosophy: the two natures of Christ (divine and human), the two testaments, the dualism of the Church and the Synagogue; the Old and the New

Covenant; life on earth and in heaven; spiritual and temporal power. If these dualities lie behind the pattern, the symbolism would be recognized by all religions. The idea of a universal church would be conveyed to all who enter the cathedral.

The next pair of columns moving east is emblazoned with a bold chevron pattern. The scallop capitals are decorated with nailhead-like flowers, a common Romanesque detail.

The chevron became particularly important during the last phase of construction at Durham, but what does this pattern mean? There are numerous suggestions. Possibly it is a reference to pre-Norman, pre-Christian Britain, for chevron patterns are found on prehistoric monuments, such as New Grange in Ireland, where they are thought to symbolize the power of the sun. Others believe they represent the female deity, the Great Goddess, who was worshipped in Britain in ancient times, or that they are in some way geometrical symbols of the sound waves that reverberated through the cathedral as the monks chanted. If the chevron was regarded as a traditional sacred symbol in the early twelfth century, it is possible that the monks introduced the pattern in the nave, the most public part of a monastic cathedral, to make the local people feel more at home. But the overt pagan associations make this unlikely.

A simple analysis of the columns offers another answer. The pattern is formed by 12 bands on each column, and each band has eight points, four pointing up and four pointing down. The key or prime number here is four because eight and 12 evolve from four, and four is the number of the square. In fact, the chevrons on this pattern can easily be explained in relation to the square. Take a square and then place a second square on top of it but rotated 45 degrees and you have an octagram or eight-pointed star. Turn alternate points up and down and you have one of the chevron bands on the column. This pattern seems, then, also to be proclaiming the importance of the square in the design of Durham – this time in the form of an eight-pointed star. The column, based on the circle, and the chevron, based on the square, are in combination perhaps another exercise in squaring the circle.[6]

If the coded message of the column is to do with squaring the circle of the material world leading to the spiritual, it was an appropriate one to give to believers as they progressed east towards the altar and St Cuthbert's body.

The third pair of columns is the most enigmatic of all, and arguably the most important, for between them rose the famed Jesus screen. This, with its great altar, stood at the east end of the nave. Here Mass was celebrated for pilgrims, and it marked the start of the most sacred part of the church to which laymen had only limited access.

The columns are covered with lozenge or diamond shapes. The individual lozenges measure 12 x 12 inches (30 x 30 centimetres), so each has a surface area of 144 square inches (936 square centimetres). The inch as we know it relates directly to Norman measurements, so this is the numerical value each lozenge was originally intended to have. In addition, the columns are 12 lozenges

high and 12 lozenges in girth, so the surface area of each column is covered with 144 lozenges.

As already established, geometry and numbers had great symbolic significance to the medieval mind, so the recurrence in these columns of the related numbers 4, 8, 12 and 144 cannot be coincidence.

The Bible, the guide to understanding the cathedral, offers a clue in the Book of Revelation. Chapter 21 describes the New Jerusalem: 'And I saw a new heaven and a new earth…and…the holy city, New Jerusalem, coming down from God out of heaven…and the wall of the city had twelve foundations…and the City lieth four square and the length is as large as the breadth, and he measured the city with a reed, twelve

Right: A lozenge column. Note the cushion capitals, with their semicircular lunettes, on the smaller shafts in the background.

thousand furlongs: the length, and the breadth, and the height of it are equal… And he measured the wall thereof, an hundred and forty and four cubits, according to the measure of a man, that is, of an angel.'

So here are all the numbers found in these columns. The New Jerusalem is a mighty cube, which suggests that the geometrical form underlying the design of the cathedral is the square. It seems clear that the Benedictines were not just creating a temple in the image of the body of Christ, but were also in a more abstract, essential and mystic way realizing the prophecy of the Book of Revelation. They were creating the New Jerusalem, the celestial city 'coming down from God out of heaven' as the dwelling for St Cuthbert's shrine.

But there is more. The lozenge pattern that now appears most striking, forming the 'positive' shape on these columns, might originally have been the 'negative' if the framing bands of stone were painted a stronger colour. In this case the framing pattern would have looked like a net, suggesting that the man who devised it had not just the New Jerusalem in mind but also the Temple of Solomon. I Kings 7:13–20 describes the columns of the temple as having '…nets of chequerwork…wreaths of chainwork…and the two rows round about upon the one network.'

While having the appearance of a net, the frame can be read as a double spiral or double helix. Recent discoveries about DNA have given this form special meaning because it is known to be the geometry of life itself. It was between these columns during the Middle Ages that people sought salvation and new life as they

prayed at the altar set in front of the massive Jesus screen.

The more this pair of columns is contemplated, the more it seems to reveal. The lozenges are diamond shapes, so when painted the column could have had a gem-studded appearance. Precious stones are frequently referred to in the Book of Revelation. The rainbow beside which Christ sits in judgement – as featured in St Cuthbert's shrine – is likened to an emerald, and the foundations of the walls of the New Jerusalem '…were garnished with all manner of precious stones. The first foundation was jasper; the second sapphire; the third a chalcedony, the fourth an emerald… the eighth beryl… the ninth a topaz… the twelfth an amethyst'. The mineral world expresses a very pure volumetric geometry. For example, beryl is hexagonal, halite cubical and quartz trigonal. This passage from Revelation must, like the gem-studded Durham columns, be invoking the varied qualities possessed by these different geometries.

The Nave Vault

The nave columns, the areas of wall they support, and the piers between which the columns stand were designed and built to support a stone vault. For example, the triple shafts that rise from the floor were designed specifically to support the three ribs that spring from their top, so it is reasonable to suppose that a stone rib vault was intended from the very start of construction. The vault could have been a high, ribbed groin vault with semicircular transverse arches like that which survives in the north transept. But by

about 1128, when, according to Symeon, work on the nave vault (*testudo*, literally 'tortoise shell', as he called it) started, a profound change had taken place in the way construction was conceived. This change must have been the result not only of new technological knowledge but also of changing aspirations. The change must surely have been driven by the desire for a different sort of architecture – one that was more logical and that more fully realized the monks' scheme for the completion of their New Jerusalem.

The one word that sums up this new desire is 'light'. The monks wanted a structure that was lighter, both actually and visually, so that the nave would look more elegant, aspire more movingly up towards heaven. They also wanted a structure that would allow more light to flood into the interior of the cathedral because light, the medium inhabited by God, was sacred. The Bible makes two famous references to light (Genesis 1:3–22 and John 1:1–9) in both of which light is clearly seen as a gift of God. The reference in John 1 is particularly powerful: 'And the light shineth in darkness, and the darkness comprehendeth it not… that was the true light,

Above: A nave vault bay. Pointed transverse arches rise from shafts while semicircular diagonal arches rise from corbels.

which lighteth every man that cometh into the world.' It is clear why the Benedictines wanted their New Jerusalem to be flooded with light. But more light meant bigger windows, and bigger windows meant a potentially fatal weakening of the walls that were the main support of the semicircular groin vault that had been built in the choir and transepts. Clearly, if bigger windows were to be achieved, a new type of vault, incorporating a new structural system, was needed – one that would relieve the wall of some of its structural role.

There is no record of the process by which this leap of imagination was made, where the inspiration came from or who was responsible. All that is known is that Bishop Flambard, the man who had been in charge of the construction of the cathedral for 29 years, died in 1128, the year in which the vault started to rise above the nave. We can only speculate as to who undertook the challenge of covering the nave (201 feet/61 metres long and 72 feet 9 inches/22 metres high) with a stone vault constructed to an experimental and pioneering system calculated to flood the interior with light. Whoever it was demonstrated the new possibilities of engineered construction in a most spectacular fashion. The transverse arches running between the nave walls and dividing the rib vault are no longer semicircular in shape, as in the choir and nave, but pointed.

Pointed arches had been used before – in Muslim architecture and in the Benedictine monastery at Monte Cassino in the 1060s, and by 1128 the abbey church at Cluny in France had a pointed barrel vault and pointed nave arches. But never till Durham had pointed arches been used

in such a bold and structurally breathtaking manner, and as part of a coherent system of engineered architecture. The cathedral's high-level vault, incorporating pointed transverse arches, was the first in Europe and thus anticipated, even heralded, the age of Gothic architecture. The designer here made a leap of faith and created something that was to change the nature of architecture for ever. By using a pointed arch he revealed a great understanding of the potential offered by this new type of engineered construction, and opened an entire world of new possibilities. He realized that the pointed arch can carry loads with greater efficiency and elegance than the round arch, and that it can soar higher than a round arch of the same span, with no structural weakening. This was important, for it meant a vault formed with pointed arches would appear loftier and lighter than a barrel vault, be more beautiful and more 'aspiring'.

The form of the pointed arch is derived from a simple geometrical construction called the vesica piscis – a pointed oval created when two circles of equal size overlap each other through their centres. From this piece of geometrical construction much is possible. By simple extension the square, the double square, the equilateral triangle, the hexagon, the six-pointed star, root two and the golden section proportion can be created and defined. It's no wonder that the vesica became one of the basic forms of sacred geometry, just as the aureole (its equivalent in art history) became the form in which Christ was often depicted in Romanesque and Gothic art (see Windsor Castle, p. 64).

But this was not only a form with pleasing geometrical consequences. Its use reveals that its designer had, through observing nature or studying newly available material from the East, realized that building material can be given added strength through design. The analogy with the humble egg is useful. Eggshell is a brittle material, and an egg is easily broken if squeezed along its short axis. But if that same egg is squeezed along its long axis, a massive amount of pressure is required to break it. Its domed or arched shape gives the shell amazing additional strength. The mason of the nave vault must have learnt the lessons of nature well. At a stroke, the pointed arch solves many of the structural problems of ribbed vaults and gives the structure greater strength. First, its pointed form means that more of the weight – the thrust of the vault – is taken vertically down through the walls and shafts than horizontally outwards. So, since the walls do not act as abutments to restrain so much outward thrust, they can be lighter in construction, which means that more wall can be cut away to allow for larger windows. This is exactly what happens in Durham, where the windows lighting the nave through the triforium are far larger than the similar windows in the transepts and choir.

And this new structural system, which made far better use of God's gift of geometry, led to the construction of a more logical and beautiful building. And beauty was an important thing in the medieval church, for the achievement of beauty – whether in music, stained glass or architecture – was a way both to affirm the glory of God and to realize the gifts offered by His creation.

The beauty of the pointed transverse arch lay not just in the geometry of its construction and in the elegance of its structural performance but in the way it solved the great aesthetic and functional fault of the semicircular ribbed groin vault. The differing heights of the wide diagonal ribs and of the narrower transverse arches could be happily reconciled. In the Durham nave the diagonal ribs are still of semicircular form and here can be true semicircles. They rise to the height dictated by their geometry – they are not flattened as in the choir and transept vaults – and the pointed transverse arches are simply scaled to match the height determined by the semicircular arches formed by the diagonal ribs. Both types of arch are true to their nature, and the result is that the vault looks, and actually is, stronger, as well as visually better.

The structural role played by these different types of ribbed arch, and their relation to the walls from which they spring, is also startlingly logical. The diagonal ribs spring partly from mere corbels, so they brace the vault only against side movement, while the real supporting role is played by the powerful, pointed transverse arches, which rise from the shafts attached to the mighty nave piers.

But even pointed arches exert some outward thrust, and this was also dealt with in a remarkable manner, which shows that the designer of the nave wanted to make the whole structure work in a harmonious and related manner. Within the triforiums of the choir and transepts are heavy round arches that help to transfer some of the outward thrust exerted by the ribs of the nave vaults on to the outer walls of

the aisles. In the nave, however, this system was developed in a subtle but significant manner. Round arches were replaced by slender and elegant quadrant arches placed near the springings of the ribs of the high vault. These dealt with the outward thrust exerted by the ribs of the nave vault in a more sophisticated manner. Rather than simply transferring the thrust to the outer aisle wall, these quadrant arches attempt to contain, or neutralize, the thrust by meeting it with an equal and opposite counterthrust. This was a daring solution, which demanded a confidence based on the ability to calculate loads, to understand the structural potential of stone ribs and pointed arches, and to create a state of poise in an arched structure, which is intrinsically dynamic, by achieving a series of finely balanced counterthrusts. This system was not pioneered at Durham. Arches based on half tunnel vaults were used at St Etienne in Caen and in the choir gallery at Gloucester (1089–1100). But for the first time this system was realized in a minimal and elegant manner in combination with a vaulting system incorporating pointed arches. This, arguably, introduced the structural principle behind that later and most characteristic of Gothic structural forms, the flying buttress. This move towards an engineered architecture – with a structural frame formed by stone pointed arches, ribs and proto-flying buttresses, and with a wall area giving way

Above: Quadrant arches within the nave triforium help to counter the outward thrust of the nave vault.
Opposite: Putlog holes, which supported scaffold during the building process, remain open within the north-west tower.

to large areas of glass – makes Durham Cathedral the pioneer of all steel- or reinforced-concrete-framed and glass-walled modern architecture. (The Durham quadrant arches were thickened in the early twentieth century.)

The walls of the cathedral are constructed of two skins of square-cut sandstone blocks, the core being filled with a mix of rubble and lime mortar. This construction method was quick, cheap and stable, for the rubble core gives the walls a flexibility, allowing them to settle and move without serious structural consequences. When the concrete-like lime mortar and rubble mix was poured into wall voids above arches, timber shuttering had to be constructed to hold the mix in place until it set. Incredibly, oak planks from this shuttering survive *in situ* in a number of the nave triforium arches.

The construction of the vault was a pioneering business. Close inspection today reveals that its builders learnt rapidly and grew quickly in confidence and knowledge. It is still possible to see evidence of the invention, experimentation and innovation that characterized the construction. By the time the masons reached the west end, in about 1133, they had greatly refined their techniques. The thickness of the stone cells between the ribs decreased as they realized that strength could be achieved by the minimal use of materials. Weight was created only when required for structural stability. Masons had long realized that a tall clerestory wall above the nave arcade added weight where it was needed to help counter the outward thrust of a nave vault. Likewise, at Durham the voids above the hollows of the vaults were filled with stone rubble to help direct the thrust of the vault downwards rather than outwards.

The consequence of the Durham nave vault was rapid and dramatic. Abbé Suger and his masons at St Denis near Paris must have heard of Durham's vaults and the pointed arches used in the nave arcade in Cluny Abbey. Suger certainly had close contact with Abbé Bernard of Clairvaux, and would have known of the new knowledge coming from the East, and from this mix High Gothic was born. The west front of St Denis, completed in 1137, was still essentially Romanesque, but the choir, rebuilt in 1140–4, is (according to architectural historian Sir Banister Fletcher) 'probably the earliest truly Gothic structure' in the world.[7] If St Denis is the pioneer of Gothic architecture, then Durham is, without doubt, the pioneer building behind Abbé Suger and St Denis.

The revolutionary architecture of Durham and St Denis was refined and developed at Bourges Cathedral *c.* 1190–1275, Sens Cathedral *c.* 1140–1200, Notre Dame in Paris *c.* 1163–1250 and Chartres Cathedral, 1194–*c.* 1220.

Mysteries of Construction

Who designed and built Durham Cathedral? There are no records, but the Benedictine monks, with bishops Walcher, St Calais and Flambard, were able and more than willing to undertake such a challenge. They must have worked with at least one master mason, who, at the very least, would have supplied technical expertise. But his identity and experience are unknown, although the physical evidence of the building suggests he was English rather than Norman. The Romanesque style flourished in England before the Conquest, and Durham, although it contains elements that could be seen as French in origin, has much that is in the English tradition, notably the column capitals. Similarly, we know nothing about the workforce. They have left their masons' marks on the building but these are also mysterious. Perhaps these abstract signs are their lodge or guild marks – signs to show that they had a hand, albeit anonymous, in the making of this great house of God.

Geometry

Although the names of the designers and builders of Durham Cathedral are not known for certain, one thing is clear. Whoever created the cathedral had a great belief in geometry. As they would

have reasoned, it is geometry that holds the universe together, so that the same geometry would be capable of holding the cathedral together and of creating a building in harmony with God's cosmos. A cathedral was the geometry of the heavens realized in stone.

The designers would have combined the authority of the Bible, in which the size, form, proportions and geometry of sacred buildings and structures are discussed in some detail, with a deep-rooted, pre-Christian belief in the sacred power of numbers, which were seen to embody divine and malign qualities. Three represented the Holy Trinity; four, the number of the elements and the material world; five, the number of man; six, as represented by two triangles forming a hexagram, stood for the Holy Trinity; seven, a holy number, being the sum of three and four, indicated the marriage of sacred and material; eight, the number of new life and of the final resurrection inspired by baptism; 12, the number of the universal church, the number of Apostles. This belief in the virtue of numbers goes back to the earliest days of the Church and was inherited from the Neoplatonic school of the first century AD, which venerated and promoted the works of Pythagoras. It is probably for this reason that the Bible contains so much numerology and implies that geometry and ratios are the building blocks of God's creation, from which come power, harmony, beauty, energy and life. St Augustine expressed the belief well when he stated that numbers are the thoughts of God.

But perhaps the biblical text that most impressed the designers of Durham is less direct in its reference to geometry: 'Look not at the things which are seen, but at the things which are not seen: for the things which are seen are temporal; but the things which are not seen, are eternal.' (II Corinthians 4:18)

Geometry (the unseen aspect of a cathedral) was more important than the stones (the seen), which would eventually wear away. To the medieval mind, aware of the sacred importance of light, the fact that the intangible was spiritually more significant than the material would have been an easy concept to grasp. And in grasping this idea, another, bigger idea and understanding emerges. The space inside a cathedral – the volumes defined by its geometry and revealed by its walls and vaults – is as important as the walls themselves. In the Middle Ages it was accepted that it is in space flooded by light that God dwells with the community of saints, awaiting the Last Judgement.

The question now is how does this information and these insights help us to read the cathedral, to unlock the secrets of its stones, to see it through the eyes of the men who made it and the people who first used it?

The starting point is to examine the basic dimensions of the cathedral – to construct a geometric model or hypothesis based on those biblical texts and theories of sacred numerology that seem to best fit the physical evidence offered by the cathedral, and then to test this hypothesis against the cathedral fabric (see diagram, p. 40).

Another passage from the Book of Revelation (21:6), when read in the context of medieval sacred geometry, offers a clue to understanding the meaning of the 'odd' column in the south transept: 'I am Alpha and Omega, the beginning and the end.' It was common in the Middle Ages to illustrate God, the great architect, creating order out of primeval chaos, a task achieved by using a pair of compasses. The 'beginning' is the point of the compass and the 'end' is the arc it describes. If, on a plan, the point of a compass is placed on the 'odd' column and opened to the furthest point of the cathedral – the north wall of the north transept – the arc that it describes is most revealing. From the north end of the transept the arc marks the original east end of the cathedral, the south wall of the prior's lodging, a corner in the cloister and the most westerly column in the nave. It is clear that the 'odd' column marks the centre of a sacred world formed by the cathedral and the related monastic buildings. The 'odd' column therefore marks a very important place indeed – the centre of a micro cosmos, a heaven on earth, the New Jerusalem of the Book of Revelation.

What this geometry also reveals is the importance of the prior's lodging, for this building defines the southern extent of this little Holy Land. The prior's lodging is now occupied by the dean and contains twelfth-century fabric much altered in the early to mid-thirteenth century. It was a fairly conventional, high-quality domestic building that included a great hall. But it also contains something more unusual. The current dean is proud of one of the building's more mysterious features – a thirteenth-century window that originally lit the double-height great hall and is still framed by early, presumably thirteenth-century, decoration. This, the dean reveals, is traditionally referred to as the Sufi decoration. The scheme shows plant forms that

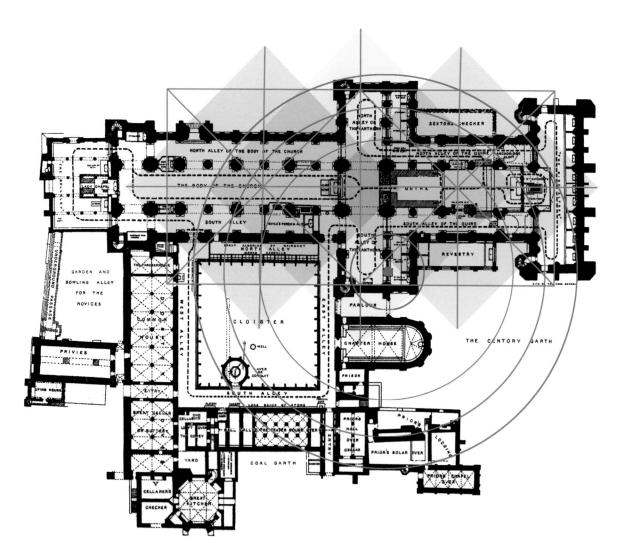

Studying the cathedral plan above suggests one of the geometrical structures that might have been used in the design of Durham. The two western bays of the nave (to the left) are architecturally distinct from the rest of the cathedral (for example they have no columns) so they can be seen as a narthex or baptistery outside the sacred space of the cathedral. Moving east from the font, over the cross in the nave floor, the cathedral proper is entered – and its plan fits within a double-square (shown in blue). This reaches from the font in the west to the apse of the original east end of the cathedral and from the north wall of the north transept to the south wall of the south transept. Geometry based on the square and its permutations is known as *ad quadratum*. This system, which seems to underlie the design of the cathedral, was in common use among Norman masons.

Ad quadratum is based on the square and its derived figure, the octagram, which is created by overlaying a square with a second square of the same size turned at 45 degrees to the first to create an eight-pointed star. The blue overlay shows two second squares turned at 45 degrees on the double square with a third 45-degree square placed centrally, its edges going through the points where the first pair of 45-degree squares cross through the edges of the double square. This central square is slightly larger than its flanking diagonal squares and has, at its centre, a small square (shown in dark blue) where all the diagonally placed

squares overlap. The irregular 12-pointed star produced by this geometric exercise is called the dodecaid.

During the Middle Ages this was a figure rich in Christian symbolism. Its numbers – four (the square), eight (the octagram) and 12 (the dodecaid) relate to key numbers in the Book of Revelation and the three diagonal squares represented the Father (the central larger square), the Son (the east square over the choir) and the Holy Ghost (the west square from the font and including the nave). The small central square where all three diagonal squares overlap symbolizes Godhead – all in one. In the cathedral plan this marks the area below the crossing tower: the heart of the cathedral.

In red are concentric circles radiating out from the 'odd' column in the south transept. This column marks the centre of the monastic and cathedral world. The outer circle defines key elements that form the perimeter of the monastery, including the north edge of the north transept, the original east end of the cathedral and the outer, south, wall of the prior's (or dean's) lodging. Circles are also drawn through other important points in the monastic complex. This creates a diagram like a medieval chart of the Ptolemaic cosmos, which showed the movement of planets around the centrally placed earth. Such charts were used to investigate the alleged relationship between planetary movement and tones – the music of the spheres.

are stylized but not geometric, something not generally associated with Islamic decoration. The traditional association with the Sufi seems unlikely since the design appears so unIslamic – until the mosque in the great Sufi centre at Balkh is remembered. Around its massive columns are stylized plant forms hauntingly similar to those shown in the prior's lodging.

The Virgin Mary and Women in the Cathedral

In the Middle Ages women and Durham Cathedral simply did not mix. It all went back to that ancient misogynist, St Cuthbert, who was said to have promised God that he would have nothing to do with women. From its completion in about 1133, the main body of the cathedral was closed to women. All they were allowed to enter was the narthex, or baptistery, at the west

Above: This decoration in the dean's lodgings is though to be Sufi-inspired. It compares with the mosque at Balkh.

end. Women could be baptized in Durham and thus enter the Christian Church, but they could not enter the sacred parts of Durham Cathedral itself. A band of dark marble was let into the nave floor immediately to the east of the font to mark the boundary that women were forbidden to cross. This strange boundary stone survives, a perplexing reminder of female subservience and spiritual inferiority in the Middle Ages. This segregation and slighting of women throws light on one of the most intriguing religious paradoxes in medieval Britain. Women were regarded, and often treated, as little better than the spawn of the Devil. They were seen as a source of sensuous temptation, evil imps lost in original sin, and dedicated to the simple objective of beguiling men into sins that would lead to the damnation of their souls. This jaundiced view, promoted by celibate male clerics, was derived from Old Testament writings rich in the antics of femmes fatales, including Delilah, Bathsheba and, of course, Eve herself.

Yet that epitome of female and motherly virtues, the chaste and loving Virgin Mary, was venerated and worshipped with such a passion that England was generally regarded in Europe as the Virgin's chosen land.

These conflicting attitudes to females in the Middle Ages are starkly revealed at Durham for built to the west of the narthex in 1170–80 is a spectacular chapel dedicated to the Virgin. Most English cathedrals possess Lady Chapels, usually built at the sacred east end, beyond the high altar. But at Durham the exclusion of women from the cathedral meant that this chapel, from which women could hardly be banned, had to be

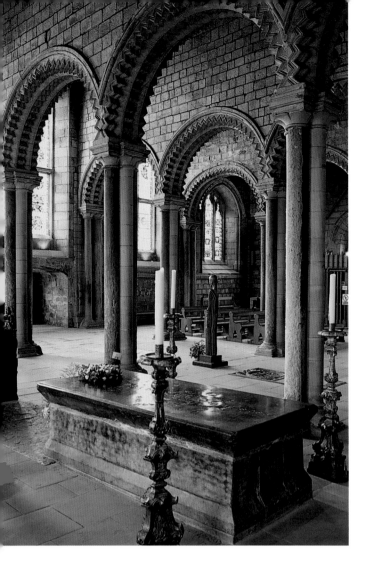

surely the most obvious monument in England to the influence of Islam. With proportions of 2:3, it comprises five aisles of equal height and width separated from one another by arcades that were originally of daringly minimal dimensions. It looks much like a Muslim prayer hall in Cordoba, and in its usual function – crowded with women banned from the cathedral – echoed the organization of a mosque, in which women are segregated from men. The bishop in power when the Lady Chapel was built was Hugh Pudsey, but, as with earlier parts of the cathedral, the designer is unknown.

The Cult of St Cuthbert – Pilgrimage and the Chapel of the Nine Altars

When the remains of St Cuthbert were moved into the newly completed chancel in 1104 the cathedral immediately became an important place of pilgrimage. The saint put the cathedral on the spiritual map of Europe and provided it and the town with a steady source of income from pilgrims who were, in a sense, the tourists of their time. Revenue also came from the business of praying for the souls of the dead. A key tenet of the medieval Roman Catholic Church was that the living could intercede for the souls of the dead. All who died went to purgatory – but for how long, and how intense would the suffering of the soul be while working its penance? People could lessen their time in purgatory by doing

constructed on the only site that was acceptable – to the west of the narthex and in front of the west door and west front of the cathedral. It was an extraordinary, almost desperate, decision that compromised the appearance and function of the west end of the nave. But what could have been a disaster was salvaged by the astonishing design of the chapel and by its dual function as a Galilee porch – a place outside the main volume of a cathedral and used during Sunday processions or as a refuge for penitents. This was a particularly apposite double use at Durham because here the status of women and penitents was more or less synonymous.

The Lady Chapel is still robustly Romanesque in detail – indeed, it is something of a shrine to the chevron – but it is also something more. It is

good works in life, and since spending money on founding colleges, almshouses or churches counted as good works, it seemed in the Middle Ages that the rich had a better chance of shortening their stay in purgatory than did the poor. This transference of worldly status into the spiritual afterlife was emphasized by another popular medieval practice. The rich would build chantry chapels, particularly in great churches that, like Durham, had the bones of a saint in residence. In these chapels priests would pray or chant for the soul of the departed. But the priest from the cathedral chapter or monastic order had to be paid to do this, usually from an endowment left by the deceased.

Chantry chapels were built within the nave at Durham, the most famous being that of the local and powerful Neville family, but virtually all trace of these once-ornate structures has long since been swept away.

However, evidence of the increasing importance of pilgrimage is clear. The number of visitors swamped St Cuthbert's shrine, and in about 1240 the monks took the decision to build a massive additional transept to the east of the cathedral. This was to provide a large and impressive setting for the shrine, and space for the hordes of pilgrims wanting to see, and process around, the saint.

This lofty space, set at a lower level than the chancel, was started in 1242 and not completed until 1274. It is a spectacular piece of Gothic design in the style that became known as Early English. Here light is supreme. Using newly improved engineering and constructional skills, the masons took the design of the nave to its logical conclusion. Areas of wall were reduced to a minimum and window areas enlarged to the maximum. Sensible use was made of buttresses to reinforce the slivers of wall that support the stone vaults, but the structure of the massive window on the north side of the chapel literally defies understanding. Added in the 1280s, it is a supreme example of stone engineering, incredibly bold, with the design working on the very edge of what is structurally possible. There are two layers of tracery linked by horizontal stone ties, with the interior tracery acting to brace the minimal exterior tracery and glass against wind pressure. As Christopher Downes, the architect now responsible for the cathedral fabric, explains: 'The window is working at the extreme of its structural capacity – it can't be altered or reduced by even

Left: Detail of the north window, showing stone horizontal bracing linking the inner and outer tracery.

one stone without danger of collapse. We simply wouldn't be allowed to build it now.' Medieval masons were daring, indeed: structures like this were an act of faith and a declaration of belief in the power of God's geometry to allow man to pull off structural miracles. The window is, in a way, an act of worship in itself. The name of its designer, Richard of Farnham, is recorded as *Architector novae fabricae* (Architect of the new building), and the name of the mason may be Thomas Moises, which is carved on a buttress at the east end.

The transept is called the Chapel of the Nine Altars because it contains nine altars dedicated to various saints along its east wall. Pilgrims would have prayed at these, probably in turn, while circumambulating the shrine and cathedral in much the same way as Muslims circulate around the Kaaba at Mecca. But why nine altars? Nine has a potent meaning in Christian symbolism. It represents the Trinity, and is the last number in the denary system. This east altar is the final and most spiritually 'high' part of the cathedral, so nine appears to be an appropriate number for its altars. Or is this number yet another obscure reference to the influence of the Koran and the Mosque of the Nine Domes at Balkh?

At the same time as the Chapel of the Nine Altars was constructed the stone vault over the choir was rebuilt. The early twelfth-century semicircular transverse arches were replaced with pointed arches, and the splendid new vault furnished with an array of Gothic detail. These arches, although created over 150 years after the cathedral was designed, appear to confirm the original meaning of the building's sacred geometry. The centre point of the diagonal square

symbolizing Christ (see diagram, p. 40) is marked by a vault boss carved with the figure of a lamb holding a banner, the Lamb of God, the universal symbol of the Son of God. More enigmatic is the carving on the vault boss that stands over the western edge of the choir, marking the most easterly point of the diagonal square symbolizing the Holy Ghost (see diagram, p. 40). This boss is carved with a scene that shows Christ holding a blanket or net from which protrude the faces of what appear to be children. Is this Christ, the fisher of men, carrying souls into heaven at the point where the most sacred part of the cathedral starts? Perhaps, but a biblical text might throw light on this imagery: 'As newborn babes desire the sincere milk of the word, that ye may grow thereby. If so be, ye have tasted that the Lord is gracious, to whom coming, as unto a living stone, disallowed indeed of men, but chosen by God, and precious. Ye also as lively stones are built up a spiritual house, an holy priesthood to offer up spiritual sacrifices, acceptable to God by Jesus Christ. Wherefore also it is contained in the scripture. Behold, I lay in Sion a chief cornerstone, elect, precious: and he that believeth in him, shall not be confounded. Unto you therefore which believe, he is precious: but unto them which be disobedient the stone which the builders disallowed, the same is made the head of the corner.' (I Peter 2:2–7) This is a strange text, but one that touches on much of Durham: the babes in the boss, the 'lively' or living stones from which the cathedral is built, the 'holy priesthood' of the Benedictines offering up prayers 'acceptable to God', and the 'disallowed' stone or 'odd' column, the symbol of Christ, that is in fact

'elect, precious' and the 'cornerstone' of the new 'Sion', the cathedral at Durham.

Fire and Sword

The crossing, where the north–south axis of the transepts crosses the east–west axis of the nave and choir, is one of the most spiritually charged places in the cathedral. It is at the physical centre of the building and, in the analogy of the cathedral as Christ's body, it marks the heart, the omphalos or navel that draws sustenance and sacred power from above. This abstract role was made tangible by the construction over the crossing of a mighty tower and spire. This, an aspiring finger pointing to God, was to act like a lightning conductor, to capture and bring spiritual force into the cathedral.

In fact, in 1460 the tower was hit by lightning and very badly damaged – proof, it may have been thought, of the power of God's energy that lurks in the heavens. The upper stages had to be rebuilt, and here the stones speak – almost

literally – of the world as seen by the fifteenth-century mason and monks at Durham. And it seems a very different world from that of the twelfth- and thirteenth-century monks who created the earlier phases of the cathedral. Now there appears to be uncertainty, a sense of worldly frivolity and lack of deference, even, perhaps a questioning of Christian values and the omnipotence of God. There seems to be a revived interest in the old religions of the north. The high-level carvings tell the tale. There are mischievous imps and devils, mocking portraits of monks, an ironic image of a one-legged beggar, a cat with a diminutive woman, suggesting witchcraft, and a lascivious mermaid clutching her breast and holding a comb, striking an image of worldly vanity – the *belle femme* – and perhaps making a joke at the expense of the man behind the rebuilding of the tower, Prior Bell. There are also darker, less playful or witty images: the Angel Gabriel, with a claw-like hand, reading the book of doom on Judgement Day; a strange creature with a cat's face and wings, perhaps a siren or a succubus, set on the capture of men's souls; and a green man, familiar pagan personification of a nature spirit that hibernated through the winter and appeared refreshed with new foliage in the spring. Here the green man is shown asleep, grasping a sapling that has yet to sprout new life, perhaps implying that the old religion merely sleeps and is not yet dead.

But the most extraordinary thing about this tower is its size. At 218 feet (66 metres) high, the distance from the top of the tower to the floor of the nave is the same as the distance from the nave floor to the river bed below the cathedral's clifftop site.

Whether a recreation of the thirteenth-century tower or a new idea in the fifteenth century, what does this relationship mean? It could just be a conceit, an attempt to achieve a notion of visual harmony, but few things in a cathedral – certainly of such scale and importance – would be done for visual reasons alone. To someone, this relationship must have had a very important symbolic or even tangible importance. We cannot know for sure now, but we can speculate. Perhaps it is to do with forging a connection between the elements – the water of the river, the air in the sky, the earth of the site and stones of the cathedral, and the heavenly fire delivered by lightning. The sacred geometry of the cathedral, if indeed organized around a square, does suggest that the fusion of the material world, as represented by the four elements, with the spiritual world was of crucial importance to its creators.

The Church in the Middle Ages

Medieval churches, such as Durham Cathedral, were many things apart from being places of worship. Their plan could accommodate festivals with their various rituals (particularly Easter and Christmas), when the building became a representation of Jerusalem, the sacred or heavenly city around which the congregation would parade. The stained-glass windows and the strong colours on the stonework would have made the interior a splendid place far removed from the humble buildings generally experienced by the majority of those who entered it. The interior of the cathedral was strictly divided to reflect the earthly status of worshippers. At Durham women were very restricted as to the parts they could visit, rich were divided from poor, laity were divided from clergy, and the clergy were themselves divided according to their role. Churches were ornamented and laid out to inform, control and inspire these different types of user. For most, services would have been remote. The general lay worshippers would have stood around in the nave, divided from the clergy in the choir (virtually a church within the church) by a massive screen. Grander lay members of the congregation would be in the transepts. The laity took little active part in the main service: they merely witnessed the clergy at work reading and chanting in Latin, and hoped to benefit from the spiritual 'fall-out' generated by the act of divine worship. More intimate acts of worship took place in the many chapels that most large churches contained.

Durham Cathedral would generally have functioned in this manner, but it had two potentially conflicting roles. First, it was a great monastic church serving the special requirements of its Benedictine monks, so public access had to be limited. Second, it was a place of international pilgrimage, so it had to admit flocks of pilgrims to St Cuthbert's shrine. A compromise was reached through strict physical control of the interior.

The appearance and organization of the interior of Durham Cathedral in its Roman Catholic heyday, just before the Reformation in the 1530s, is hinted at in the text of *The Rites of Durham.*

The interiors would have been brightly coloured, with the patterns on the columns emphasized. Small areas of red and black survive, including painted chevron decoration.

At the west end of the nave was a chamber where people seeking sanctuary from criminal prosecution were lodged. Anyone who could reach the sanctuary knocker on the north door would be given shelter in the cathedral for a limited period (about a month), and so gain a chance to organize his or her defence. When the time had expired, the accused would then have to face trial or leave the kingdom.

Between the piers next to the font were small altars that were accessible to women. At the east end of the south nave aisle was the Neville chapel, where prayers were sung for the souls of this powerful local family. This chapel was a large and lavish affair, with the aumbry (the cupboard in which sacred vessels were kept) still visible and marking the location of the lost altar. The astonishing Neville screen, a multi-pinnacled Gothic tour de force of the 1370s, still survives in the choir. It has the dual function of displaying the wealth and power of the Nevilles in a way that beautifies the cathedral and also literally lays up treasure in heaven for them, and perhaps buys respite from purgatory.

Between the most eastern piers of the nave and aisles was the massive and famous Jesus screen. On it was placed a huge rood or crucifix that towered above the Jesus altar. Here, close to two columns decorated with 144 lozenges, pilgrims could hear Mass and live out yet another passage from the Book of Revelation (7:1–4): '…I saw four angels standing on the four corners of the earth, holding the four winds of the earth… And I saw another angel…having the seal of the living God: and he cried with a loud voice to the four angels…hurt not the earth…till we have sealed the servants of our God in their foreheads. And I heard the number of them which were sealed: and there were sealed an hundred and forty and four thousand.'

The Jesus screen marked the beginning of the more sacred part of the cathedral, the monks' preserve, but it did not entirely bar laymen from the east of the cathedral. Pilgrims could pass through it on their way to St Cuthbert's shrine and the Chapel of the Nine Altars. Beyond, to the east, was the world of the monks.

In the aisles of the transepts was a series of chapels, while the choir held the bishop's throne, the high altar and the most astonishing of the cathedral's furnishings – a massive, multi-branched candlestick erected each Easter, which virtually filled the height and width of the choir.

The Rites of Durham also reveals how the cathedral was used. Each Sunday the monks would progress around the building, like blood coursing through a body. They moved from the choir nave, chanting and praying, went around the north transept, west along the nave, around the Lady Chapel, through the south nave door, into and around the cloister, back into the nave, around the south transept, along the south choir aisle, around the Chapel of the Nine Altars and then back into the choir nave. Progressing through and around a sacred site or object had great significance in medieval Christianity, as it still does in Islam. The monks were walking through the body of Christ and measuring out significant distances, various dimensions having great symbolic and sacred importance. Typical is the fact that the distance from the cross in the floor at the west of the nave – the line over which women were forbidden to cross and which marks the start of the sacred portion of the nave – to the high altar is about 365 feet (110 metres). Since the cathedral was seen as a microcosm of God's creation, walking the length of the cathedral, from the cross to St Cuthbert, was perhaps regarded, in terms of grace, as the equivalent of a year-long pilgrimage.

Apocalypse

The apocalypse promised in the Book of Revelation and long awaited by the servants of St Cuthbert finally arrived. In 1534 Henry VIII broke with Rome. Chantry chapels, rood screens and shrines that promoted ancient saints like Cuthbert were swept away. Virtually overnight, Durham's most sacred possession, the shrine of St Cuthbert, which had been venerated in the cathedral by tens of thousands of people for nearly 450 years, became a religious

embarrassment. It was destroyed, although the body of the saint was saved.

The consequence of the Reformation is that the cathedral lost much of its meaning. Rituals that it was created to accommodate were banned, shrines and images it was meant to house were smashed, and the sacred ideas that gave the building power and presence were rapidly forgotten.

The nagging question of who designed the cathedral remains unanswered. People puzzle over this mystery but miss the obvious conclusion. The anonymity of the designer is intentional. If the name were known, it would detract attention from the cathedral as the house of God, as the work of God.

Cathedrals were not to be monuments to the ego of an individual. They were the corporate creation of many dedicated people working under the inspiration of their belief in God. Only in this way can they be what they set out to be – truly universal churches.

Right: Grotesque, high up in the crossing tower, showing a cat and an old woman – perhaps signifying witchcraft.

2

Windsor Castle

The history of Windsor Castle is the story of England. The castle's spaces and interiors offer an unparalleled theatre of history, having witnessed many varied and dramatic events as the building has pursued its career from fortress, palace, prison, shrine, royal burial place and lunatic asylum, to barracks, country house and museum. Extending over 13 acres (5.2 hectares), Windsor is Europe's largest occupied royal palace and the biggest inhabited castle in the world.

Windsor Castle, even on an international scale, is matchless. Its very special artistic qualities have been recognized since at least the mid-seventeenth century. Samuel Pepys called it 'the most romantic castle that is in the world', and in 1724 Daniel Defoe described it as 'the most beautiful, and most pleasantly situated castle and royal palace, in the whole isle of Britain'.[1]

Due to the castle's diverse roles and functions over many centuries, it now offers a particular and very revealing vignette of the evolution of English architecture. It is, in a sense, the architectural epitome of the English nation. Its fabric provides an insight into evolving ideas about kingship and related rituals, about techniques of military defence and about developing expectations of domestic comfort and convenience.

But despite its familiar appearance, nothing at Windsor is quite what it seems. Behind its imposing walls and gates lie centuries of secrecy, intrigue and forgotten visions of grandeur.

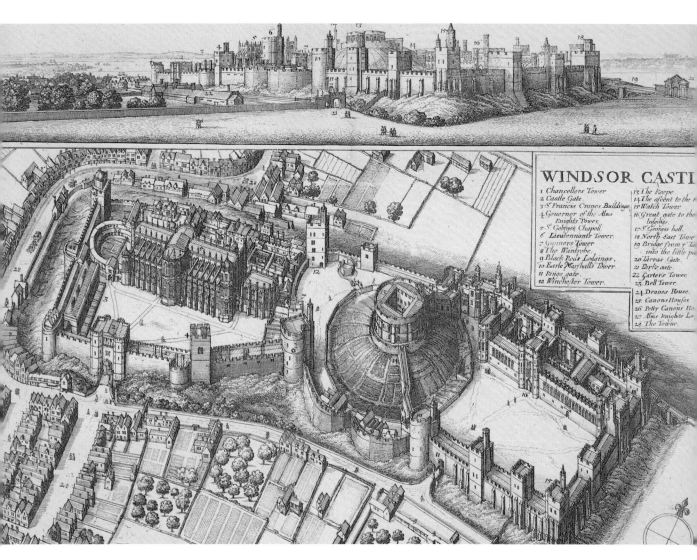

WINDSOR CASTI

1 Chancellors Tower
2 Castle Gate
3 St Francis Cranes Buildings
4 Gouernor of the Alms Knights Tower
5 St Georges Chapell
6 Lieutennants Tower
7 Gunners Tower
8 The Wardrobe
9 Black Rods Lodgings
10 Earle Marshalls Tower
11 Kings gate
12 Winchester Tower

13 The Keepe
14 The ascent to the
15 Watch Tower
16 Great gate to the lodgings
17 St Georges hall
18 North East Tower
19 Bridge from the into the little pa
20 Tarras Gate
21 Dyke gate
22 Garters Tower
23 Bell Tower
24 Deanes House
25 Canons House
26 Petty Canons Ho
27 Alms knightes Lo
28 The Towne

The castle is a manifestation of three distinct worlds – the royal, the military and the religious – embodied by the Upper Ward, the Middle Ward and the Lower Ward. Each has dominated the others at different periods of English history.

Although now a byword for suburban gentility, Windsor is a place steeped in myth. In ancient times it was believed that Herne the Hunter, a demon with magical powers and antlers growing from his temples, prowled the thickly wooded park, terrorizing hapless travellers. Perhaps more significantly, legend has it that Windsor is one of the mythical sites of Camelot, where King Arthur held court and set up his Round Table. This was a potent myth that

Previous page: The Long Walk through Windsor Park.
Above: Hollar's seventeenth-century bird's-eye view of Windsor with the Lower Ward and St George's Chapel on the left, the Middle Ward in the centre, and the Upper Ward on the right.

successive monarchs sought to exploit in a number of dramatic ways.

Origins

The origin of Windsor is primarily military. The first substantial castle on the site was built by William I in about 1070 as part of a defensive ring around newly conquered London. The high ground above the Thames was selected as a naturally strong site. A motte – an earth mound surrounded by a ditch – was thrown up, and a round wooden stockade was placed on its summit. To the east of, and attached to, the mound an area was enclosed by another stockade to form a bailey. Thus were defined the Upper Ward, and the Middle Ward (which was to have the motte as its focus).

Between 1105 and 1110 Henry I enlarged and strengthened what had in effect only been a temporary castle, part of the emergency measures William had introduced to hold his conquest. Henry's major contributions were the creation of a walled enclosure to the west of the motte – the future Lower Ward – and the construction of a great hall in this new bailey and a substantial house for himself – the *domus regis* – against the north wall of the Upper Ward. Thus was established the site of the castle's main royal apartments. Henry I may also have replaced the timber stockade on the motte with a stone-walled shell keep. Certainly by 1160–80, during the reign of Henry II, this work had been completed and the main characteristic of Windsor Castle – a round stone tower on a conical mound – was in place. Henry II also installed a garrison in the Lower Ward, although the

defensive wall was probably still timber. However, the timber stockade of the Upper Ward was replaced by a stone wall with mural towers, and the *domus regis* enlarged, with ranges set around a central courtyard. Windsor was now beginning to gain its status as one of the largest and strongest stone-built castles in the land, and a residence fit for a monarch.

The strengthening of the castle was timely indeed, for in 1216 it was to face the ordeal of a lengthy and serious siege. In that year Prince Louis of France invaded England – at the invitation of various disgruntled Anglo-Norman barons – in an attempt to oust King John and enforce the French king's claim to the throne of England. The French troops, with their English supporters, initially swept all before them, with only the great fortresses at Dover and Windsor Castle holding out for King John. His death in October 1216, and the accession of his infant son as Henry III, unified the English, but Prince Louis remained determined to acquire the throne for his father. Following a defeat at Lincoln, and still unable to breach the stalwart defence of Windsor and Dover, Prince Louis withdrew. The invasion was over. The hero of the hour was Hubert de Burgh, the justiciar of England. He had held Dover Castle against two French sieges, and soon after 1217 set about repairing and reinforcing the defences of both Dover and Windsor.

In the 1220s Windsor Castle acquired the splendid walls and towers that protect its Lower Ward. These reflected the latest military technology and myths. The towers project far forward from the walls, allowing them to be more effectively defended by flanking fire, and their curved form deflected missiles thrown at them by heavy catapults of the type the French had used in their recent sieges. The most impressive of these works, although now much altered and repaired, is the mighty Curfew Tower. The stone-built curtain wall is ornamented with bands of larger, lighter-coloured square stones – in the manner of the towering fifth-century Theodosian Walls of Constantinople – which, at the time, were thought to be impregnable and a potent symbol of ancient and stable kingship. A wall was also constructed to the south of the mound on which the shell keep stood, and its junctions with the existing walls of the Upper and Lower Wards were reinforced by great towers, the origins of the Henry III and Edward III towers that still stand today. These works defined the extent of the Middle Ward. De Burgh may also have built or repaired the stone walls of the keep, and perhaps established a chapel in the Lower Ward. During the mid-thirteenth century, Henry III took the first, if somewhat tentative, step towards making Windsor one of the great royal palaces in his kingdom. He extended the hall in the Lower Ward, including a chapel for his own use, and in the Upper Ward greatly increased the size and grandeur of the *domus regis* for use by his queen and children.

It was Edward III who, from the 1340s, was to complete the castle's transformation from battle-scarred fortress to enchanted palace, and in the process launch Windsor as the new Camelot and himself as the new King Arthur. Windsor was to be a powerful statement of English kingship, in the ascendant after the early triumphs of the Hundred Years War with France.

The New Camelot

Edward III's transformation of the castle into a symbol of political power, dynastic ambition and military triumph is one of the most extraordinary stories of the Middle Ages.

The Hundred Years War with France – a combination of territorial struggle, a fight for power and commerce raiding – took coherent form in 1337. At stake were the English possessions in France, the control of profitable sources of trade and custom revenues, prestige within the community of European monarchs, and, ultimately, the crown of France itself.

The war had started as a mere feudal squabble between Philip VI of France and Edward III of England. Edward, as Duke of Aquitaine, was the vassal of the French king, and had to acknowledge his dominance and pay him homage. After a series of bloody confrontations, Edward hatched a plan, psychological as well as military in nature, for the defence of England and defeat of France.

In 1343 he decided that he would hold a mighty tournament at Windsor Castle, and invitations were issued throughout much of Europe to lords and their ladies, knights, esquires and high-born damsels. Windsor was suddenly the centre of the military and social map of Europe. To minimize the travel problems created by the war, Edward offered to ensure safe passage to all who wished to attend.

At the end of the tournament Edward made a momentous announcement. He was going to recreate the brotherhood of the Round Table: he was the new King Arthur, and Windsor Castle was to be the new Camelot.

This new order was to be served by 300 knights, the boldest in Christendom, and they were to gather at a massive round table housed in a new round hall – 200 feet (60 metres) in diameter – to be built in the Upper Ward of Windsor Castle. It was to be a romantic evocation of the golden age of chivalry. The knights were to pledge allegiance to Edward, and thus to England, and stand with him against France. This move to enlist the myth of King Arthur and his knights in the battle against France was a shrewd, indeed cunning, move on Edward's part. By claiming to be the new Arthur, heading a new Round Table, Edward was implying that his cause was not only just but almost holy, and that he was seeking to realize God's will by fighting for his rightful inheritance.

That the new Round Table had a powerful spiritual dimension is confirmed by the fact that the Virgin Mary was chosen as its protectress.

After announcing the foundation of the new order, Edward set about making Windsor the new Camelot. Soon after 1344 the Crown started to pay large sums for the construction of the round building that was to house the order. Work certainly started because materials were delivered, and masons and carpenters paid, but this great enterprise was never completed. The war in France demanded ever more of Edward's time and money, and he appears to have lost interest in the New Round Table and its building.

But then came the Battle of Crécy.

In July 1346 Edward mustered an army of 10,000 men, English and Welsh, and they sailed from Portsmouth for the Cotentin peninsula. The strategic aim of this force remains something of a mystery, but if provocation was Edward's plan it worked admirably. Like a swarm of hornets, Philip and his 30,000-strong army set off in pursuit of Edward, eventually catching up with him at Crécy.

The battle was a trial by ordeal, and Edward and his army were the clear winners – thanks, claimed the English, to the just nature of Edward's cause and to the support and protection of the Virgin and of St George. Against frightful odds, the French army had been crushed, Philip had been humiliated and the door was opened for the capture of Calais – the city and port that was to be the jewel in England's collection of French possessions for the next 200 years, and an invasion route into France.

Victory led Edward to turn his attention once more to Windsor and his New Round Table. He wanted to offer thanks to his protectors, and the moribund order of the New Round Table provided a means of doing this. At some point in 1346 or 1347 Edward decided to revive his order, to give it an even more sacred character and to dedicate it to his blessed protectors – the Virgin and St George.

The order was changed in both composition and name. It was to be called the Order of the Knights of the Garter, and its membership was to be limited to 26, two of whom would automatically be the monarch and the Prince of Wales. Its base, however, was to be the same – Windsor Castle and its thirteenth-century chapel in the Lower Ward.

The exact details about the origin, purpose and meaning of this new order, with its perplexing name, are highly confused and uncertain. The

original statutes and ordinances were lost, destroyed or hidden, and the earliest surviving documents date from 1415. What is known for certain is that on 6 August 1348 letters patent were issued for founding the College of the Blessed Virgin Mary, St George and St Edward at Windsor.[2] As explained in *The Most Noble Order of the Garter* by Peter J. Begent and Hubert Chesshyre, 'The college was clearly intended to prayerfully support the Order and to staff and maintain the Chapel within Windsor Castle.' The letters patent made it clear that the structure of the college was to shadow the structure of the order it was to serve. It was to be two worlds, the spiritual and the secular, working in harmony. As it contained 24 picked knights, so there would be 24 priests or canons to maintain the spiritual life of the chapel, and these would be supported by 24 bedesmen (poor and aged knights living at the expense of the order), who were to attend the chapel to pray for the souls of the knights, living and dead. Clearly, the Order of the Garter was to fight its battles both on earth and in heaven.

But what is not explained in any contemporary documents is the meaning of the insignia and motto of the order, and why 24 was such an important number. Were the answers to these questions so strange, so potentially provocative or open to misunderstanding that by 1415 all evidence had been destroyed?

The insignia of the order is a blue garter edged with gold. The motto, in old French, is '*Honi soit qui mal y pense*', which means roughly

Left: Windsor Castle from the Eton bank of the Thames. The Upper Ward stretches to the left of the round tower.

'Shame on him who thinks evil of it'. But what evil of the order could anyone have been thinking? And why should their punishment be shame? Does the answer to this question lie in the emblem itself?

A garter, possibly a lady's, was a curious, rather intimate, symbol for knights to wear. And when buckled up the garter formed a circle or, more precisely, an oval.

The colours – blue and gold – were the colours of the French king, and it was common practice in medieval chivalry to adopt the colours or emblem of a defeated enemy. But blue was also commonly used in medieval paintings as the colour for the Virgin's robe, so when the Knights of the Garter donned their blue robes, they were cloaking themselves in the colour of their patron.

A rare surviving example of English medieval sacred art (most was destroyed during the Reformation) throws fascinating light on the relationship between the Virgin, Windsor and the Knights of the Garter. Called the Wilton Diptych and dating from *c.* 1390, the painting shows Mary holding Christ and surrounded by 11 angels, a total of 13 figures, each wearing a deep blue robe, like the mantles of Knights of the Garter. Above the Virgin floats a banner emblazoned with the red cross of St George; above that is an orb showing an island, standing on which is a large castle. This is thought to represent England as a place under the special protection of the Virgin, and the castle must be the recently rebuilt Windsor. On the panel opposite the Virgin are Richard II, St John the Baptist, St Edward the Confessor and St Edmund. The Diptych therefore shows or alludes to all three patrons of

the Garter – the Virgin, St George (through his banner) and St Edward.[3]

What does the order's close affinity with the Virgin signify? The surviving annals are silent on the matter, but there is a little near-contemporary comment that sheds some light on this, and on the meaning of the garter emblem. In 1463 an Italian ecclesiastic called Mondonus Belvaleti made an intriguing statement in a book about the Order of the Garter (*Tractatus ordinis serenissimi domini regiis Angliae vulgariter dicti la Gerratiere*), claiming that it 'took its beginning from the female sex'.

By giving birth to Jesus, the Virgin gave mankind its saviour. As a result, she and the parts of her body through which Christ entered the world were venerated in the Middle Ages. Typically, one of the few surviving English Gregorian chants of the twelfth century – the Worcester fragment – praises the womb of the Virgin. The Virgin and the birth are also associated with an oval shape, symbolic of the female genitals, and this shape is often seen in medieval art.

The oval, pointed at top and bottom, is called a vesica piscis (literally 'fish-shaped vessel'), which is a simple but profoundly influential geometric figure produced when two circles of equal size are overlaid through each other's centres. In medieval painting and sculpture Christ is often shown within a vesica piscis. Indeed, the early Christian symbol of the fish is in fact a vesica piscis with two of the arcs extended to imply a fishtail. So, arguably, one of the earliest and holiest of all Christian symbols is the vesica piscis – the symbolic representation of the generative power of the female and the place

through which the saviour of mankind entered the world. Edward, a man of the world, realized that the feminine symbolism of the order, if recognized by non-initiates, could provoke ribald jokes or thoughts, so he built a warning into the motto: 'Shame on you if you think any shame in this.'

The Virgin also offers an explanation for the number of knights.

The moon is traditionally a feminine symbol that relates to the monthly cycle of the female body, and is thus related to the act of birth. The moon goes through 12 cycles each year, with between 12 and 13 full moons, making between 24 and 26 full and new moons each year.

It may have been the lunar cycle, and its link to the Virgin, that inspired St John the Evangelist when, in Revelation 4:3–4, he described Christ as sitting in judgement surrounded by a rainbow 'and round about the throne were four and twenty seats: and upon the seats I saw four and twenty elders sitting'.

This biblical text may have been the immediate cause of Edward choosing to surround himself (and his son) with 24 'elders'. This implied division of the Garter Knights into two teams of 12, each headed by the monarch and the Prince of Wales, has tempted some to see the order as no more than two jousting teams and the king and his son as team captains.

Above: The Wilton Diptych (c. 1390) shows the Virgin under the banner of St George. Barely visible, England and Windsor Castle are depicted on the orb at the top of the banner.

Little now survives of the buildings Edward III created in the 1340s and 1350s for his orders of the New Round Table and of the Garter. If the huge round building in the Upper Ward were ever completed, it has left no archaeological trace behind. The form such a massive building could have taken in the fourteenth century is a mystery since the technology to roof such a large structure in an elegant manner did not then exist. One possibility is that the building was to take the form of a circular amphitheatre (not unlike the Colosseum in Rome) built of stone and timber frame, with the central space covered by a huge tent supported by posts and guy ropes. Certainly, the expertise for creating such massive fabric structures existed for tournaments, and military camps took the form of huge tent cities, including massive marquees.[4] What does survive in the Upper Ward are the lodgings for the 24 or 26 canons of St George's Chapel. These are timber-framed buildings, incorporating a modest, cloister-like open arcade, organized around a courtyard – rather like an Oxford or Cambridge quad or court. The lodgings were built in 1350–4, and it is just possible that they incorporate materials – particularly timbers – from the huge round amphitheatre/hall that Edward had by then abandoned. Edward linked these lodgings to the thirteenth-century chapel dedicated to St George with a rebuilt and grander cloister, along the east side of which rose a building containing the chambers of the dean and the college chapter house.

Against the south wall of the Lower Ward Edward built lodgings for the poor knights, or bedesmen (extended in the 1550s), while in the Upper Ward he extended the *domus regis* to create a fascinating and complex royal palace incorporating the king's and queen's lodgings, state reception rooms and service buildings organized around three courtyards. The basic plan and scale of Edward's palace determined future developments in the Upper Ward and are directly reflected in the existing state apartments. It was at this time – probably in the late 1350s and the 1360s – that the great hall was enlarged and a chapel built to its west (thus together creating the volume of the existing St George's Hall), with the king and queen each having a multi-roomed apartment arranged around the central and western courts. Encircling the court to the east were service buildings, including a massive kitchen dating from 1360 that survives little altered. Lodgings were built against the south and east walls of the Upper Ward.

These works, supervised by William of Wykeham, Bishop of Winchester, who was to develop a talent for pioneering architecture (such as New College Oxford, 1379), cost a vast sum – at least £44,150. In fact, the new palace was the most expensive secular building project undertaken in Britain during the Middle Ages. Much of the money, along with the determination to create such a prestigious and modern palace, came from the wars in France. In 1356 the English won another astonishing victory (at Poitiers) during which the French king was captured and brought to England, staying for a while at Windsor. Ransom for the release of the French knights taken at Poitiers, and eventually for the French king himself, provided the royal exchequer with funds to complete this fantastic enterprise.

The buildings that Edward III created in the Upper Ward during the 1350s and 1360 have been greatly altered, mostly beyond recognition. But the fragments that survive do offer a fascinating insight into the lost palace. The misnamed Norman Gate, guarding entry into the Upper Ward from the Middle Ward, survives from Edward's defensive work. It is a fine piece of construction comprising a pair of stout round towers (one rebuilt in the early nineteenth century) flanking an entry passage defended by gates and portcullis, and murder holes in the stone vault down which missiles and boiling oil could be showered on attackers. At ground-floor level, beneath St George's Hall, is a boldly detailed rib-vaulted undercroft that served as storage space and as a strong support for the floor of the great hall above. To the north of this undercroft is a vaulted passage, built by Edward to support the northward extension of the earlier great hall above, which has more delicate detailing than the larger undercroft itself. Clearly, this was a passage of some importance and, fascinatingly, the decorations include vault bosses each carved with a rose (the first recorded use of the rose as a symbol of kingship in a royal building).

That the use of the rose here was no mere mason's decorative whim is confirmed by the other major survival of Edward's palace – King John's Tower, originally known as the Rose Tower. This is a remarkable fragment. It adjoined Edward III's great chamber, and contains the king's private staircase and a series of closets that would have been used by the king for private meetings. One of these closets at ground level is stone vaulted, with a huge central boss embellished with a massive, 10-petalled rose. From this date (1360) the rose became one of

the main symbols of the English monarchy.

Why did Edward III choose a rose as an emblem? One answer relates to the Order of the Garter: the rose was one of the traditional symbols of the Virgin Mary, with the Catholic rosary now being the best-known expression of the connection between the Virgin and the rose.

The thirteenth-century chapel of St George, the spiritual home of the Order of the Garter, has long gone, except for its west door, to be replaced by a purpose-designed structure that really is one of the most extraordinary religious buildings in Britain.

Above: The 1360 undercroft beneath St George's Hall is the best surviving interior of Edward III's palace.

The Chapel

The monarch behind this building enterprise was Edward IV. Planning of the new chapel started in 1472–3, and it was to be built immediately to the west of the existing chapel. Construction started in 1475 but was not completed until 1528, by which time Edward was long dead and England transformed almost out of recognition. In 1498 the old chapel was largely demolished, and a massive chapel dedicated to the Virgin Mary was started on its site.

The role that Edward IV envisaged for St George's Chapel was complex. It was to be a shrine and chapel for the Knights of the Garter, where living knights would gather, dead knights would be buried and commemorated, and where bedesmen would pray for their souls. It was to be a royal chantry chapel, the burial place of monarchs with chapels erected over their tombs, and it was to mark the triumph of the House of York in the Wars of the Roses.

Within a year of his decisive victories at Barnet and Tewkesbury in 1471, Edward IV commissioned the design of the new chapel. Not only would the chapel celebrate Yorkist power, but it would also provide an impressive spiritual home for the Knights of the Garter – Edward thereby rewarding and flattering the most influential members of England's ruling elite. And the order, in its much enhanced setting, would be an even more powerful diplomatic tool to entice allies and supporters at home and abroad. It was a shrewd move: at a stroke Edward would honour both the Virgin, the protectress of England, and the Knights of the Garter, the men on whose support his survival depended.

Edward put the design and construction of the chapel under the control of Richard Beauchamp, who had been Bishop of Salisbury since 1450. Beauchamp was made master and surveyor, with Henry Janyn engaged as master mason, and letters patent for the 'new chapel in honour of the blessed Mary and St George the Martyr' were issued by Edward in 1472.

Beauchamp was an accomplished architectural client by the 1470s, and must have been well versed in the mysteries of sacred architecture. During the 1450s he had reconstructed the east end of Salisbury Cathedral, including the shrine of St Osmund and a fine chantry chapel for himself.

In a chapel dedicated to the Virgin it is likely that the vesica piscis – one of the most sacred of symbols representing the Virgin Mary's gift of Christ to the world – would be the generating geometrical form,[5] and research at Windsor seems to prove the case.

An obvious clue, a starting point in attempting to understand the geometry underlying the design of the chapel, is the width of the nave: this is the same as the height of the nave arcade, to the point of the springing of the vault. Because the width and height of the nave are the same they can be defined by a circle of about 35 feet (10 metres) in diameter. This establishes a relationship between the plan and the section and elevations of the building, and could be the module around which the geometry of the chapel was organized. It is tempting to see this circle as the symbolic round table of the building – invisible but all-powerful in creating the world that is seen.

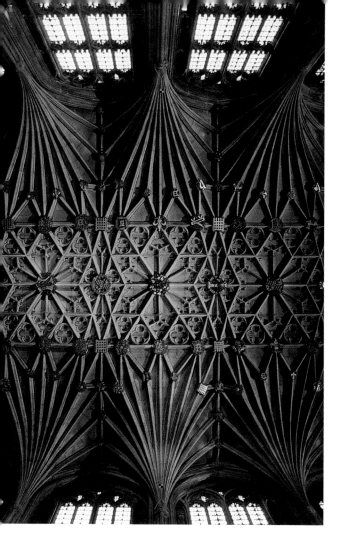

It is possible to test this theory.

A circle 35 feet (10 metres) in diameter, with its centre set where the chapel axes cross, defines the space below the crossing, with its circumference fitting between the crossing piers. The round table therefore sits within the sacred heart of the building.

From this circle the vesica piscis is defined by drawing two larger circles, their radii being equal to the diameter of the first circle, with their centres formed by the two points where the first circle crosses the main east–west axis of the chapel.

These two larger circles, and their overlap forming the pointed oval of the vesica piscis,

Above left: Detail of the St George's Chapel nave vault, with ribs arranged around centrally placed six-pointed stars.
Above right: Looking east along the nave towards the choir. The nave and choir both have widths similar to their heights.

relate in a most revealing manner to the fabric of the chapel, suggesting that this could indeed be the geometry underpinning the design of the building. The points of the vesica mark the north and south edges of the main volume of the chapel, while the arcs of the large circles pass through the centres of the four crossing piers.

The points of the vesica also define the north–south axis of the chapel, and the points where this axis passes through the circumference of the first, smaller circle mark the centres for a second set of larger circles, which create a second vesica piscis set at 90 degrees to the first. These second circles also make fascinating connections with the built fabric of the chapel. For example, they define the outer edges of the north and south transept chapels that give the chapel a characteristic cruciform shape, making it a

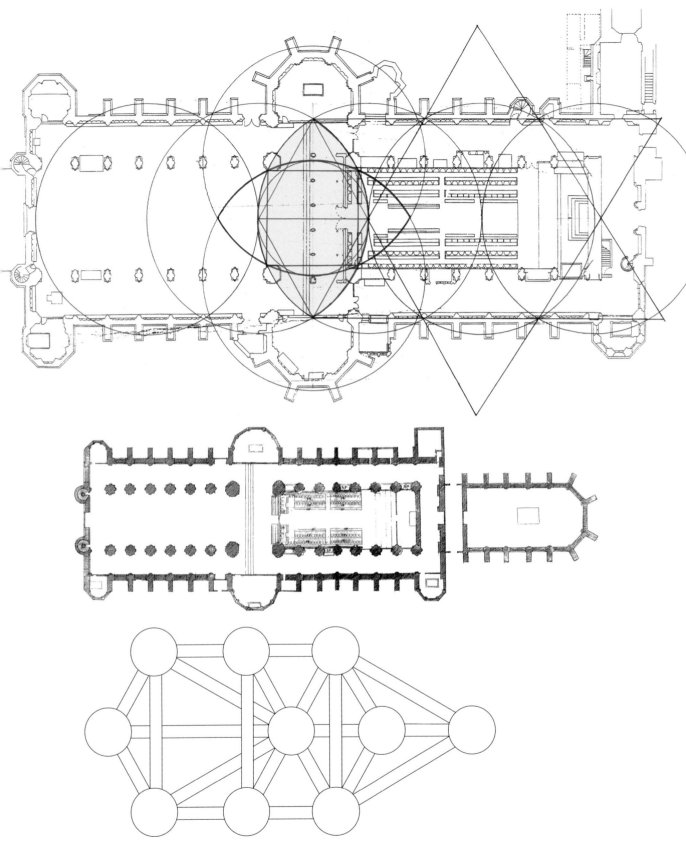

Top: Plan of St George's Chapel, showing the geometry – derived from a central vesica piscis (shaded) – determining the form of the building's fabric.

Centre: St George's Chapel with the Lady Chapel on the right.

Above: The general dispositions of the corner chapels, transepts and the Lady Chapel relate to the form of the Sephiroth – or Tree of Life – from the cabbala.

representation of Christ's body on the cross. This second pair of large circles also marks the centres of piers in the choir and the nave, establishing the rhythm for the placing of piers in the chapel.

From these vesicas a geometrical configuration unfolds, which appears to determine the design of the fabric of the chapel (see diagram opposite). These forms include north- and south-facing equilateral triangles overlapped by a square within the vesicas, double squares defined by the outer points of the vesicas, repeated large circles defining the lengths of the nave and the position of the altar in the choir, hexagons and hexagrams, these last being the six-pointed star known as the Seal of Solomon. This geometrical evolution was very important to the medieval church designer. In sacred geometry the vesica piscis is the construction from which straight-line geometry, such as the equilateral triangle and the square, is derived from the circle. So, as well as symbolizing the Virgin birth, the vesica piscis also represents the connection between the circle, the traditional image of the spiritual world, and the square, the image of the material.

If the geometry of the chapel is derived from the vesica piscis, the fabric tells additional stories, and hints at the symbols and meanings that obsessed Edward and the Bishop of Salisbury.

First let's consider the external imagery.

The eaves of the chapel are crowded with grotesque carvings – devils, imps, weird figures and strange beasts. Some are clearly restorations, but others could be original. They must represent the world of evil expelled from the interior of the sacred place.

The motifs at the west end of the chapel are also very strange in their symbolic meaning, and to understand them it is necessary to understand the construction history of the chapel.

By the time of Edward IV's death and burial in the chapel in 1483, the walls and roof of the east end of the building (the choir) had been completed, the nave was in hand, but, in all likelihood, construction of the west front had not started. Vertical straight joints to the east of the two small west chapels show where the building stopped in the 1480s.

Indeed, at the time of Edward's death even the exact design of the west front may not have been determined, but it was obviously going to be a very important element of the building. It was to contain the main door through which the knights were to enter their chapel on special occasions, and a great window carrying important messages in stained glass. The significance of the architecture of the west end is revealed by its setting. The Horseshoe Cloister was built to the west of the chapel in 1479–81. Its function was to provide lodgings for minor canons and vicars, but its main purpose was sacred. In a sense, it forms an extension of the chapel, its cloister defining a temple courtyard that would form a fitting setting for rituals that involved processions through the west door.

Work on the chapel virtually ceased during the three-year reign of Richard III: he had more urgent things to worry about. His main contribution to the chapel was the body of the rival to the House of York, the former monarch Henry VI, who had been murdered in the Tower, probably on Richard's orders. In 1483 Richard moved Henry's body from Chertsey Abbey to join Edward IV's body in the chapel, an action that might have been intended to help heal the rift between the Houses of York and Lancaster but which was also probably calculated to gain funds for the completion of the chapel. Henry was venerated as a saint, and miracles of healing were said to take place at his tomb. Within a decade of his death, Henry VI's tomb was a centre of pilgrimage, and where there were pilgrims there was money.

Richard was killed in 1485 at the Battle of Bosworth, and with him fell the House of York. For seven years St George's Chapel, the shrine to the Yorkist cause, lay desolate. Then, in 1492, the new king and heir to the Lancastrian cause – Henry VII – got things moving again.

Work on the west front was finally started in about 1496, but its images and symbols celebrate the new Tudor dynasty. They include a hemp bray, a machine for processing hemp. This unlikely detail is a rebus – a visual pun on a name – in this case, Sir Reginald Bray, a Garter knight and friend of Henry VII. Bray gave a lot of the money towards completing the chapel during the early sixteenth century, so this rebus dates the works.

Another symbol on the west front is a portcullis – a badge used by the Tudors and adopted from the Beaufort family (Margaret Beaufort was Henry Tudor's mother). Rather oddly, the portcullis is supported by a devil. Does this perhaps signify family friction? Other, more conventional motifs include a Tudor Welsh dragon, a rose – the symbol of the Virgin and of kingship, which the Tudors made their own preferred insignia – and the ostrich feather of the Prince of Wales.

But spaced at distances along the north, south and east walls of the chapel is the strangest symbol of all. It shows a crown set above a 10-petalled rose with a sunburst behind it. It clearly dates from the time of Edward IV and is said to be one of the badges used by the king, thus explaining the opening words in Shakespeare's *Richard III*, where Edward IV is called 'this sun of York'.

Perhaps it is Edward's badge of ownership and nothing more. But there is something odd about it. In the centre of the rose is a crucifix. This could be a consecration cross, as many historians claim, but there are only six of these symbols placed around the outside of the chapel, with one east of the altar inside, instead of the usual 12, and there is no evidence that the chapel was ever consecrated.

However, these badges could mean something else: they could offer a code for understanding the meaning of the chapel.

The rose was the symbol of the Virgin and the English monarchy, but the rose with a cross at its centre was the symbol of a curious body called the Brotherhood of the Rosy Cross – the Rosicrucians. This Christian brotherhood, dedicated to the discovery and application of ancient and esoteric religious rituals, mysteries and knowledge, including alchemy and the Hebrew and Christian cabbalas, flourished from the early seventeenth century but traced its origins back to the fifteenth century and earlier. One suggestion is that the brotherhood dates back to the early fourteenth century when the Knights Templar were suppressed, and that the knights attempted to continue their existence,

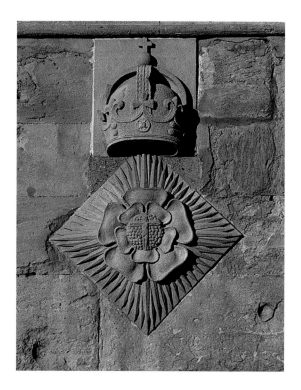

and their quest for knowledge, by founding the Rosicrucian Order.

The Rosicrucians were fascinated by legends that had, or seemed to have, profound spiritual meanings. One story that gripped the imagination of the brotherhood was that of King Arthur, the Knights of the Round Table and their quest for the Holy Grail. This story was the focus of renewed interest in the 1470s with the publication of Sir Thomas Malory's *Le Morte d'Arthur*, the most compelling and powerful of all the Arthurian romances.

So can Edward and Beauchamp have conceived their chapel, its design and symbols as a repository of ancient knowledge focused on the

Above: Badge, including rose and crucifix, fixed to the outer walls of the chapel.

Virgin Mary and Arthur's Round Table and expressed through the rituals of the Garter ceremonies?

With this question in mind, the details inside the chapel take on added meaning. At eye level, running around the interior of the nave, is a band containing three repeating motifs. The rose – the Virgin? The crown – worldly power? And a star formed by sunrays – some with a rose and cross at the centre.

Inside the chapel the star is everywhere. The vault over the nave, completed by 1506, has at its centre a six-pointed star – the Seal of Solomon – that is one of the forms generated by the vesica piscis. In the Middle Ages this six-pointed star, composed of two equilateral triangles, signified the Holy Trinity, and it was to the Holy Trinity, along with the Virgin and St George, that the chapel was dedicated.

In the nave, immediately to the west of the north door, is something most strange, which is described in no guidebook. It is a bold piece of graffiti, the style of lettering suggesting that it is late fifteenth or early sixteenth century in origin. It is now impossible to make out the first word, but the rest appears to read '– made me for thy secret'.

Who is 'me', who is 'thy', and what is the 'secret'? A shape scratched below the letters may be a clue. It is a vesica piscis, perhaps surrounded by rose petals, the symbol of the Virgin Mary.

Can the indecipherable word be the name of the mason who built this section of the nave in the 1480s? If so, then 'me' is the chapel and 'thy' is the Virgin. Perhaps the 'secret' refers to the true meaning of the Order of the Garter and to

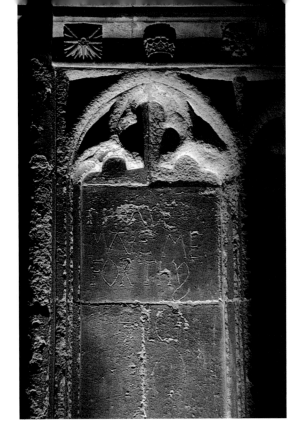

the ancient mysteries enshrined in the design of the chapel. Examination of the plan of the chapel may help to solve this mystery.

At the east end is the choir containing the stalls of the Knights of the Garter, and to the west is the nave. This long hall is given a cross-like plan by the addition of large octagonal chapels or transepts that are attached to the centre of the building and protrude to the north and south. In addition, at both the east and west ends of the building are smaller, octagonal chapels.

This long hall with six chapels attached really is a most unusual arrangement, and it is significant that all the chapels are linked by a choir of carved angels in a continuous, ribbon-like scroll. So there are hierarchies of angels inside the chapel to counter the orders of devils outside.

Richard Beauchamp was a learned man well aware of the mystic ideas that influenced religious thought and architecture in the late Middle Ages. One idea that was current in late fifteenth-century England was the Tree of Life – the Sephiroth – which was derived from the cabbala, a system of cosmology and theology evolved among the Jews in Spain from the sixth century to explain the nature of God, the origin of the world and the character of man's destiny. The cabbala, which means 'received wisdom', is the inner doctrine concerning the scriptures that, by tradition, was known to Moses and handed by him to the 'select' of Israel to provide a means of interpreting the scriptures to reveal the inner meaning of the texts of the Old Testament. The search for this meaning was based on the belief that not only are the scriptures the word of God,

but that language – specifically the 22 letters of the Hebrew alphabet – is itself divine, for it is the medium through which God's thoughts are made known to man. When contemplating the alphabet, the cabbalist was contemplating both God and his works.

Creation was conceived as emanating outward from God as a series of 10 elemental forces, connected each one to the other in varied sequences to form a tree-like structure. These 10 forces were thought to express the attributes – the full power – of God. The traditional configuration of the Tree of Life (see diagram, p. 64) could explain the unusual placing of the chapels. These, with the main body of the chapel, seem to reflect the traditional form of the Tree of Life. This is, perhaps, not so surprising since a Christian version of the cabbala, utilizing Latin and offering insights into hidden meanings in the New Testament, was well established by the 1470s.

Above: Enigmatic graffiti on the interior wall of the St George's Chapel nave.

The chapel was intended to be a very powerful place indeed – the epicentre of the monarchy, its military and spiritual base, and its sacred sepulchre. To organize the building in the image of God's Tree of Life would clearly be appropriate.

The traditional explanation for the creation of the Tree of Life was that 'God wished to behold God'. In St George's Chapel the English monarchy – God's anointed rulers exercising power by divine right – wished to behold itself in all its spiritual, temporal and dynastic glory.

The chapel was, and remains, a glorious place, not just because of its powerful but enigmatic geometry and details, but also because of its architectural and engineering achievements. It is one of the masterpieces of the late Gothic age in England. The wall area has been reduced to the minimum: the outward thrust of the internal stone vaults is gathered on to small sections of wall and then restrained or balanced by external flying buttresses so that windows can be as large as possible to allow God's light to flood inside.

Arthur's England

In 1528 the stone vault above the crossing in the chapel was finally put in place. It bears the arms of the reigning monarch, Henry VIII, and of the then Garter Knights. So, on the eve of one of the periods of greatest change in England's history, this wonderfully engineered piece of construction was completed. Within a few years virtually everything it stood for would be challenged or dramatically overturned.

In 1534 Henry broke with Rome and the symbols and images enshrined in the chapel were disowned or devalued. The Protestant Reformation rejected the veneration of saints and their images as expressions of superstition and idolatry, and even the Virgin Mary, after almost 1000 years as England's most adored sacred figure, was abandoned. The Reformation hit St George's Chapel far less hard than it did many other religious buildings throughout the land. It was classed a Royal Peculiar, which meant that it did not come under the control of any diocese, so it was not swept along in the wholesale changes that resulted in the spoliation and destruction of most monasteries and many cathedrals. But even if much of its ritual and beauty was left intact, such as the splendid carved choir stalls of the 1480s which still survive, the relegation of the Virgin and the saints meant that the meaning and symbolism of the chapel were obscured and diluted.

Despite this fatal schism, Henry VIII managed to maintain the English monarchy's association with Arthur and the Round Table. Indeed, the Tudors had made it almost a matter of principle to give their reign pedigree and security by association with the mythical king of the Britons. When Henry's father had become Henry VII in 1485, he and his supporters claimed that the Tudors marked the return of the first true British monarch since Arthur's time. To make the claim clear Henry VII called his eldest son Arthur, but this future Arthur II died before reaching the throne, opening the way for his younger brother to become Henry VIII.

From the time of his accession Henry VIII made use of Windsor and its Arthurian associations to legitimize his reign. In 1511, his second year on the throne, Henry embellished the Lower Ward of the castle with a splendid new gate that was to act as a grand processional entry point for St George's Chapel. And as early as 1517 he announced that Windsor was to be his burial place, the rightful setting for the sepulchre of a rightful king, the new Arthur.

Henry VIII was to have been buried in the centre of the Lady Chapel that his father had started to build in 1498 to the east of St George's Chapel. This was to have been a mausoleum for Henry VII and the Tudor dynasty, but work stopped when Henry VII chose instead to be buried at Westminster Abbey. Henry VIII took on his father's original idea and started to build a mighty tomb of marble and bronze for himself in the chapel, but he died when work was still under way. No one felt inclined to complete the grandiose project, and the unfinished and unoccupied monument was demolished during the Civil War. Its bronze was melted down for cannon, while the Lady Chapel itself was turned into a powder magazine.

By then royalty had been swept from Windsor Castle and the Order of the Garter largely abolished.

The Civil War

The Civil War arrived early at Windsor. In February 1642 there was unrest in the town and attacks on the park, with fences torn down and many of the king's deer slaughtered. Some of the local anti-monarchists were imprisoned, but the atmosphere remained hostile, and early in 1642

Charles I and his queen left Windsor as the political situation in London worsened. In July of that year the townsfolk of Windsor formally declared their support for Parliament, and money was raised to support Parliamentary troops. What must have been a long-simmering conflict between castle and town had now reached boiling point. In October Parliament instructed Colonel John Venn to march to Windsor with 12 companies of foot soldiers to take possession of the castle as governor. This move anticipated a similar plan by the king and his supporters, who had been planning to take Windsor as a base for an assault on London. This pre-emptive strike by Parliamentary forces did not prevent the Royalists from making plans to take Windsor by storm in early November 1642. The castle had first been built as a military stronghold, and its strength and location on the River Thames, commanding the routes between London and Oxford, meant that it was once again of great strategic and military importance.

Prince Rupert of Bohemia, nephew of Charles I and leader of the Royalist forces, planned a night assault by a body of musketeers, who were to assail the walls and open the gates to a large number of their troops.[6] This was all very dashing, but the Royalist forces never quite screwed up the courage to launch such a bold and risky direct attack. However, negotiations over the future of Windsor were opened but any chance of the Crown regaining the castle by peaceful means was shattered in late November when the king suddenly advanced to Brentford. Talks collapsed, Charles retreated and Windsor remained firmly in the hands of Parliament, which quickly gave the castle a key role in the defence of London and in the future conduct of the Civil War.

In January 1643 Parliament established its military headquarters at Windsor under the command of the Earl of Essex. In a dramatic reversal of fortune, the nerve centre of England's monarchy and bastion of knightly privilege suddenly became a republican stronghold. Essex brought 60 Royalist prisoners with him, including Sir Charles Bowles, Sir Francis Dodington, Sir Edmund Fortescue and Sir William Valentine. These cavaliers left their mark on the castle, carving their names, the dates of their imprisonment and the reason for their incarceration in the rooms where they were imprisoned in the fourteenth-century Norman Gate. Fortescue, whom the king had made sheriff of Devon and who was captured in late 1642, carved above the fireplace '…held prisoner in this Chamber… Pour l'Roy'.

During 1643 the people of Windsor probably started to regret their early and generous support for Parliament. The garrison looted and pillaged the district and committed acts of vandalism inspired by Puritanical iconoclastic ideology. St George's Chapel was despoiled by Governor Venn, and this freebooting was put on an official basis in December 1643 when orders came from Parliament to 'remove scandalous monuments and pictures' in the chapel.

The unruly behaviour of the garrison came to a head in November 1644, when it mutinied because of lack of pay. The consequences of such alarmingly unmilitary behaviour in a key fortress could have been disastrous for the Parliamentary cause. In order to keep closer control of the castle, Oliver Cromwell decided to make it his base of operations for the army.

Cromwell and his generals worshipped in St George's Chapel, a royal structure that was spared when so many less provocative religious buildings throughout the land were being destroyed. It is recorded that from nine in the morning until seven in the evening on 21 December 1647 Cromwell and his generals prayed in the chapel 'reverently and pathetically'. They were, no doubt, seeking God's blessing on their new determination – to kill the king. But it would take over a year of intrigue and trial, during which time Charles was briefly imprisoned at Windsor, before this bloody resolve was achieved.

Charles became convinced that, through his Christ-like martyrdom, the monarchy would be reborn. The people of England, he believed, would be shocked by his public execution and thereby see the error of their ways, rediscover their love of the Crown and demand its restoration.

If he could not live like a king of England he would, said Charles, die like an English gentleman. And this he did, very publicly and very bravely, in Whitehall on a cold January morning in 1649. As the axe was about to fall, it seems that his last thoughts were of Windsor and the Order of the Garter. Charles handed his insignia of the Garter to Bishop Juxon with the instruction that it should be given to the Prince of Wales together with one whispered word: 'Remember'.

The Order of the Garter was, for Charles, the ultimate expression of kingship.

A week after the execution his body was returned to the castle for burial, and he was laid to rest without ceremony alongside the bodies of Henry VIII and his queen Jane Seymour.

Britain's Lost Baroque Palace

During the 1650s, Windsor became something of a dosshouse. Virtually abandoned by Parliament, many of its rooms were appropriated by the poor of the parish, and the chapel, with its royal tombs, became decayed and forgotten.

But if Charles had made many miscalculations, there was one thing he had got right. His brave and brutal death, combined with the lack of direction shown by republican rulers in the late 1650s, did lead to a restoration of the monarchy. In 1660 his son was invited back to reign as Charles II, but the political controls and popular rejection of the myth of royalty that Charles I had refused, dreaded and eventually fallen victim to, were imposed on his son. Charles II did not rule by divine right, nor was he master of the country. He was a constitutional monarch, with strictly limited powers; even the expression of his opinions was controlled. The country was ruled by a Parliament elected by a small section of society.

Although Charles had little power and little money, he did have palaces and pomp, and he decided to transform long-neglected Windsor – the prison and burial place of his martyred father – into the centre of the restored monarchy.

Tradition was all-important, and the Order of the Garter was revived. Its outward splendour was increased and given a special Stuart identity through emphasizing the eight-pointed Garter star or sunburst introduced by Charles I.

The order's Arthurian connection was not lost on Charles II, who, like so many monarchs before him, desired to associate his rule with that of Arthur in an attempt to give his dynasty a sense of tradition, solidity and increased legitimacy. So, in 1683, Charles commissioned Sir Christopher Wren to build a new royal palace in Arthur's city of Winchester, but even more importantly, the royal apartments in the Upper Ward at Windsor Castle were remade in the manner of French aristocratic and royal palaces. Charles, the constitutional monarch, was determined to have the trappings, if not the actual power, of an absolute monarch.

In 1674 the architect Hugh May started the transformation of the medieval buildings.

The works were radical and destroyed or obscured much of Edward III's fourteenth-century palace, but they were the very height of fashion and grandeur. The king and the queen were each to have their own apartments, each comprising a sequence of interconnecting rooms of different sizes and uses. These apartments, with their carefully chosen emblematic schemes of decoration, were to be the physical mani-festation of the values and hierarchies of the royal court.

The rooms were relatively large and public at the start of the sequence, becoming increasingly intimate, rich and private the deeper one penetrated. And the depth to which visitors could penetrate this set of rooms revealed their status at court and in society. These rooms were a mirror of the world – the fixed, hierarchical and status-conscious world of the revived Stuart court.

It is now more rewarding to investigate the queen's apartments, for they are far better preserved than those of the king.

A grand and now long-destroyed flight of stairs brought visitors up from the central court in the Upper Ward to a large, first-floor room. This was the first room in the sequence – the Queen's Guard Chamber – and, like most of the rooms in these royal apartments, it was altered and redecorated in the early nineteenth century. A good idea of its original appearance is given in *Royal Residences* by W.A. Pyne (1819). In this chamber Yeomen of the Guard were stationed to keep out the lower classes, but anyone looking like a lady or a gentleman was allowed to loiter in this room and to pass into the next room on the route – the Queen's Presence Chamber.

The Queen's Presence Chamber retains much of its original decoration, which is loaded with allegorical meaning. The ceiling, painted by Antonio Verrio, shows Charles's Portuguese queen, Catherine of Braganza, seated beneath a canopy supported by zephyrs (gods of the winds), while figures of envy and sedition retreat before the outstretched Sword of Justice. The point being made is that the queen, despite her foreign and Catholic origins, was the personification of loyalty, and just in her dealings with everyone she received in this room.

It was here that ladies and gentlemen could watch the court in action and see royalty going about its business, such as receiving deputations. Charles II specified that entry to his and his queen's Presence Chambers was limited to 'persons or gentlemen of quality and good fortune' and 'all wives and daughters of the nobles, and their women that attend them…and all other ladies of good rank and quality, but not their servants'.

The Queen's Presence Chamber was guarded by gentlemen ushers, who would eject anyone who misbehaved. They also controlled entry into the next room, the Queen's Privy Chamber. Anyone permitted to cross the threshold of this room had received a privilege available only to the elite of the land.

Again, the character of the events that took place in the Queen's Privy Chamber is reflected in the subject matter of Verrio's ceiling painting. It shows the queen in a chariot drawn by swans towards a temple of virtue. All around are pastoral scenes, so the message is that the queen is virtuous and innocent in her dealings, an embodiment of benign nature itself.

Above: The Upper Ward, with St George's Hall on the left. The elevations were mostly transformed from the 1820s to the designs of Wyatville.

The next room in the sequence was the Queen's Gallery or Ballroom, now much altered. Then came the Queen's Drawing Room, where courtiers and 'people of quality' would assemble each morning to greet the queen when she was at Windsor. From here the holy of holies was approached – the Queen's Bedchamber and Closet. Right of access to the bedchamber was strictly limited to the highest in the land. In the case of the king, whose own Great Bedchamber was located four rooms away from the queen's, those with right of entry included the Lord Steward, the Lord Chamberlain, secretaries of state and the rest of the Lords and Privy Council.

But it is highly unlikely that the king or queen actually slept in these bedchambers: they were really rooms of state. In fact, where the king and queen slept is something of a mystery. The king might have slept in his Little Bedchamber, a more private dressing room that adjoined his Great Bedchamber. More to the point, the king's apartments had a backstairs – and backstairs played an essential role in the private and political life of the court. They permitted people to enter the king's apartments in secrecy and with great discretion, hence the term 'backstairs intrigue'. These meetings could be political or

Above: The Queen's Presence Chamber, created in the 1670s by Hugh May, with a painted ceiling by Verrio.

amorous, and they probably took place in the closet or cabinet that adjoined the king's Little Bedchamber. The closet was the most private room in the apartment, where not even princes of the blood had automatic right of access.

While backstairs allowed privileged visitors to come and go discreetly, they afforded the king the same advantage. At one time Charles II's mistress, the Duchess of Portsmouth, had a bedroom at Windsor reached directly by the king's backstairs. Nell Gwyn, the mother of two royal bastards, was lodged in Burford House, just outside the castle walls, and the backstairs allowed the king to visit her most discreetly.

In addition to the king's and queen's chambers, the new apartments in the Upper Ward contained two spectacular state rooms that, in their scale and decoration, were comparable to the great baroque interiors of Europe. There was the Chapel Royal, with its vast painted ceiling and splendid, if illusionary, monumental architecture, and then there was St George's Hall. Both of these were created within the chapel and the great hall of Edward III's palace. Charles II's St George's Hall was the climax of baroque Windsor. In fact, it was one of the great rooms of the world. William Pyne in 1724 called it 'one of the most spacious and magnificent apartments in Europe'.[7] Within the splendour of the remade St George's Hall Charles dined and gave receptions in a style worthy of a prince of absolute power.

The works to the castle were to have included an elaborate mausoleum for Charles I that, with an appropriate funeral procession, was to cost £70,000. In 1678 Parliament granted Charles II the money to rebury his father with the pomp

and ritual denied in 1649. He took the money – and kept it. Charles I never did get his funeral procession or monument, and his body still lies where it was placed in haste one cold and sad February evening.

With Charles II's own death in 1685, Windsor Castle's star went once more into decline.

The Squire of Windsor

The ceremonies and prestige of the Order of the Garter and of St George's Chapel were maintained, but succeeding generations of monarchs preferred not to live in the state apartments at Windsor. The accommodation was majestic enough but seemed increasingly undesirable as tastes changed and standards of comfort and convenience rose during the eighteenth century.

But monarchs had to appear at the castle from time to time and, symptomatically, in the early eighteenth century Queen Anne purchased a comfy little house just outside the walls of the Upper Ward, and stayed there when obliged to be in Windsor. Called Garden House, it became the happy Windsor home of George I and George II.

Meanwhile, the apartments in the castle were left to decay – draughty and musty reminders of the eclipsed Stuart court. The Hanoverian monarchs, troubled as they were by Stuart-led rebellions through the first half of the eighteenth century, no doubt loathed these great rooms with their unsubtle allegorical decoration evoking Stuart glories. They must have seen them as vacuous and vainglorious monuments to years of

posturing and misrule. But such was their lack of interest in Windsor that the early Hanoverian monarchs didn't even bother to have this Stuart propaganda removed.

Things changed for the better after George III came to the throne in 1760. He, and more particularly his wife, Queen Charlotte, grew increasingly fond of their rambling and ramshackle castle. The artistic tastes of the time favoured the romantic and the picturesque. While mock medieval castles and gimcrack neo-Gothick pretend-priories were rising around the land, the king and queen found themselves the happy possessors of one of the great and genuine medieval monuments of Europe – perhaps even the home of King Arthur. As with earlier dynasties, owning the castle gave the Hanoverians a pedigree. It was a noble possession, a badge of

hereditary legitimacy, a thing of ancient beauty. But it was still uninhabitable.

George gave Charlotte Garden House in 1776, and then enlarged it, probably to his own designs with architect Sir William Chambers, so that the ever-growing royal family could recline in comfort in their convenient modern home and contemplate the mighty castle only a few steps away.

In Windsor the king and his family cultivated charmingly suburban manners. George's ill-tempered intolerance and dictatorial attitudes may have contributed to the alienation and eventual loss of the American colonies, but at Windsor his relations with his fellow citizens were

Above: St George's Hall, created in the 1670s by May and Verrio, as it appeared in 1819.
Opposite: George III and his family parading with local worthies on the South Terrace of Windsor Castle in the 1780s.

positively democratic. He was, when acting in his private capacity, merely a local gentleman and head of a family. He and his wife, Mr and Mrs King, were remarkably free and open with their neighbours. The king would saunter around the town and pop into the shops.

The good-spirited George would often watch the town boys playing cricket in the royal park. As Charles Knight, the son of a Windsor shopkeeper, later wrote: '…many a time had he bidden us good morning, when…he was returning from his dairy to his eight o'clock breakfast. Everyone knew that most respectable and amiable of country squires, and His Majesty knew everyone.'[8] There were few places in the town, recalled Knight, 'in which strangers or neighbours might not gaze upon…or jostle' the king and his family.

The king made much of the castle available to the curious public. The Lower Ward became virtually the town square, where, among other things, the inhabitants of Windsor grew accustomed to celebrate Bonfire Night, often in a riotous manner. And when in town the royal family would join the local worthies in their daily promenade up and down the South Terrace, which lay between the walls of the Upper Ward and the Garden House, by now renamed the Queen's Lodge. The Sunday promenade on the South Terrace became something of a national institution. The royal family would be joined by socially ambitious and fashionable families from London and the south-east of England, and all would nod sedately to each other as they paraded up and down, while the band played on the nearby East Terrace.

This pleasant period in the life of the royal family was dogged by the king's bouts of so-called 'madness'. He first became incapacitated in 1788, and was confined for most of the time at the royal palace at Kew, although also at Windsor. Upon returning to good health in 1789, the king put a long-cherished ambition into motion. The royal family would no longer merely enjoy a fine prospect of their fairy castle – they would actually inhabit it.

In 1800 the fashionable country house architect James Wyatt was commissioned by the king to remodel parts of the north and east ranges of the Upper Ward in an attempt to create sets of apartments that were both comfortable and sympathetically Gothic in character. The royal family took up occupation in the winter of 1804, but Wyatt does not seem to have been completely successful in his task, or at least not according to Queen Charlotte, who wrote to her friend Lady Harcourt: 'Not to shock you…with

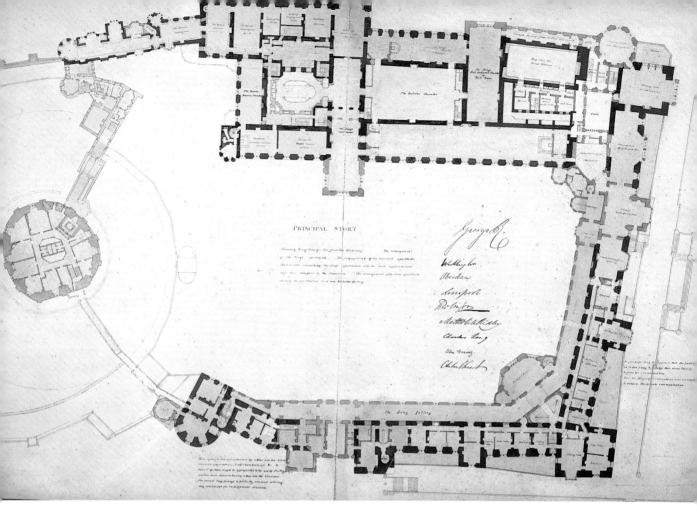

PRINCIPAL STORY

Above: The Upper Ward buildings, at first floor level, as reorganised from the 1820s by Wyatville.

my opinion on this subject I will briefly tell you that I have changed from a very comfortable and warm habitation to the coldest house, rooms and passages that ever existed.'

The best surviving example of Wyatt's Gothic additions is the Grand Vestibule he created in the state apartment on the north side of the Upper Ward. It is a Gothick fantasy, theatrical and far from authentic in feel.

When George III died, his body made the short journey to St George's Chapel, where he was interred in the generous, neo-Gothic ribbed vault that Wyatt had been ordered to create below the Lady Chapel. George, like monarchs before him, had resolved to turn St George's Chapel into a dynastic mausoleum.

Triumph

George IV could easily have hated Windsor Castle. He loved light, bright, fashionable and witty architecture, and Windsor was decidedly old-fashioned and, despite the recent works, gloomy and uncomfortable. In addition, it held painful memories of the father with whom he had fought for so long. He must have wanted to turn his back on the place, even to demolish it. But, despite his many faults, George IV was not a brute and he did not lack a sense of history or wonder. He loved the rambling castle and its romantic Garter rituals, so evocative of the chivalric values of the Middle Ages. In 1824, therefore, it was Windsor that George decided should be made into the new great palace for the monarch. Britain, victor in the Napoleonic Wars and of the decisive Battle of Waterloo, the richest and most powerful country in the world, should house its king in a splendour appropriate to its new status. This is what George and his advisers said, and Parliament agreed. Some £250,000 was voted for the works, which, when completed 15 years later, were to have cost £800,000 – a truly colossal sum.

The proposal was to create accommodation within the Upper Ward that would include a spectacular new state apartment, in which the great and powerful of the world could be received. It would also include new, highly fashionable, comfortable and convenient private rooms. This was to involve the destruction of most of the works by Hugh May and Verrio, and the demolition or restoration of a good deal of what remained of the medieval fabric.

The proposal also envisaged the creation of new rooms within what had been open courts in Edward III's palace. The most impressive of these new rooms was to be dedicated to the Battle of Waterloo and the victory over Napoleon.

In the same way that the Order of the Garter and St George's Chapel commemorated the early victories in the Hundred Years War with France, the Waterloo Chamber, where an annual celebratory dinner was held, acted as a triumphal memorial to the recent victories over France and Napoleon. This military triumphalism was to characterize the new Windsor. A dramatic manifestation of it was the increased importance given to the seventeenth-century Long Walk. George IV swept away the old Queen's Lodge to create a heroic route from the new South Gate of the Upper Ward. Three miles (5 kilometres) long, it cut straight through the park and terminated in

a fantastically overscaled equestrian statue of George III. Known as the 'Copper Horse', the statue was commissioned by George IV, made by Richard Westmacott and erected in 1831. It shows George III as Marcus Aurelius, the epitome of the just ruler. Carved on the base is the unlikely inscription 'to the best of fathers'. This statue, echoing the grandeur of Rome, is one of the most extraordinary works of its age.

Despite such romantic posturing, evoking the glories of past ages, the new palace George created within the ancient walls of Windsor was essentially pioneering – in fact, almost ruthlessly modern.

The remaking of Windsor Castle represents a key moment in the development of domestic and public architecture in Britain. The mastermind behind this transformation was a courtier named Sir Charles Long, the man who had organized George's complex and theatrical coronation. The architect chosen to execute the king's and Long's vision was Sir Jeffrey Wyatville, nephew to James Wyatt and the leading architect to the aristocracy.

During the first decades of the nineteenth century, new ideas about comfort and convenience had been speedily and often experimentally reconciled with older ideas about display and pomp. The Wyatt family was in the forefront of these developments. For example, the cloister-like Gothic corridor added by James Wyatt to the medieval and seventeenth-century Wilton House in Wiltshire between 1801 and 1811 had, at a stroke, made the house comfortable and convenient, removing the need to reach one room by walking through several others.

The early nineteenth-century corridor, conceived as a well-lit gallery for the display of art, as an area for informal gatherings and as a means of connecting rooms in a convenient manner, was the single most important device in the new breed of country house.

The additions and alterations to ancient Belvoir Castle in Leicestershire after 1801 by a whole bevy of Wyatts had shown the Prince of Wales, as George IV then was, the way forward. These works included a new kind of grand interior that helped the prince to see how privacy and informal comfort could be integrated with the formality of state apartments in an old castle.

The prince first tried his hand at the making of a modern country house with the Brighton Pavilion, built to the designs of John Nash in 1815–21. But it is in the Upper Ward at Windsor Castle, in the marriage of the state and private apartments, that this new type of interior is fully realized for the first time. The Upper Ward at Windsor is, in many significant ways, the prototype

for the Victorian, or modern, country house.

In the Upper Ward two worlds had to be integrated: the quasi-public state apartments on the north side, and the private apartments on the east and south sides. And these two worlds are linked by one of the wonders of Windsor – the Grand Corridor. It provides a route to the medieval rooms it adjoins, meaning that all the rooms and apartments can be entered independently rather than by having to pass through one to the other. It also acts as a route for parade, as a gallery for displaying various works of art and furniture, and as a convenient, well-lit and relatively informal sitting area. It is a brilliant solution to a difficult problem, and works on both the functional and aesthetic level.

This grand processional route is echoed by a more mundane but equally vital subterranean tunnel system that supports the life lived in the ornate world above. The tunnels allowed servants

carrying food, fuel or waste to reach various parts of the grand upper world quickly and without being seen en route.

Wyatville also made use of the newest building technology to make sure that the castle was as fireproof as possible. In these tunnels shallow brick arches span between cast-iron beams, and similar, supposedly fireproof materials were used in the construction of the grand rooms above.

The decoration that George chose for the main interiors reflects exactly the exquisite and eclectic tastes of the time in which Greek, Roman, Renaissance and even Gothic are happily mixed and playfully juxtaposed. These interiors were created partly by Wyatville, but mostly by firms of decorators and furniture-makers, notably Morel and Seddon, working very closely with the prince and his advisers.

The main state apartments, including the Waterloo Chamber, the Grand Reception Room and St George's Hall, are divided from the private apartments by several rooms that acted as both private drawing rooms and more intimate state entertaining rooms as occasion demanded. These are the Crimson Drawing Room, the Green Drawing Room and the White Drawing Room, and they epitomize George IV's taste – a French-influenced classical mix, with lots of Greek and a little Egyptian, that has become known as the Regency style.

By way of contrast, George chose Gothic style for the dining room – a decision that probably

dismayed the architect Wyatville, who was not known for his love of the medieval. The sideboards and side tables were designed in 1827 by the 15-year-old Augustus Pugin, who was later to pioneer the revival of authentically built and detailed Gothic architecture in Britain.

St George's Hall was the focus of George IV's reconstruction of the Upper Ward. It was created by ripping out May and Verrio's work and by knocking through the old St George's Hall and the adjoining Chapel Royal to form one massive space 180 feet (54 metres) long. As in Charles II's day, the hall was the great room of state, but more than that – especially in its neo-Tudor Gothic decorative scheme – it was dedicated to the rituals and symbols of the Order of the Garter.

George also made use of Windsor Great Park. While his father had built model farms and sensible houses for workers, he built fantasies.

Above: The Green Drawing Room, one of George IV's more exquisite and intimate additions to the castle.
Opposite: Wyatville's Grand Corridor wraps round the rooms on the east and south sides of the Upper Ward.

His most exotic creation was at Virginia Water, the mighty lake within the park. It is an extraordinary place, created for George by Wyatville, using Roman period columns, capitals and pedestals from the ruins of Leptis Magna, a gift from the Bashaw of Tripoli to George III.

George IV did not live to enjoy the lavish rooms he had commissioned for Windsor Castle, and when they were at last ready for occupation they were to serve a very different style of court and monarchy.

George's younger brother, William IV, presided over perhaps the dullest court in English history, and spent much of his time in a somnambulant reverie at Windsor. Life in the gorgeous and fashionable Crimson Drawing Room was definitely not as its sophisticated designers had envisaged.

William's successor, Victoria, had bad memories of Windsor. It was a sprawling and gloomy place haunted, for her, by unpleasant associations. She remembered the arguments between her uncle, William IV, and her mother, and she must have reflected upon the dismal last decade of her grandfather, George III, whose unhappy presence must still have haunted the apartment in which he had been confined during his last illness.

But all this changed in 1839.

The Heart of Empire

It was at the head of the Sovereign's Staircase, leading up to the Grand Corridor, that on 10 October 1839 Victoria resolved that Albert was the man for her. She had met him in 1836 and recorded a favourable impression in her journal. Albert was, she wrote, 'extremely handsome… has a beautiful nose and very sweet mouth and fine teeth… full of goodness and sweetness, and very clever and intelligent'.[9] Despite reading rather like a description of a fine horse, these sentiments reveal that Victoria was already starting to fall for the man. Just over three years later, she saw Albert again as he ascended the Windsor staircase. She wrote in her journal: 'It was with some emotion that I beheld Albert – who is beautiful.' Five days later, while still at Windsor, Victoria sent for Albert: '…he came to the closet where I was alone, and after a few minutes I said to him, that I thought he must be aware why I wished [him] to come here, and that it would make me too happy if he would consent to what I wished… We embraced each other over and over again, and he was so kind.'[10]

From being a sort of purgatory for Victoria, Windsor became an earthly paradise, the ultimate royal refuge. It was, once again, the monarch's fairy castle. But although Victoria and Albert loved Windsor, it never really became the family home. They built Osborne House on the Isle of Wight and Balmoral in Scotland as their private homes in which they could lead the grand and secluded life of great landowners.

Windsor was the queen's official residence and as such played a key role in affairs of state. It was in the apartments in the Upper Ward that many ideas evolved and were developed about the role a constitutional monarchy should play in the mechanism of a modern state. For example, the notion of formal and highly ritualized state visits, used to cement political relationships between Great Britain and foreign governments, first took root here during the 1840s. Before that time, monarchs had generally stayed at home, or visited the palaces of other monarchs only as prisoners or by accident.

But everything changed after the French Revolution and the Napoleonic Wars, which either toppled monarchs or obliged them to adopt a more mobile frame of mind as they got into the habit of fleeing bloodthirsty republics. The most dramatic of the early state visits to Windsor came in 1855 and was, as all present perceived, an eerie interlude in England's centuries-old struggle with France which many at the time believed would soon resume.

The visitor was Napoleon III, the Emperor of France and nephew of the great Napoleon Bonaparte. Victoria received him and his wife, the Empress Eugénie, for a state ball with supper in St George's Hall. With admirable tact, the Waterloo Chamber was temporarily renamed the Music Room. Distant as Napoleon III's relationship was with the 'Bogey Man', it was enough to make Victoria nervous. When she eventually danced with the emperor, Victoria was very excited. 'To think,' she later wrote in her journal, that 'the granddaughter of George III, should dance with the Emperor Napoleon, nephew to our great enemy…in the Waterloo Room too.'[11] Prince Albert merely observed that precautions were being taken in the Royal Crypt to prevent George III turning in his grave.

This happy world came to a frightful end for Victoria in December 1861. Albert died of typhoid fever in his bedroom off the Grand Corridor in Windsor, only yards from the scene of his fateful meeting with her 22 years earlier.

Victoria's grief was overwhelming. Death and mourning now became the keynote of life at Windsor. Victoria had the room in which Albert died photographed so that it could be preserved exactly as it was at the moment of his death. At her command, a memorandum was issued by the Lord Chamberlain ordering that the room 'should remain in its present state and not be made use of in the future'. Albert's dressing gown and fresh clothes were to be laid out on his bed each evening, and a jug of steaming hot water placed on the washstand. His pen and writing pad lay open on his desk, as if he were to appear and start writing, and guests were required to write their names in his visitor's book. 'Calling on a dead man,' as Disraeli put it.

Victoria's behaviour set the tone for decades to come. A morbid fascination with the paraphernalia of death and with the rites and rituals of burial characterized the age. Her uncontrolled indulgence in grief provided a most respectable model for her subjects to follow, and follow it they did. The Victorian cult of death remains one of the most curious and puzzling phenomena in Britain's history. It influenced dress – widow's weeds became essential fashion items – and created an entire industry focused on funerals, monuments and mourning.

At Windsor the new cult of death was expressed in a most dramatic form. The late fifteenth-century Lady Chapel at the east end of St George's Chapel was transformed into a memorial to Albert. It became the very epicentre of the Victorian cult of death. Renamed the Albert Chapel, it was embellished by George

Designed by Alfred Gilbert, it has a smouldering, bizarre sexuality. It is as if death is the ultimate excitement – the moment of final, tumescent climax when all passion is spent, when the tortured soul is set free, a moment of blessed liberty and release.

Victoria's prolonged seclusion after Albert's death, when she became known disparagingly as the 'Widow of Windsor', may have launched a thousand funeral businesses, but it also made her increasingly unpopular. By refusing to undertake any public duties she seemed, to many, simply to be failing to do her job. Even when her own son Prince Albert Edward was married in St George's Chapel in March 1863, Victoria was only glimpsed, hidden in the first-floor and very private royal pew. In her journal she explained her strange conduct and revealed her emotions on that wedding day: 'Oh! What I suffered in the chapel, where all that was joy, pride, and happiness on January 25th, '58 [when the Princess Royal was married at St James's] was repeated without the principal figure at all, the guardian angel of the family, being there. It was indescribable. At one moment, when…the flourish of trumpets…brought back to my mind my whole life of twenty years at his dear side, safe, proud, secure, and happy, I felt as if I should faint.'[12]

Gradually, Victoria re-entered public life. She, and the Empire, finally weathered the emotional storm. But given the obsessive nature of her grief, it is perhaps predictable that Victoria's only significant contribution to Windsor is the architecture of death – the interior of the Albert Chapel and the Frogmore Mausoleum. Strangely

Gilbert Scott for Victoria between 1863 and 1873 in a polychromatic High Gothic manner to house the tombs and memorials of her lost loved ones. First and foremost is the cenotaph to Albert, which shows him clad as a medieval Garter Knight, while on the plinth on which he lies is a miniature statue of Victoria praying and weeping in perpetual grief.

The most astonishing monument is that to Victoria's grandson, the Duke of Clarence.

enough, as early as 1843 Victoria and Albert had talked of building a mausoleum for themselves, and only four days after Albert's death Victoria set the plan in motion. The mausoleum is a curious building in the thirteenth-century Italian style as seen by German architects in the nineteenth century, and realized in the leafy setting of Windsor park. Inside lie the bodies of Albert and Victoria, with their memorial showing them forever locked in cold, white marble intimacy.

Windsor today is where the royal family still chooses to build its tombs and bury its dead. It is the one way they can leave their mark on a place where new building has become virtually impossible. When fire swept through the state apartments in the Upper Ward in 1992, some argued that here was an opportunity for a radical modern design, particularly of the gutted St George's Hall. There is no doubt that this is what former monarchs in earlier ages would have done. Charles II swept away Edward III's great hall to realize his baroque vision, only to have his spectacular rebuild swept away by George IV. But what was eventually decided upon was a compromise. St George's Hall was not faithfully restored to its appearance before the fire, nor is it a daring example of contemporary design. It is safe and traditional, with a beautiful new oak roof that has little to do with Wyatville's roof and looks as if it were designed 600 years ago.

This caution and conservatism should come as no surprise. The days of Windsor Castle as a royal plaything are gone for ever: no longer is it a stage set to be put up or pulled down in pursuit of a monarch's dream. There is a sense now that the nation, as much as the royal family, owns the castle, and the nation does not want it changed. History, for this House of Windsor at least, is over.

Opposite: Inside the Albert Memorial Chapel – the epicentre of the Victorian cult of death.
Right: St George's Hall as reconstructed after the 1992 fire. Wyatville's work has been restored with the addition of a newly designed oak-built hammer beam roof.

Holyroodhouse

The story of Holyroodhouse is closely bound to the formation and fate of Scotland. As with Windsor Castle, Holyroodhouse, in the Scottish capital city Edinburgh, has provided a stage on which many dramas of state have been played out. Kings and queens of Scotland have been born, crowned, married and died there, and architecturally it is a patchwork of styles, reflecting the aspirations and personalities of monarchs stretching back over several centuries. In its current manifestation it is the Queen's official residence in Scotland.

In its first incarnation, the palace of Holyroodhouse embodied the rivalry between England and Scotland. It was built by James IV to receive his Tudor bride, Henry VII's daughter Margaret, in 1503, in an ostentatious display of power and wealth. This subtext of conspicuous consumption is the strand that binds each major phase of rebuilding at Holyrood as successive monarchs have brought their own identity to the palace, while positioning it firmly at the head of a 'Nation to Be Reckoned With'.

The fluctuating fortunes of the palace hold up a mirror to the strength and pride of a nation through the ages. In its sixteenth-century heyday, before Crown or legislative union, it was a true powerhouse. It was a permanent royal residence and also the heart of Scottish government, as it accommodated the main ruling body, the Privy Council.

As such, however, it suffered heavily in the late medieval political intrigues, and it was not spared in the revengeful attacks by the English in 1544 following the 'revolt of

Arran'. The palace and abbey were sacked and burnt, along with Edinburgh town, to 'deface it as to leave a memory for ever of the vengeance of God upon their falsehood and disloyalty'. However, Holyroodhouse rose again to receive Mary, Queen of Scots in 1561, forming the eye of the cyclone for six turbulent years, during which time it became soiled by the blood of her secretary's murder, plotted by her weak and jealous husband, Lord Darnley.

When her son, James VI, realized his highest desire – to ascend the throne of England – Holyroodhouse was largely abandoned, as a succession of monarchs chose to live and rule south of the border, and for many years it was largely retired from royal life. It was lavishly restored by Charles II in the 1670s, to become once again the jewel in Scotland's crown, but its fortunes again declined. It was, by turn, ignored then made the focus of ill-judged attention as it became synonymous with both religious divide and political struggle. The fate of the nation was hotly debated at Holyrood as the Bill of Union subsumed Scotland into an English-dominated Great Britain at the start of the eighteenth century. A generation later Scotland's 'last best hope', Bonnie Prince Charlie, captured Edinburgh and set up court for seven glorious weeks at Holyrood, that potent symbol of Stuart monarchy, only to ride out into the darkness, never to return.

As though somehow intertwined with the fate of the Stuarts, the decaying palace was accorded the unsavoury status of debtor's sanctuary, and then became a safe haven for the French nobility during the French Revolution – an ironic commentary on the final years of the Young Pretender in exile on the Continent. It was only when George IV ascended the throne in 1820 that its significance was once again fully appreciated, and the ancient walls began to receive the attention and respect they so richly deserved.

Origins

The palace has its origins in an Augustinian abbey founded by the 'chaste' and 'humble' David I in 1128. One of three abbeys to have been established in Scotland that year, its foundation was said have been an apology for a day's illicit hunting by King David on Holy Rude Day – the feast of the Exaltation of the Cross (14 September). The legend, which is almost certainly not contemporary with the founding of the abbey, had passed into the collective consciousness by the reign of James I (1406–37), when the Holyrood convent seal featured a stag's head supporting a cross between the antlers. This is still the symbol of the palace of Holyroodhouse.

In the years following 1128 the abbey thrived and at the end of the twelfth century it devoted its wealth to an ambitious building programme. It became a grand Romanesque building, of which only a doorway at the south-east angle of the present ruin remains. Its early history is shrouded in mystery, though the scanty abbey records provide a tantalizing glimpse of what life within its environs would have been like.

Previous page: Entrance elevation of Holyroodhouse with the seventeenth-century entrance screen and tower in the foreground. The Great West Tower is in the distance.
Opposite: The abbey ruins.

The abbey was inextricably linked to royalty from the very beginning. In medieval times throughout Europe there was a great tradition of kings sojourning within monastic walls, possibly because these would have been the only institutions large enough to accommodate a sizeable itinerant court. Despite the honour of receiving a king, it must have placed a huge strain on the abbot, and thrown the daily life of the monastery into disarray, for when the king travelled, he took with him as much of his court as he deemed necessary to his comfort – perhaps a hundred or more people and their animals, plus possessions such as silver and tapestries. The monks were expected to lead an ascetic and humble life of prayer and devotion, and one can only imagine the disruption caused by a rumbustious court seeking the best food, wine and entertainment.

There is some evidence that even prior to the building of the palace in the sixteenth century, the king would have enjoyed his own personal accommodation at Holyrood, separate from the abbey lodgings. In 1329, during the reign of Robert I, Exchequer grants for wine and kitchen utensils suggest that Holyrood was already a royal residence as well as an abbey. The relationship between Holyrood and the Crown, which was always close, burgeoned with the nomination of Edinburgh as the chief Scottish burgh in 1452, and the need for separate royal lodgings must have become especially pressing as royal visits increased in both frequency and duration. The Stuart king James II was born within the abbey walls in 1426, crowned there in 1437, married there in 1449 and buried there in 1460. Although there is no clear indication of where his quarters at Holyrood were situated, or how they would have appeared, there is evidence to suggest that purpose-built rooms existed at least from 1449, when the Exchequer rolls record that building materials were brought to Holyrood '*ad fabricam regis*' (for the royal construction); and in 1473 the Exchequer recorded payment of a glasswright for repairs to a window in the 'Queinis chalmire' (Queen's chamber).

At first sight, Holyrood appears to be an unusual choice for the site of a medieval royal guest house. Edinburgh Castle, with its solid bulwark of defences, would seem to have been a more appropriate choice. However, the castle's elevated position evidently had its drawbacks, as one bishop was driven to describe it as 'windy and richt unpleasand'. Furthermore, the very nature of the legend accompanying the foundation of the abbey, and the features of the abbey seal, suggest that a major attraction of Holyrood was the parkland, rich with sport. While the abbey did not perhaps occupy the best position defensively, it at least offered the benefit of an entire cloister of monks to pray for one's soul, should the worst come to the worst; and its close proximity to the 'Drumselch', or hunting hill, must surely have made it especially attractive.

The tradition of the royal hunting lodge has a rich heritage on both sides of the Scottish border, and few pastimes would have compared to the physical and mental challenge of the chase. The requirements for a good day's hunting were simple, and with Scotland's wild and dramatic scenery and richly stocked parkland, this is one occupation in which the Scottish nobility could equal if not exceed the English in the quality of their pastime.

Building an Image

Residentially, however, 'keeping up with the Tudors' proved far more problematic. At the start of the sixteenth century, when James IV was betrothed to Margaret Tudor, the manner in which he would marry and keep his young bride became a matter of personal and national pride. It was crucial to emulate, if not surpass, the opulence of high society south of the border, and it seemed entirely logical to situate the Stuart court in the burgh recently deemed the capital of Scotland – Edinburgh. However, the castle offered only the most basic accommodation, and as a symbol of power and nobility, a guest house attached to an abbey would have been wholly inadequate.

James IV therefore began the programme of building that would see the secular royal buildings encroach upon and finally supersede the monastery that had provided their foundation. He essentially converted the royal lodging into what was described in a document of 1503 as 'the kings palace near the abbey of Holyrood', and in 1513 as the palace of Edinburgh. Building work did not begin until October 1501, and as the marriage was due to take place in 1503 the whole scheme had to be completed within two years – a scant amount of time in which to plan, design and build a grand royal status symbol.

There has been some dispute as to the extent of the work he carried out, some attributing the surviving Great West Tower to him, and some crediting his son James V with its creation. Certainly, the relatively small amount of money spent on James IV's building programme would appear inadequate to cover an ambitious project such as the tower, and it is much more likely that it is of later construction. What is clearer is that James IV was responsible for the building of a chapel, gallery, royal apartments and gatehouse in a quadrangular plan west of the abbey cloister, a position suggested by the earliest representations of Holyroodhouse, such as the 'English Spy' drawing of 1544 and Gordon of Rothiemay's 'bird's eye' view of 1647.

The work was undertaken by a variety of craftsmen, including carpenters, glaziers and masons, under the superintendence of a master of works who was responsible for planning and carrying out all the operations on site and paying all the workmen. The Treasurer's accounts, a contemporary source, reveal this man to have been one Leonard Logie, who eventually received £40 Scots (about £3 sterling) as reward for 'his deligent and grete laboure made by him in the building of the Palace beside the Abbay of the Holy Croce'.[1] Walter Merlioun, the king's master mason, built the 'Foirwerk' (gatehouse) and the 'New Hall' (chapel), while a man called William Turnbull built the 'Gallory' and Michael Wright (probably a wright by trade as well as by name) was responsible for building and fitting out the Queen's Great Chamber, for which vast quantities of wood, glass and plaster were imported.

Despite the timescale, most of the work was completed on time, although the all-important blazoning of the royal arms on the gatehouse was completed just as Margaret was crossing the Scottish border in the last days of July 1503. In all, the accounts record an expenditure of approximately £3800 Scots (£320 sterling) on the work, excluding decorations, which seems

inexpensive in comparison to the £6125 Scots (£510 sterling) spent on the week-long nuptials celebrated there.

Following the entries in the Treasurer's accounts for 'bigging' (building) are those for furnishing the interior of the new palace and clothing the king. As only the very best and most ostentatious would do, many of the materials appear to have been imported from Flanders, which was the height of fashion in the early sixteenth century. The orders included '35 tymir of ermine' (one tymir being 40 skins)[2] and five 'chairs of estate' (described at length), to be covered in gold cloth and velvet, with wood and iron details, fringing and ribbons.[3] There are also transactions recorded with an Edinburgh merchant called James Homyll, who imported furniture 'furth of Flandrez'.[4]

King James was obviously determined that his queen should lay down her head in comfort, as her chamber was to be hung with red and purple-blue velvet, costing approximately £340 Scots (£30 sterling), and her 'bed of state' was covered with a 'cloth of gold' costing the princely sum of £386 Scots (£32 sterling).

It is fortunate that an account of the prestigious wedding, which took place in August 1503, has survived in the form of a report made by a herald, John Young, who came north of the border in Margaret's train. From Young's account we can catch a glimpse of the celebrations, which comprised seven days of music, feasting and jousts. King James received his English guests,

Above: Aerial view of Holyroodhouse in the context of Edinburgh.

seating the Archbishop of York on his right hand and the Earl of Surrey on his left, 'So that it was a noble thing to see the said chamber so nobly furnished'. From this minutely detailed account, we can also recreate certain elements of the palace furnishings. We know, for example, that the Great Chamber was hung with a tapestry representing 'the ystory of Troy towne', the King's Chamber was 'haunged about with the story of Hercules, togeder with other ystorys', the King's Hall was 'haunged of the ystory of old Troy', and the tapestry hangings on the walls of a fifth room depicted the exploits of Hercules.

It must be assumed that James IV succeeded in providing the luxury to which his young bride had become accustomed, for very little building took place after the wedding. However, as an intriguing footnote to his architectural achievements, the king took the unusual step of enriching his palace with a lion complete with its own personal keeper. Although it is impossible to tell where the lion originated, the accounts list payment to 'the man that brocht the lioun to the King…for bering of the lioun in his cradill fra Leith to the Abbay' and also payment to 'Andro Broun that kepis the lioun in the Abbay'.[5] Evidently, the unfortunate creature either managed to adapt to its chilly new environment, or a successor was found to replace it, because in 1513 payment was made for work on the lion house, which suggests that the unusual pet was by then a permanent feature at Holyrood: 'to Schir Johne Sharpe, to pay for…maissone feis one the lione house, and all utheris expesis maid be him one all werkis within the Palace of the Abbay gardingis.'[6]

From Palace to Fortress

For much of his reign, James IV presided over comparative peace, both at home and abroad, but it was not to last, and he died fighting the old enemy – outsmarted by the Earl of Surrey's troops at the Battle of Flodden in 1513. He left an 18-month-old heir, and the Duke of Albany took up residence in Holyroodhouse as regent to the boy king. When James V began his personal rule in 1528 aged 16, it was a time of growing civil and religious unrest, and seething unsettled scores with the English. He must have anticipated the need for a place of greater fortification at the royal palace, and in 1529 he began a building project, the principal result of his efforts being the surviving Great West Tower.

The tower, which hardly sounds a comfortable place, was built with local stone walls, 7 feet (2.1 metres) thick, gun ports at ground-floor level, and windows (since enlarged) all barred with iron. The building also appears to have been approached by a drawbridge: 'received from William Hyll, this 12th day of February, a great Iron gate, for the principal entrance, and drawbridge of the new Tower, with two great bolts for the closing of the slot of the said iron gate and the great bar of the same'.[7] This suggests that the tower was originally at least partially moated. As an ornamental touch, the turrets were completed with finials in the form of lions and miniature turrets, all brightly painted and gilded. The total cost of the work, which took place between 1529 and 1532, amounted to over £4500 Scots (£375 sterling), almost a quarter more than James IV devoted to the building of an entire palace.

The tower, which still dominates the palace frontage, is of great architectural interest, and its design reconciles influences from both James's great ally, the French, and his rival, the English, while remaining a unique example of its type. In the late medieval period there was a trend throughout Europe to build conspicuous towers to adorn the façades of castles and palaces, as a bold statement of the eminence and wealth of the owner. Thus, similarities can be seen between the Holyrood tower and that of Tattershall Castle, Lincolnshire (1430–5) and Raglan Castle, Monmouthshire (1430–60). However, the Holyrood tower is perhaps more closely aligned to certain prominent French examples, such as the Château of Vincennes (1365–73). The scale of the fortifications, and the means by which entry to the rest of the palace from the tower could be strictly controlled, is more original, possibly being

an innovation of the king working in conjunction with his master masons, John Ayton and John Brownhill.

In 1535, after the first phase of building, James sailed to France and married Madelaine, the daughter of Francis I, in Paris on 1 January 1536. The couple returned to Scotland in May, where, according to a contemporary chronicler, Queen Madelaine enchanted the Scots with her 'loving countenance and comlie behaviour', but her enjoyment of her new home was to be short-lived, as she died within 40 days of landing at Leith.

Holyroodhouse was now the main palace in Scotland, and, as such, it was not long before

Above: Holyroodhouse as shown in 1544 'English Spy' drawing.
Opposite: View after Gordon of Rothiemay's 1649 perspective of Holyroodhouse.

James V, poor health notwithstanding, began the second phase of enlarging it. Like his father before him, he may well have been preparing to impress a prospective bride. If this is the case, however, once again the 'poor relation' did not miss the opportunity of producing a conspicuous status symbol in the style of, but rather greater than, something produced south of the border. As can be seen from Gordon of Rothiemay's drawing of 1649 (below), the large expanses of glazing and cresting in the sixteenth-century Holyroodhouse draw heavily on the design of Tudor buildings, such as the palaces at Richmond and Hampton Court.

Between 1535 and 1537 the master of works' accounts show that James V spent over £5760 Scots (£480 sterling) on 'biging [building] of the new foir werk [gatehouse], reforming and beting [improving] of the remanent of the Palace of

Holyrood House, with the great foir hous, gardens, dykes [walls], biging and repairing'.[8] This is the largest amount of money spent on any of the three phases of building in the sixteenth century, and for it the king received a palace of the highest quality and fashion. Not only was the house remodelled and a new porch or gatehouse added to the forecourt, but the gardens were now laid out and enclosed within walls, creating the more cultivated air of a stately home. The palace also became strictly self-sufficient at this point, distancing itself completely from the abbey with the erection of a chapel within the palace quadrangle.

The best representations of the early palace remain the drawings of Gordon of Rothiemay, and the 1544 'English Spy' drawing (although it is difficult to discern any level of detail from the latter). What we can see, however, is in sharp

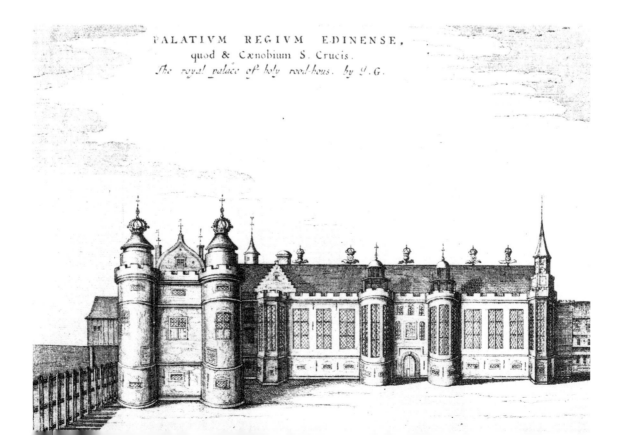

PALATIVM REGIVM EDINENSE,
quod & Cænobium S. Crucis.
The royal palace of holy roodhous. by J.G.

contrast to the type of dwelling inhabited by the ordinary sixteenth-century Scots family. Scotland in this era was a relatively primitive country, with little industry compared to its English neighbour. It relied mainly upon very basic agricultural methods, which left food production at the mercy of the elements. Money was scarce, and the greater proportion of society comprised cottars or peasants, who farmed small areas of land tied to their dwellings. They also worked for the tenant farmer, who in turn rented land from the baron, a representative of a greater laird, or sometimes even the Crown.

The country people of Scotland occupied modest houses made from materials available locally, and the general arrangement of their homes varied little. Houses were generally supported by floor to ceiling beams called 'cruck timbers': if the family moved, then the crucks went too, leaving the walls of the house to crumble into the ground. Walls were constructed from turf, rough stones, and wattle and daub (a twig and clay paste). The houses were low, virtually windowless, and consisted of a single smoky living room for up to three generations of one family. Sharing the same roof space as this room was the byre or stable for the precious cattle on which the family relied, and, for the sake of convenience, the dung heap was likely to be situated close by the front door. It is equally likely that the family washtub – a large container of stale urine rather than the washing vessel that the name suggests – would be close by. (Urine was an essential aid in the preparation of cloth.) Such was the harsh reality of life for many of the king's subjects.

Troubled Neighbours

With his palace complete, the widowed James V turned his thoughts to finding a suitable bride. Once again he sought her out in France, much to the dismay of his uncle, Henry VIII of England. Henry would not tolerate any challenge to his authority, and with James V evading his requests for a meeting, he viewed Scotland as something of a 'loose cannon' from which an invasion could easily be launched against England. Despite Henry's disapproval, James V married Mary de Guise, the wealthy widow of the first Duke of Lorraine, in 1538. The new queen was crowned at Holyrood the following year. Their marriage cannot have been entirely happy, as the couple suffered the loss of their twin boys within two days of each other, and by 1540 the disease that was to claim James's life was taking hold. In 1542 the king 'tunit his bak into the lordis and his face into the wall', leaving as his successor a five-day-old girl, Mary Stuart, who would become the most notorious of Scottish monarchs – Mary, Queen of Scots.

The death of James V set off a chain reaction of power struggles among the Scottish nobility. The task of maintaining government during a royal minority was daunting, as it became evident that the aristocracy was split into two rival factions – the pro-French and Catholic group who rallied around the Queen Mother, Mary de Guise, and the pro-English and ultimately Protestant group, initially led by the Earl of Lennox. Henry VIII, meanwhile, craved neither the Catholic nor the Lutheran, but desired a reformed Scottish Church based on the model he had created in England, setting his sights once again on dynastic union. He lost no time in betrothing his son, Prince Edward of England, to the child Queen Mary. State papers record that this was 'solemnly done at the High Mass, and solemnly sung…in the Abbey church of the Holyroodhouse'.

Religious battle lines were being drawn. In the following years, Scotland was to become deeply insecure, both in terms of religion and politics. In turn, that great symbol of the Catholic Stuart line, Holyroodhouse, enjoyed a heyday of only seven short years before both it and the attached monastery fell victim to the turbulence of the times. The betrothal celebrated at High Mass in the abbey church of Holyroodhouse was ultimately to seal its destruction. The royal union between Scotland and England, so contrary to the true inclination of most Scots, was withdrawn in the 'revolt of Arran', which precipitated Henry's vengeful strike of 1544. The Earl of Hertford and his men were instructed to 'burn Edinburgh town, and so deface it as to leave a memory for ever of the vengeance of God upon their falsehood and disloyalty'.[9] The same source records that 'Also we burned the Abbey called Holy Rood House and the Palace adjoining to the same'.[10]

The monastery was pillaged and burnt, and although the church of the abbey was patched up within a year, the monastery was never restored. Thus suppressed, and with the monks driven out never to return, the assets of the monastery were secularized to the Crown and then made a lordship for one of Queen Mary's half-brothers, Lord Robert Stuart. The abbey suffered yet further physical damage in September 1547 when the English again occupied Edinburgh. Sir Walter Bonham and Edward Chamberlayne were granted a somewhat unnecessary licence to repress 'Hollyroode Abbey'. They arrived to find the buildings empty, so they compensated themselves for their time and effort by stripping the lead from the church and most of the lodgings, and taking down two bells.[11]

The palace, locked and guarded by 'men-of-war', was deserted by the court for 10 years. Although it is difficult to assess the level of damage sustained by the palace in the 1544 raid, it cannot have been rendered entirely uninhabitable as the Treasurer's accounts record that a parliament was planned there only months later.[12] What is clear, however, is that before Holyrood Palace was deemed fit to receive Mary de Guise when she was appointed regent in 1554, a further programme of restoration was undertaken by Sir William Macdowell, then master of works, who was paid £1796 16s 2d (£150 sterling) for his trouble. The abbey church, which was also restored, was subsequently assigned to the burgh of the Canongate as its local parish church, while the palace, as restored by Mary de Guise, became the house in which Mary, Queen of Scots lived during the years she reigned in Scotland.

Throughout her regency Mary de Guise fought against the reforming tide, raising armies from France and Italy to rally to her cause. Protestant armies gathered force, however, and eventually forced a victory with help from the English, which culminated in the Treaty of Leith in 1560, abolishing the Roman Catholic Church in Scotland. In that year Mary de Guise died, and within a year her daughter, Mary, returned to Scotland from France, where she had been raised from early childhood. She had ascended to the highest echelons of the French court, marrying the dauphin, later Francis II, and thus ruling as queen for several years. However, she left France as a widow, and upon her arrival in Scotland, she was greeted by a country in the throes of massive religious and political upheaval.

Mary, Queen of Scots

In many ways, the fame of Mary, Queen of Scots far outweighs the influence of her reign. She ruled for only six years, during which the Reformation continued to evolve without royal support, yet largely unchecked. Mary herself was a Catholic, but on the advice of her ministers she did not attempt to influence the rising Protestant trend, and tactfully continued to worship as a Catholic privately. In many ways she entered Scotland as a figurehead of times past – of a religion and dynastic house that were rapidly becoming obsolete. It is therefore ironic that she lived in a palace conjoined to a decaying monastery. The force of her personality, her lurid adventures, troubled marriages and her ghastly fate, all interesting in their own right, have made her Scotland's best-known monarch, and she lived through many of her best and worst times within the walls of Holyroodhouse.

Mary Stuart arrived in Scotland in August 1561, and immediately took up residence in the palace built by her grandfather. As the widow of the king, and a former queen of France, she expected to live in luxury and does not appear to have been disappointed. A respected Frenchman of the time, the Seigneur de Brantôme, who came over from France in her train, declared her new dwelling to be 'undoubtedly a fine building, little in keeping with the country'. Under Mary's ministrations, Holyroodhouse once again came alive and flourished. She was a wealthy, stylish woman, used to the trappings of life within the French court, and she supported her lifestyle by spending lavishly. On 29 December 1565 the Register of Privy Council records that the enormous sum of £35,000 Scots (£3000 sterling) was involved in 'furnishing' the palace to make it

Left: Bird's-eye view of Holyroodhouse and grounds in 1647.
Opposite: Mary Queen of Scots in 1558 by François Clouet.

It is the relationship between Rizzio, Mary and Darnley, and its violent conclusion, that has made Queen Mary's apartments on the second floor of her grandfather's tower the most famous rooms in Scotland. Given the country's long narrative tradition, it is now difficult to disentangle fact from fantasy, but it is clear that either in a fit of jealous pique, or in a lamentable attempt to reinforce his nominal kingship, Darnley joined forces with his friend Lord Ruthven and conspired to murder Rizzio. On the night of 9 March 1566, a heavily pregnant Queen Mary, plus Rizzio and various members of council, was taking supper in the room adjoining the Queen's bedchamber when the conspirators rushed into the room via a concealed stairway and dragged Rizzio, screaming, into the chamber. He was stabbed 56 times, then his lifeless body was hauled into the next apartment.

fit for a queen, although it does not record how this money was used.

The ruin of her reign began in 1565, when she resolved to take her first cousin, Henry Stuart, Lord Darnley, as her husband, when she was 22 and he was just 19. Darnley was the nephew of Henry VIII, and the marriage was seen as a confirmation that Mary still sought to claim the English Crown. Her proposed union therefore brought howls of protest from London and stony silence from Catholic Europe. The Scottish Protestant nobles also took umbrage against the man whom they regarded as an arrogant, English-born playboy. But Mary followed her own counsel, and married Darnley in the chapel of Holyroodhouse in July 1565.

Unfortunately the queen's interest in and respect for her new husband rapidly withered as the king spent his time solely 'in hunting and hawking and such other pleasures as were agreeable to his appetite'.[13] Consequently, Mary began to favour a young Italian called David Rizzio, whom she made her private secretary.

Following this atrocity, Mary was left virtually a prisoner in the hands of the small Protestant party who had organized it 'for the good of religion'. Although she regained control and was publicly reconciled with Darnley, Holyroodhouse ceased to be her home for several months following the murder. Later in the year she gave birth to her son, James, in Edinburgh Castle. Meanwhile, Darnley became ill and withdrew from public life, meeting a dramatic end on the night of 9 February 1567, when the house in which he was recuperating was blown up with gunpowder. The crime was blamed on the Earl of Bothwell, who seems to have organized the murder from Holyroodhouse, where he was lodging at the time.

A widow once again, Queen Mary did not learn from past mistakes, and embarked on

another lamentable marriage, this time to her husband's murderer, Bothwell. This was seen as being a step too far by an outraged Calvinist Scotland. Following the quiet wedding in Holyrood chapel, Protestant nobles imprisoned Mary and forced her to abdicate in favour of her infant son. There followed a resumption of hostilities between Mary's largely Catholic supporters, led by the Earl of Argyll, and the Protestant barons, but Mary's army was finally defeated at the Battle of Langside on 14 May 1568. She then retreated south of the border, where captivity, intrigue and eventual execution awaited her.

Partly by accident and partly by design, Mary's suite of rooms in James V's tower at Holyrood has survived virtually unaltered since her time. Of particular interest is the oak-panelled ceiling, which is almost certainly contemporary with the building of the tower.

Subsequent decoration depicts the arms of Mary's parents, her own arms and those of her first husband, the dauphin of France. Mary's bedroom, with its faded fittings, has a melancholy atmosphere. Certain of her possessions, including a sewing-box and a bed that has almost certainly never seen royal use, give the rooms a haunted feeling, a sense of perpetual mourning for the ghastly deeds that unfolded within them.

Decline Sets In

Between 1568 and 1587 Holyroodhouse was again a palace without a monarch. But in the year that Mary was executed, her son, later King James VI, came of age. James had formed no attachments to the Stuart home where his

Above: Mary Queen of Scots' bedchamber. Rizzio was murdered in the adjoining supper room.

disgraced mother had lived. He had been raised in Stirling Castle, undergoing what was considered to be an appropriate education for a Calvinist monarch. However, he chose to celebrate his adulthood with a feast at Holyroodhouse, which served also as a peace-offering to some of those who opposed him: 'The King reconciled the noblemen who were at variance and upon the Lord's day, the 14th of May, made a bankett unto them. The King drank to them thrice; willed them to make concord and peace, and vowed to be a mortall enemie to him who first brake.'[14]

James VI was a man of patience and cunning. His highest ambition was to ascend the throne of England, and as time went on and Elizabeth I failed to produce an heir, it became increasingly likely that his dream would be realized. For the greater part of his reign in Scotland, he ruled with only one clear aim – not to antagonize England. In 1589 he left the country for six months and made an uncontroversial marriage to Anne, younger daughter of the king of Denmark. She was later crowned in the abbey church of Holyrood, which was fitted up for the occasion. James was content to contain the ever-present religious troubles whenever they threatened to become too dangerous to crush, supporting the formal Presbyterian organization of the Church in 1592 against his Episcopalian inclination.

His reward came late in the evening of Saturday 26 March 1603, when Sir Thomas Carey brought the news of his accession to the English throne. In comparison with England, Scotland was disorderly and poverty-ridden, and offered little to attract the monarch of the stronger nation. James VI of Scotland, now also James I

of England, lost little time in packing up and heading south. His intention never to return to Holyrood was clear. When an inventory was taken of the furnishings left at the palace following his departure, it listed just one clock, two pieces of tapestry, a Turkish carpet, a broken bed and assorted pieces of old furniture; everything else had been carried off to London.

By establishing the royal base south of the border following the union of the Crowns, James VI sealed the fate of Holyrood, precipitating its ignominious slide into decay. The days preceding his departure from Edinburgh on 3 April 1603 were to be the last that Holyroodhouse would serve as a permanent residence to the Scottish royal family. In their absence, the palace received minimal attention to maintain its 'face of a court'. The doors were locked and the keys handed over to Thomas Fenton, 'keipar of the said palace'. Holyrood was now without a king, and Scotland without a monarch, as the reins of power were handed over to Parliament and the Privy Council. For the foreseeable future, Holyrood would become a political backwater, serving as a symbol of the monarchy rather than as a royal residence.

The next monarch to ascend the throne did little to reverse this trend. Charles I was crowned king in Westminster Abbey in 1625, but he did not head north to be formally inaugurated in the country of his birth until eight years later. There was some discussion as to where his coronation would take place, given the 'ruinous' condition of the abbey church of Holyrood, but Charles settled the matter by ordering extensive renovations to be undertaken. A comprehensive royal mandate instructed master masons James Murray and

Anthony Alexander as follows: To '…take down the East Gable within the great arch, where the old window is and to erect and build up ane fair new window of good stone work; and also a window in the East end of the North aisle; and further, to build up the North West steeple with stone, timber and lead, and make it fit to receive a peal of bells; and also to help and repair the South West steeple as far as it must be in sight; and to repair the whole West gable with some lights to be struck out therein, with the two turnpikes to be partly taken down, and well repaired and thacked in good order. As also to remove the whole lofts and desks and to repair the whole breaches and defects of all the pillars and to help the plastering of the North aisle, and to sweeten and set it off in good sort conform to the South aisle.'[15]

This extensive array of work was ordered on 26 January 1633 for completion by June, so the workmanship was not of the highest quality and did not stand the test of time.

Charles I took up residence in Holyroodhouse on 15 June, and left again for London on 18 July. By all accounts, his first visit to Scotland was not auspicious, and the nature of his coronation did little to endear him to his subjects, breeding within the staunchly Protestant nation a 'gryt feir of inbringing of poperie'.

Charles ruled in much the same manner as his Stuart ancestors – stating his own ideas and opinions, and assuming that Scotland could be brought into line to match them. His opponents, however, could not fail to appreciate that their 'true religion' and the king's wishes were incompatible. In 1641 Charles made a humiliating return to Holyrood, during which he was forced to make numerous concessions to his opponents. He subsequently retired to London, defeated and discredited, never to return.

Rising from the Ashes

It is ironic that the salvation of Holyrood should have come in the form of a monarch with only the slenderest attachment to it. Charles II never lived there, and probably never even slept within its walls, but the neglected palace enjoyed a renaissance during his reign. Before it was to rise again, however, it had to fall yet further by becoming embroiled in the Civil War.

When his father, Charles I, was executed at Whitehall in 1649, the future Charles II was offered the Scottish Crown on condition that he sign a covenant. This he did as he hoped the Scots would help him to regain the English throne. At this point, Scotland was divided into irreconcilable factions fighting with great bitterness, but royal supporters held Edinburgh and Leith, surrounded by a chain of defensive works, which Cromwell had thus far not managed to penetrate. When Charles rode north with his army in 1650, this was perhaps the only chance he had to catch even a glimpse of his official royal residence. The opportunity did not last long. Cromwell triumphed at Dunbar shortly after Charles arrived, and began the process of subduing Scotland. This was rough work and much of the country suffered under fire and sword. For a time, Holyroodhouse became a barracks, providing genteel quarters for Cromwell's men. The palace was damaged by fire

in 1650, but it is impossible to ascertain the full extent of the devastation as there is a gap in official records.

Some portion of the palace remained habitable because the council for Scottish affairs convened by Cromwell met at Holyrood in the 1650s. Money was taken from the public purse for a programme of renovation in 1658, but this cannot have been extensive, as only £1000 sterling was pledged for this purpose. Thus, for nearly 10 years, the palace must have been left to moulder in its sorry, fire-damaged state.

With the Restoration in 1660, the Privy Council once more returned to its chamber, and Holyroodhouse returned to the centre of Scottish affairs, although it was not yet home to a king. Charles did not choose to return to Scotland, making the Earl (later Duke) of Lauderdale secretary of state in his place. It is under Lauderdale's influence that the curious process of

Above: Portrait of Charles II painted by Sir Peter Lely (1680–80).

regeneration at Holyrood began. A plan by the king's master mason, John Mylne, dated as early as 1663, outlines the design for a second great tower, which had apparently been proposed by James V, but was for some reason left to his descendant to implement.

Lauderdale was a man of great architectural taste, as displayed in his earlier remodelling of his family home of Lethington at Thirlestane, and he lent his considerable ability to the royal cause. He appointed Sir William Bruce of Kinross as architect in January 1671, at which point Bruce was appointed Surveyor-General and Overseer of the King's Buildings in Scotland. A royal warrant for Bruce's plans was obtained in June of that year. When work commenced in 1672, no part of the old palace escaped improvement. Even the great tower constructed by James V was to some extent remodelled, with the iron grates removed, gun ports blocked, and the windows and doors enlarged.

This was a building intended to impress – a grand celebration of the restoration of the Stuart monarchy, and the architectural showpiece of Scotland. To a large extent, the palace provided for Charles II is still the building that survives today. A new tower was built opposite the old one, giving the palace a more symmetrical appearance. The old and the new towers were linked by a lower balustraded range incorporating a Doric entrance portico that established the rebuilt palace as essentially and fashionably classical. But Bruce did not attempt to deny or conceal the ancient origins of the palace completely. Indeed, he made a virtue of the situation by carefully juxtaposing his brand of

simple classicism with retained major Gothic features, such as the towers, to give the rebuilt Holyroodhouse a very strong character distinctly reminiscent of many a French château of the period. He also introduced a new restraint in Scottish classical design, which until then had been characterized by very exuberant and mannered forms and detailing. Bruce's restrained classicism, also French in origin, is particularly apparent in the elevations of the new courtyard, created by the removal of old palace buildings that formed two irregular courtyards. Bruce's additions to the palace are of great significance not only because they confirmed Scottish artistic reliance on France for inspiration but also because they introduced a new and sophisticated accent into Scottish classicism.

Charles II's rebuilding programme also put an end to the curious dualism of religious practice on the Holyrood site, by reclaiming the abbey church from the Canongate and putting it to use as the Chapel Royal. Thus ended the two separate lines of clergy that had officiated at Holyrood since 1567 – the King's Minister for the palace and the Minster of the Canongate for the abbey (parish) church. 'Suting to his Majesties pious and religious disposition', a way was formed from the new palace into the abbey church, which was declared to be 'his Majesties chappell royeall in all tyme comeing'.[16] As a consequence of this act of 1672, the abbey church is still designated the official Chapel Royal of Scotland, despite the fact that it has since collapsed into ruin.

The building programme was largely complete by the spring of 1675, one and a half years later than its scheduled conclusion. With the exterior complete, Lauderdale sacked Bruce (largely for political reasons) and invited talented artisans to create a beautiful interior. Chief among their achievements are the ceilings of the state rooms, executed by two London craftsmen, John Halbert and George Dunsterfeld. These works were created using a mixture of plaster, horsehair and egg white. Each detail was hand-moulded and dried before being applied to the ceiling. Equally impressive are the paintings by the Dutch artist Jacob de Wet, which include a number of personal and witty touches, such as portraits of King Charles's spaniels peeking over the edge of an historical scene on the ceiling of the king's bedroom. In contrast to the French-inspired exteriors by Bruce, the interiors are in the the Anglo-Dutch style of the London Restoration.

State papers record that the amount voted by Parliament for the enrichment of Charles II's palace totalled £360,667 Scots (about £30,000

Above: Courtyard elevation, designed in erudite classical manner in the 1670s by Sir William Bruce.

sterling) – a fabulous amount of money at the time, and even more incredible when one considers that the king was not interested enough even to view the result.

With so much grandeur at his disposal, the king carved up the palace into a series of apartments in which he installed favoured people. Among those honoured in this way were Lauderdale, Bruce and the third Duke of Hamilton, Hereditary Keeper of the Palace. The Privy Council reconvened at Holyroodhouse on 14 September 1677 following an absence of three and a half years.

Rome Arrives in Scotland

A string of famous visitors began to descend on Holyrood. In 1679, the palace played host to the Duke of Monmouth, whose name has become synonymous with the bloody repression of the 'Westlan' Whigs by the covenanters. More importantly, the king's brother and heir to the throne, James, Duke of York and Albany, spent three months there that same year while English tempers cooled down following his very public adoption of Roman Catholicism. When his presence in England continued to be discomforting, he was encouraged to return to Edinburgh with his family, and lived there until 1682. Despite the brilliance of his court, his behaviour scandalized the Presbyterian Scots. Not only did he convert one of the rooms in the palace for Roman Catholic worship (one of the most offensive actions he could possibly have taken), but he also established a theatre in one of the buildings in the North Garden, a move that

was seen as the embodiment of sin. A contemporary Scottish judge, Lord Fountainhall, wrote in his diary what appears to have been a thoroughly sensible character assessment of the Duke of York: 'he had neither great conduct, nor a deep reach in affairs, but was a silly man'.[17]

Nevertheless, this second son of Charles I became James VII of Scotland and James II of England in 1685. His reign, which lasted less than four years, is remembered chiefly for his catastrophic attempts to wipe away the struggles of the past century and a half, and reconvert Scotland to the Roman Catholic faith. Holyroodhouse had the misfortune to take centre stage in this drama. It became, in effect, a microcosm of the Counter-Reformation. The Treasury register of 1686 records first of all the king's wishes that 'the great room in our said Palace which formerly was designed to be the Council Chamber to be made up as our own Chappell', which James furnished with an altar, vestments and all the accoutrements of Roman Catholic worship, which were shipped up from London in his personal yacht. The following year, he established his own 'popish' printing press in the grounds of the palace, so that his subjects might derive the benefit of Catholic tracts. The only regular customer of the shop appears to have been the king himself, who ordered publications in bulk, then instructed his chancellor, the Earl of Perth, to sell them. In 1687, James VII endowed the chancellor's house to the Jesuits for the establishment of a Jesuit college. Not only did they use part of the royal palace as a school, but the Jesuit Superior also drew an allowance from the Treasury. Finally, on 3 December 1687, the order was given to convert the Chapel Royal – still being used as a parish church, despite the congregation having been 'warned out' in the time of Charles II – into a Catholic chapel. One can only imagine the outrage of the people of Edinburgh as the work was being carried out right under their noses; but it wasn't until the church was almost ready for consecration that silent protest erupted into direct action.

In December 1688, William of Orange landed in England in pursuit of the Crown, and when the news of his claim broke north of the border the Scots were sufficiently encouraged by it to march on Holyrood and show King James what they thought of his popish innovations. On 17 December, a large crowd bent on violence assembled outside the palace and several people were killed or wounded as the palace guards attempted to restrain them. The crowd heavily outnumbered the king's men, so it streamed into Holyrood, pillaging the Jesuit college, tearing down the altars of the private chapel, destroying the printing works and wrecking the recent works in the abbey church. In addition, the royal vault was desecrated, the coffins destroyed and the royal remains scattered. The following day, the rabble gathered anything that would burn, including vestments, books and furnishings, and set light to them in the outer court.

Ashes to Ashes

After this brief and damaging return to public prominence, Holyrood once again faded from public life. It served no purpose as a royal residence, as William III was far too occupied

with Continental wars to visit Scotland, and it also ceased to be the home of the Privy Council, which removed to Parliament Close. Only the third Duke of Hamilton remained Keeper of the Palace. In 1689, he reported to the Scottish Secretary on 'the ruinous condition of this house…it having been spoyled when the rabble fell on the Earl Perth's loadging in this house and the chappell, and his stables having been burnt a little before'. The palace was patched up and retired.

When Queen Anne ascended the throne in 1702, the prospect of a legislative union between England and Scotland, for so long out of reach, was becoming a reality. The Treaty of Union was drawn up in Whitehall in the spring of 1706, and in October the Scottish Parliament began the lengthy task of debating the momentous change. Holyrood, once the power base of the Scottish state, saw action again as the conference venue for the two parties – one for and the other against the union. Nothing in the history of Holyrood has ever been simple, and in typical fashion the palace managed to become the headquarters for both sides. Living in apartments facing each other across the quadrangle were the spokesperson of the pro-unification party, the Duke of Queensburg, who was entitled to live there as Queen's Commissioner, and the fourth Duke of Hamilton, Hereditary Keeper of the Palace and staunch anti-unionist.

The parliamentary debate rumbled on into January 1707, until only four of the 25 clauses remained unresolved. It was decided at a meeting in the Keeper's apartments to launch one last great strategic attack, but when the favoured day dawned Hamilton's seat in Parliament was found to be empty – the duke was ill with toothache and had remained at Holyrood. Thus, on 16 January 1707, the Act of Union was passed by the Scottish Parliament with an overwhelming majority, and in February the following year the peers of Scotland were meeting again at the palace, this time to decide who would represent Scotland in the Parliament of the United Kingdom.

Having enjoyed a brief renaissance under Charles II, and a period of intense, if ill-advised, attention under James VII, the decay of Holyroodhouse now began in earnest. The Hereditary Keeper still lodged there, but eighteenth-century Scotland cared little for the fate of its heritage. Holyrood saw only one chink of light in a century of gloom, when the torch-bearer of Stuart hopes blazed into Edinburgh.

James VII's grandson, Prince Charles Edward Stuart, popularly known 'Bonny Prince Charlie', launched his extraordinary attempt to win back the British Crown in 1745. What started as an ill-advised adventure soon snowballed into a full-scale invasion of Scotland, supported by the Highland lairds, who saw Prince Charles as the last best hope for Scottish independence. Within a few weeks, a large army bore down on Edinburgh, and their leader had only one real choice of base from which to coordinate his campaign – that most potent symbol of the Stuart dynasty: Holyroodhouse. It was a stroke of political genius when Prince Charles took up residence in the Queen's Apartments in James V's tower. The prince was a handsome and charming man who knew how to win friends, and he lost no time in dusting down the state apartments to receive a council of officials and Highland chiefs,

and preparing the Picture Gallery for receptions and balls. For seven glorious weeks the palace rang once again to the sounds of king and court, even if the man in charge was a pretender.

Fired by his unexpected and continuing success in battle, however, Prince Charles's plans became ever more brazen and ambitious. Soon Scotland did not seem a sufficient prize, so he raised the stakes by persuading his troops to attempt an invasion of England. He had achieved a great deal by winning the hearts of some of his most accomplished fellow Scots, but now he wanted to pursue a dream. Thus, seven weeks after he had arrived, Bonnie Prince Charlie rode out from Holyrood to begin his adventures south of the border. He would never return.

As the century passed, the catalogue of neglect suffered by Holyroodhouse began to take effect. The Chapel Royal became increasingly vulnerable, having endured a number of hasty alterations with unsuitable materials that had weakened the structure of the ancient building. The old abbey church had also borne the brunt of the damage in the 1688 revolution. The Duke of Hamilton tried to save the chapel from its 'ruinous' state in 1754, but managed to extract only a paltry £7 10s per annum from the barons of the Exchequer. The roof was found to be in danger of falling in by 1766, at which point William Milne, a descendant of previous master masons who had served the kings of Scotland, was ordered to submit a report to the barons. Unfortunately, in 1768, before any action had been taken, the abbey church collapsed.

Holyrood holds up a mirror to the state of national pride following union in the eighteenth century. The celebrated English preacher John Wesley visited the erstwhile royal residence during his missionary tours through Scotland. He reported on its melancholy state shortly before the abbey church fell into ruin: 'I walked once more through Holyrood House, a noble piece of building, but the greatest part of it left to itself, and so (like the Palace at Scone) swiftly running to ruin. The tapestry is dirty and quite faded; the fine ceiling is dropping down, and many of the pictures in the gallery torn and cut through.'[18] When he revisited Holyrood in 1780 he noted that 'the stately rooms are dirty as stables', adding that 'the roof of the royal chapel is fallen in, and the bones of James Fifth and the once beautiful Darnley are scattered about like those of sheep and oxen'.[19]

Nineteenth-century Revival

As the years went by, the decrepit state of the palace and its precincts came to reflect the surrounding area, which was a popular sanctuary for debtors – a safe haven from which to avoid imprisonment for debt. This curious arrangement is connected with Holyrood's ancient foundation charter, which conferred the right of sanctuary upon it, and by 1816 it was attracting as many as 116 'Abbey Lairds' to live in rooms in houses at the foot of the Canongate. The sanctuary was nominally presided over by the Duke of Hamilton, as Keeper of the Palace, who appointed a bailiff to keep order in his place. Although the occupants avoided imprisonment, they enjoyed only 24 hours of true freedom each week, being allowed to leave the sanctuary only on Sundays.

As the nineteenth century advanced, an Act abolishing imprisonment for debt was passed, and the sanctuary faded away, but not in time to save the creditors of its most distinguished occupant, Count d'Artois. The count was the younger brother of Louis XVI, and rightful heir to the throne through the old Bourbon dynasty. He fled to England in January 1796 as a refugee from the French Revolution. Upon appeal to the British Government, d'Artois was offered assistance in the form of accommodation at Holyrood and a pension of £6000 per annum. Apart from a two-year sojourn in London between 1799 and 1801, he lived in the Scottish palace until 1814.

Ten years later d'Artois ascended the French throne as Charles X, but his monarchy was not a success, and the revolution of 1830 drove him and his family out of his home country once again. Now an elderly man, he returned to his Scottish refuge, where his numerous charitable works earned him overwhelming public affection and respect. The 'unobtrusive tenant of Holyrood' as the *Edinburgh Observer* described him, sent out his own doctor to dispense advice and medicine to the poor at a time when cholera was rife in the city, he donated money to fund schools, and he supported the 'industrious class'. But the past returned to haunt 'the despotic Monarch of the Tuilleries', and in September 1832 he moved his family and court to Hamburg, much to the regret of the people of Edinburgh. The *Edinburgh Courant* records the moving scenes outside the palace on the morning of his departure: 'By eight o'clock, the piazza of the Palace was crowded with persons anxious to get a last look of the illustrious strangers, and before nine the space in front of the Palace was nearly filled with spectators. White gloves, white ribbons and white favours of various kinds were worn by a large proportion of the people assembled, and when the Royal Exiles came out…they were greeted with loud cheers and waves of hats and handkerchiefs, and not a few ladies were in tears – those of his Majesty's own household were exclaiming 'Ah! Pauvre Roi!'– and each seemed anxious to have the honour to kiss his hand.'[20]

Holyrood, however, was designed to be a palace of the British Crown, and its rehabilitation as such can be traced back as far as the 1820s, when George IV made his first state visit to Scotland. By this time, Holyrood had sunk too far to be considered suitable as a royal residence, so the king lodged at nearby Dalkeith. However, his imagination must have been fired by Holyrood's decaying splendour, as a comprehensive and expensive programme of restoration was undertaken on his orders.

This upward trend was given a considerable boost by Queen Victoria's love of Scotland, and although she undoubtedly preferred the seclusion of her holiday home at Balmoral to life in the city eye, she became the first British monarch in two centuries to take up residence at Holyroodhouse. The Crown reclaimed many of the grace and favour apartments, and furniture was brought up from Buckingham Palace to add to that which had been provided for the comfort of the French king. The interior of the palace was renovated –

not entirely sympathetically – to suit the fashion of the time. Indeed, on inheriting Queen Victoria's 'improvements', Queen Mary was heard to declare that the old monarch had 'dreadful taste'. There were also plans to convert the old abbey church, now the ruined Chapel Royal, into a Thistle Chapel. However, the plans were never carried through, as it was felt that to do so would detract from the historic value of the building.

In modern times Holyrood is a working palace. It is the official Scottish residence of the British monarch, and now that its dignity has been restored, the wheel of fortune has turned full circle. It has gone from guest house to palace to debtors' sanctuary to decay and back again. Around it, the city has changed out of all recognition, but Holyroodhouse presides like a time capsule from another world. The palace is admired and revered, a spectacular witness to the tumultuous journey of a nation from the twelfth to the twenty-first century.

Right: The Morning Drawing Room – one of the late seventeenth-century interiors created within Holyroodhouse.

4

Blenheim Palace

Lying just outside Woodstock to the north-west of Oxford, Blenheim Palace is one of the most extraordinary buildings ever created in Britain. At the time construction started in 1705 the palace was announced as the gift of a grateful nation to its successful general the Duke of Marlborough, for victory in a crucial military campaign. In reality, it was more a private gift from one friend to another – from Queen Anne to her boon companion, Sarah Churchill, Duchess of Marlborough. This is odd enough, but the tale took stranger turns.

The shifting relationships between the main protagonists explain the complex evolution of the building. As construction of the huge-scale palace increased in cost, so the relationship between the queen and Sarah cooled. Meanwhile, the duke, once a man beyond reproach, fell foul of the particularly bitter, corrupt and vindictive politics of the time. The project lumbered into confusion and debt, and there were concerns that, despite being a Crown project, the half-built palace would stand as a monument not to gratitude but, as the Duchess of Marlborough said at the time, to 'national ingratitude'.

Hanging over this messy business, increasingly dogged by litigation, is the bizarre, almost insane, relationship that developed between the architect chosen for the job, John Vanbrugh, and the duchess. She was an unstable character, shrewd, mean-spirited, arrogant and opinionated. It was typical that her relationship with Queen Anne should end with the duchess publicly commanding the queen to silence. But Sarah was also perceptive and frugal, with a no-

nonsense approach to life. These qualities were to make any peaceful relationship between her and Vanbrugh impossible. They argued about everything from the preservation of ancient ruins in the grounds to the phasing of construction, the size of the windows and, of course, the costs. And then there was the architecture. Sarah never liked Vanbrugh's idiosyncratic fusion of what he termed the old English 'castle air' with elements of Continental baroque, all laced with his very personal, inventive and massive classical style. Blenheim Palace was, after all, a monument to military triumph, and Vanbrugh, with his great baroque swags, military trophies and stacks of arms carved and hewn into the structure, was not going to let anyone forget the fact.

Sarah was not alone in taking a dim view of his ideas. Vanbrugh, a former soldier and playwright, was a charming, intelligent and witty artist. But his architecture, self-taught and very individual, fell rapidly in public and professional esteem as the British romance with the theatricality of the baroque started to wane during the 1720s, well before Blenheim was completed, to be replaced by a passion for the more orthodox, austere and rule-bound brand of classicism that became known as Palladian. So this great palace, in a style that many might now think is a quintessential expression of English country house architecture, was lampooned and

Previous page: The south front of Blenheim Palace.
Above: The palace from the south-west, looking towards the Long Library with its central bow.
Opposite: The East Gate. A huge water cistern is located behind the inscription.

repudiated even before it was completed, not least by the duchess herself.

But despite, or perhaps because of, its origins, Blenheim Palace does hold a special place in the hearts of the English and in the history of architecture. Vanbrugh has, in the end, been vindicated. He created a magnificent monument, but a monument to more things than perhaps he realized. With its sweeping symmetry, spreading forecourts, distinct classical accents and enfilade of grand interior rooms, it is a spectacular celebration of European baroque taste of the late seventeenth and early eighteenth centuries. It is also, with its bold and cubical forms, a wonderful expression of the particularly sculptural and masculine English variation of the international

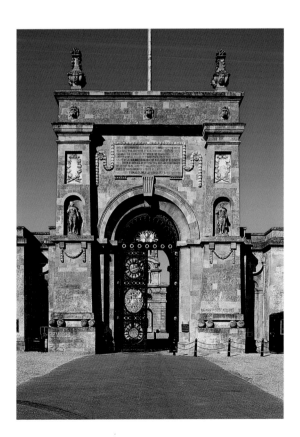

baroque school – a permutation fully realized a few years later by Nicholas Hawksmoor, who worked on Blenheim, in his London churches. But above all Blenheim is a telling monument to the quest for power and prestige. By an ironic intervention of the Fates, this celebration of a great battle became itself a battlefield as its varied array of self-obsessed and egocentric creators fought to gratify their own personal lusts for worldly rewards and visions of grandeur. Satisfactorily, this great work by a master of the theatre did itself become a theatre of the absurd and a setting for both farce and tragedy. The story of the making of Blenheim Palace is not just the story of ruthless power struggles but also, in its cut and thrust of human relations, the story of how great corporate works of art are created.

A Gift to the Marlboroughs

The inscription over the East Gate at Blenheim reads: 'Under the auspices of a munificent Sovereign this house was built for John Duke of Marlborough and his Duchess Sarah.'

This does not, of course, tell much, but it does record the generous and spontaneous spirit in which the gift was first given. The key reference here is to Sarah. Taken at face value, the relationship between Queen Anne and Sarah Jennings was close and strong. They had grown up together in the household of Anne's father, the Duke of York and future James II. Sarah had shared the tribulations of Anne's difficult and potentially dangerous youth, and in 1688 advised the Protestant Anne to abandon her Catholic father when he fled abroad. This action secured

Anne her claim to the throne, so, in 1702, when she finally became queen, she owed much to Sarah.

In 1678 Sarah married Colonel John Churchill, a protégé of the Duke of York. On Anne's own marriage in 1683 Sarah was appointed lady of the bedchamber, and when Anne succeeded to the throne she bestowed important household roles and favours on Sarah, and elevated Churchill to Duke of Marlborough for his part in the War of the Spanish Succession (1701–14).

In August 1704 Marlborough achieved his great military victory at Blenheim in Bavaria. This, at the time, was seen as the triumph of the age. It not only brought glory to English arms, but was an allied victory that was perceived as saving Europe from French domination. Marlborough was rightfully proud of his achievement, and gratified when he learnt that the queen and government wished to reward him. He concluded a letter to Sarah written immediately after the battle with the apology that 'I can't end my letter without being soe vain as to tell my dearest soull that within the memory of man there has been noe Victory soe great as this.'[1] Various ideas were considered for the reward: a statue, a square, a great London house, a great estate… Sarah leapt at this last suggestion. It not only carried a sense of nobility and grandeur, but it also offered escape. The estate offered was at Woodstock, over 60 miles (95 kilometres) from London, which Sarah imagined would free her from court life and her old friend Anne, whom she was finding increasingly tedious and irksome.

Anne seems to have been blissfully unaware of Sarah's true feelings. On 17 February 1705 she informed the House of Commons that she would

'consider of proper means for perpetuating the memory of the great services performed by the Duke of Marlborough' and had resolved to transfer to him and his heirs the Crown's interest in the manor of Woodstock. A Bill was introduced and given royal sanction on 14 March, and it was only then that any public mention was made of adding a palace to the gift. No one, however, seemed quite sure how it was going to be realized. W.C. Coxe in his *Memoirs of John Duke of Marlborough* (1820) gives a hint of the thinking that was going on behind the scenes: 'Not satisfied that the nation alone should testify its gratitude, the Queen accompanied the grant with an order to the Board of Works to erect, at the royal expense, a splendid palace, which, in memory of the victory, was to be called the Castle of Blenheim. A model was immediately constructed for the approbation of the queen, and the work was begun without delay, under the direction of Mr (afterwards Sir John) Vanbrugh.'[2]

Mystery still surrounds this early phase of the operation. No one now knows for sure whose idea the palace was, Sarah's or the queen's, and how it was intended that it should be constructed and paid for. If the queen's order to the Board of Works ever existed, there is now no record of it. Indeed, there appears to have been very little in the nature of a written agreement for the whole extravagant commission. It is in this early confusion, or perhaps brazen trickery as some would have seen it, that lie the roots to many of the problems that were later to dog the construction of the palace.

John Vanbrugh was an intriguing choice for architect. In 1686 he had obtained a commission in the army, and in 1690 was arrested for espionage and spent two years in a French prison. After his return from France he turned to writing for the stage. His first play, *The Relapse*, appeared in 1696, and his masterpiece, *The Provok'd Wife*, in 1697. But by then, when in his mid-thirties, Vanbrugh's interest had moved away from the stage to architecture. Quite why or how this happened is unknown, and it certainly mystified and amused many at the time.

His first commission was a major one – a vast country house in Yorkshire for the Earl of Carlisle. Work on Castle Howard got under way in 1700 and lasted for well over 20 years. Bold and baroque in conception, it is an astonishing achievement for one whose architectural experience was as limited as Vanbrugh's is thought to have been. Significantly, he was assisted by Nicholas Hawksmoor, some three years his senior, whose huge natural talents had been enhanced by 15 years of training and experience in the office of Sir Christopher Wren. Following this commission, Vanbrugh's rise in the architectural establishment was nothing less than meteoric. The Earl of Carlisle was First Lord of the Treasury and consequently in a position, in June 1702, to appoint Vanbrugh Comptroller of Her Majesty's Board of Works. Thus, less than two years after joining the architectural profession, Vanbrugh became the principal colleague on the Board of Works of the veteran and immensely experienced Wren. Having secured this powerful public position, which validated his architectural pretensions, Vanbrugh turned it to his advantage. He set himself up as architect-in-chief to the rising Whig aristocracy,

a position that he was to enjoy and greatly profit from over the following decade.

Perhaps, then, in 1705 it was only natural that Vanbrugh should have been commissioned to design a palace paid for at royal expense for a client who was a Whig by connection if not by upbringing or conviction. Even so, it is worth reflecting on the fact that by then Vanbrugh had designed only four buildings, two of them for

Above: Portrait of Sir John Vanbrugh, after Sir Godfrey Kneller.

himself – a house in Whitehall and a theatre in the Haymarket. The others were an orangery (in fact only a revision of a design by Hawksmoor), and Castle Howard (still 20 years from completion and for which he may have been only the front man, with Hawksmoor doing the detailed design work).

From what can now be reconstructed from contemporary documents and accounts it seems likely that the Duke of Marlborough chose, or at least willingly accepted, Vanbrugh as architect. Perhaps it was a question of two old soldiers hitting it off. Sarah certainly believed that her husband was responsible for Vanbrugh's appointment: 'I was very much misrepresented by those that said it was my importunity that prevailed for him, for at the beginning of those works I never had spoke to him, but as soon as I knew him and saw the maddnesse of the whole Design I opposed it all that was possible for me to doe… I don't know that the queen had any particular favour for Sr C. Wren, tho he had been an old servant, but 'tis certain that old Craggs, who was as ill a man as ever I knew, recommended Sr John Vanbrugh to the Duke of Marl.'³ (James Craggs, the shadowy intermediary, had once managed Sarah's business affairs and been employed by the duke as secretary of the Ordnance Office. He finally succumbed to his illness in 1721.)

Vanbrugh offered a different version of events, and suggested that his selection by the duke was not influenced by a third party: 'The Building was not conducted by her [the queen's] Board of Works, but left to him [the duke] to employ such Officers and Workmen as he should

see fit… his Grace…cast his eye upon the Board of Works, where (for Reasons best known to himself) not inclining to engage Sir Christopher Wren…he fix'd upon the next Officer to him, her Comptroller [which of course was Vanbrugh], thinking him (as such) qualified for the Business he was going upon, and so desir'd he would given him his assistance in it.'⁴

Since Blenheim was, in its way, an official commission, it is strange that Wren – still at the height of his powers in the early years of the eighteenth century and then surveyor-general of the queen's Board of Works – was not appointed. Perhaps Vanbrugh's explanation is correct and Marlborough decided to pass Wren over. This is understandable. Wren was 74 and still immensely busy in 1705. Work on the construction of the west front of St Paul's Cathedral was just about to start, and he must have been fully immersed in the technical and artistic problems of designing and constructing the cathedral's dome. Wren was also supervising the design and construction of the Royal Hospital at Greenwich, and presiding over the completion of many of his City churches.

Or perhaps Wren's Tory associations were wrong. Or Marlborough simply wanted to give the new man a chance, believing that relative youth and the desire to prove himself made Vanbrugh the better choice.

But even though Wren was passed over for the main commission, his experience and expertise were badly needed. Vanbrugh, honestly admitting his own professional limitations, agreed that Wren should go to Woodstock to undertake the complex task of estimating how much it would cost to build a palace there.

Wren reported that the queen's present would cost her nearly £100,000. Anne was satisfied by this estimate, but the duchess was appalled. It was in her nature to economize, if only for the sake of economy. Thrift was her religion. Years later, Sarah wrote: 'Every friend of mine knows that I was always against building at such an expense, and as long as I meddled with it at all, I took as much pains to lessen the charge every way as if it was to be paid for out of the fortune that was to provide for my own children… nothing made it tolerably easy to me but my knowing that she [the queen] never did a generous thing of herself, if that expense had not been recommended by the Parliament and paid out of the Civil List.'[5]

Marlborough himself seems not to have been shocked by the proposed cost of the building. While the duchess saw it as a house, the duke saw it as a great public building – an almost impersonal monument to his achievements and those of the English nation rather than as a celebration of his personal greatness. This is a subtle but important distinction.

Vanbrugh appears to have well understood the duke's feelings about Blenheim, better, indeed, than did Sarah. It seems that a great mutual liking developed between the duke and his architect. They both understood the real meaning and purpose of Blenheim and took the long view that they were building for posterity rather than for the present. This shared vision allowed them to stand in the mire of the building

site, even when all started to go horribly wrong, and together envisage a great monument of brave and majestic design when everybody else saw only a catastrophic folly. Both, at least initially, shared a great passion for Blenheim. Vanbrugh described it as his 'sort of childe', and recorded 'the more than common delight the Duke had from the beginning taken in this Work at Woodstock'.[6]

The Design

Given the hazy origins of the commission, it is now difficult to say exactly what Vanbrugh's design brief specified. However, it seems pretty clear that it was supposed Vanbrugh would design a house similar to Castle Howard, but

Right: Looking east along the enfilade of state rooms behind the south front.

Floor plan labels: SALOON, HALL, COURT, LIBRARY, KITCHEN, CHAPEL, EAST GATE, STABLE COURT (UNFINISHED), NOT BUILT

larger, incorporating such military symbolism as seemed appropriate, and providing apartments, both state and private, in which the highest and most powerful in the land could be entertained. The formula for this type of design was fairly well tried and tested by the early eighteenth century, having been developed in royal and private palaces in Britain for the previous quarter of a century. What was demanded were sets of rooms, placed in a row and with doors all aligned to create a dramatic vista through the building, along which courtiers could parade and in which royalty could receive their subjects or the aristocracy their guests. This pattern had been brought to perfection in the great houses and royal palaces of late seventeenth-century France, particularly in the Palace of Versailles from the 1670s. But there were other demands of which Vanbrugh was well aware, and which are reflected in his design for Blenheim.

The mathematical and rational classicism of the mid–sixteenth-century Italian architect Andrea Palladio had been introduced into England most successfully by Inigo Jones in the early seventeenth century, and certain of Palladio's

ideas – particularly his planning – greatly influenced essentially baroque architects such as Vanbrugh. So, in emulation of Palladio's villa planning, Blenheim has a tall cubical hall set on axis with a rectangular saloon. These two impressive rooms, each with a ceiling painted with allegorical scenes glorifying the achievements of the duke, form the core of the principal block of the palace. Stretching majestically from the saloon are a pair of state apartments comprising a reception room, a withdrawing chamber and a state bedchamber.

The early years of the eighteenth century also saw new ideas emerging about comfort and convenience. The state apartments, incorporating a state bed in which no one slept, were essential expressions of status and social hierarchy. But for ordinary daily use they were hopelessly formal

Above: The principal floor level of Blenheim Palace. The state apartments run behind the south front; the private apartments are behind the east front. To the east (left) is the kitchen court with the stable court to the west.
Opposite left: The entrance hall looking south towards the saloon.
Opposite right: The vaulted north corridor, running behind the entrance front.

and uncomfortable – indeed, practically unusable. So Vanbrugh created a wing set at right angles to the main state apartments to contain a smaller private apartment in which the duke and duchess – each with their own bedroom, of course – could live in greater comfort and privacy.

Vanbrugh also appreciated the potential of the corridor, a simple planning device that would start to transform country house living from the second half of the eighteenth century. The hall is divided from the saloon by a vestibule framed by columns supporting a great arch, a composition looking startlingly like a proscenium arch from Vanbrugh's playhouse days. This arch provided a fitting setting for the theatre of life at Blenheim, for it frames the

vestibule that forms part of the south corridor, running parallel to the state apartments along which the life of the palace bustled. The job of the corridor is obvious: it provides an individual and discreet entry or exit route to each of the state rooms, thus removing the old evil of having to walk through one room to reach another. Vanbrugh's north and south corridors, although handsomely vaulted, are fairly rudimentary. It was to be 100 years before the full potential of the corridor was realized (see Windsor Castle, p. 80), but Vanbrugh certainly grasped the essential possibilities.

In other respects, practicality was not a strong point of the Vanbrugh plan. Famously, the kitchen is not only located a very long way from

the dining room in the bow room of the east wing, but it is separated from it by an open colonnade. Dignity was clearly more important than hot food, and the aroma of cooking in the state or private apartments would have been intolerable. Kitchens, however, were notorious fire risks, so to detach this one in its own court was not, perhaps, such an impractical idea. But when it came to the water supply, Vanbrugh revealed himself to be a man ahead of his time. The vast upper portion of the East Gate was designed to evoke a sense of power and strength, but it was also to house a huge cistern from which water could be supplied under a certain amount of pressure to rooms in the house. The cistern itself was filled by a paddle-wheel engine housed in one of the arches of the Grand Bridge.

Vanbrugh's designs, presumably through discussions with the duke, also reflect the burgeoning artistic life of the age. Books were becoming cheaper and more available, so the entire west wing of the palace is given over to one gigantic room, the Long Library. Long galleries of similarly dramatic form had become common in English country houses from the mid-sixteenth century. Originally they were used primarily for winter constitutionals, but gradually, as at Blenheim, they became the place where the intellectual achievements or aspirations of the owner went on display. They became showrooms for books, or for the paintings and sculpture acquired on the Grand Tour, thus becoming the forerunners of nineteenth-century public museums or art galleries. It was in this room that the duke intended to hang his paintings; it was later used to house a library.

There can be little doubt that the duke, given his early passion for the palace, made a major contribution to the evolution of the brief. But Vanbrugh also developed a number of his own, very individual, architectural theories. He had a love of ancient buildings, if apparently little archaeological understanding of them. The romance of history was overpowering, and on several occasions he attempted to invoke the power of the past – its forms and details – in his own architecture. Vanbrugh's passion was for what he termed the 'castle air', which he explained (in reference to his 1707 remodelling of Kimbolton Castle, Huntingdonshire) made a 'very noble and masculine shew'. His most obvious excursion into mock medieval architecture was his own home in Greenwich – Vanbrugh Castle (1718) – but even here, despite the round tower and conical roof, the detailing is essentially classical rather than Gothic. For Vanbrugh the essence of the 'castle air' lay in the evocation of medieval forms, in the weighty massing of the building and in the creation of powerful and romantic silhouettes rather than in the direct duplication of Gothic or medieval details. This creative adaptation of medieval sources, combined with the more conventional baroque sense of movement and of theatrical and dramatic advance and recession of forms, give Blenheim its distinct architectural character. Vanbrugh was able to design successfully in three dimensions, or, as Wren said, in 'perspective', so that Blenheim looks striking from virtually all viewpoints and from varying distances. Like a great kaleidoscope, the building, as it is walked around, composes and recomposes itself in a seemingly endless succession of different and dramatic forms.

The most striking expressions of the 'castle air' are the squat, cubical towers that terminate and advance beyond the elevations of the main building, and that have a brooding, almost defensive, castle-like quality. The details of these towers are quintessential Vanbrugh. He preferred to use the language of classicism, but hardly ever in a conventional way. Like Continental baroque architects of the seventeenth century, and like Hawksmoor, Vanbrugh loved to give conventional details or compositions new or unexpected meaning by using them out of context in strange combinations and at unlikely scales. This was to outrage, indeed horrify, later generations of orthodox classical architects, who believed that the classical orders were literally God-given, and enshrined immutable laws of beauty and propriety that were only ignored by the ignorant or arrogant. As if to permanently alienate such pedants, Vanbrugh topped his towers with huge stone spheres resembling mighty cannon balls supported by scrolls formed by fleurs-de-lis (symbolic of France being crushed). The entire top storey of the towers were arranged to look vaguely like medieval battlements.

The central block of Blenheim is placed within a powerful architectural setting achieved by the bold but simple notion of making the kitchen court and the stable court part of the main architectural composition. This pair of courts, of equal area, although the stable court was never finished, frame the main prospect of the central building, which rises above these ornately detailed subservient buildings. By this means, and by using other related gates, walls and minor structures, Vanbrugh knitted the palace into the larger landscape. The placing of the wings and house, and their relationship to each other, is a fine example of Continental baroque planning, and is derived fairly directly from Versailles. In the court of the absolute monarch penetration was all-important. The depth to which people could progress along the royal apartments determined their rank at court and in society. The act of penetrating the outer courts of Versailles, of ever decreasing area, to the château itself was a similarly powerful expression of status. Visitors to Blenheim were clearly intended to be classified in a similar way.

Quite whose fanciful idea this was originally is hard to say. Perhaps because the house was being paid for with somebody else's money, or perhaps because it was seen as a great national building, Vanbrugh and the duke seem to have taken a fairly relaxed view about expanding the brief. Certainly Vanbrugh, the inspired artist rather than the professional architect, was quite happy to develop the final design of the house and to resolve details even after construction work had started.

Once the duke had approved Vanbrugh's plan and the queen had expressed her desire to pay for the work, Vanbrugh started to prepare the ground by digging the foundations, and opened a quarry in Woodstock Park. However, he had still not been formally appointed surveyor (that is, architect), and only nine days before the foundation stone was due to be laid he had still not been officially put in charge of the works.

Showing good sense and prescience, he began to wonder if it were wise to proceed without 'Authority in writing for what he had been directed by the Duke to Transact'.

As the duke was in Flanders, Vanbrugh turned to Marlborough's friend the Earl of Godolphin, the Lord Treasurer, to sort things out. Through Godolphin Vanbrugh received a warrant, dated 9 June 1705, that appointed him 'at the request and desire of the Duke of Marlborough...Surveyor' of all the works and buildings the duke had resolved to erect at Woodstock, and empowered him to make and sign contracts on the duke's behalf. In this document no mention was made of the queen or Crown. Given the relaxed atmosphere of the time, when the Marlboroughs were the golden couple and Godolphin was in power, this omission seemed not to worry anyone. But it would come to vex all concerned and the warrant would become a very important document in the legal wrangles that soon surrounded the enterprise.

Vanbrugh was now officially the surveyor of Blenheim, but his other commitments meant that he could not remain indefinitely on site to oversee detailed design amendments, the acquisition of materials and construction. These duties had to be undertaken by others, so two comptrollers were rapidly appointed. One was Henry Joynes, who came from the Board of Works and was to develop into an able draughtsman and architect in his own right. The other was William Boulter,

Opposite: View along the length of the Long Library – one of the great glories of Blenheim.

whom Vanbrugh was later to refer to as 'a Creature of her Grace's' because of his tendency to be manipulated by the duchess. Overseeing Joynes and Boulter, from the headquarters of the Board of Works in London would be Vanbrugh, Hawksmoor in the role of assistant surveyor, and Wren as 'unofficial advisor'. At the Treasury, controlling funds were Samuel Travers M.P., the surveyor-general for Blenheim, and his deputy, a Mr Taylor, both of whom reported to Godolphin.

The foundation stone of Blenheim was laid on Monday 18 June 1705, an event recorded in the diary kept by William Upcott, a late eighteenth-century antiquary: 'Seven gentlemen gave it a Stroke with a Hammer and threw down each of them a guinea: Sir Thos Wheate was the first, Dr Bouchell the second, Mr Vanbrugge the third; I know not the rest... The stone laid by Mr Vanbrugge was eight foot [240 centimetres] square, finely polished about eighteen inches [45 centimetres] over, and upon it were these words inlayed in pewter: In memory of the battel of Blenheim, June 18 1705, Anna Regina.' The event embraced the whole of the local community and was celebrated with 'several sorts of musick, three morris dances; one of young fellowes, one of maidens, and one of old beldames. There were about a hundred buckets, bowls and pans, filled with wine, punch, cakes and ale. From my lord's house all went to the Town Hall where plenty of sack, claret, cakes etc. were prepared for the gentry and better sort; and under the Cross eight barrels of ale, with abundance of cakes, were placed for the common people.'

The site on which construction started was daunting. Woodstock Park had belonged to the

Crown for centuries and been renowned for its game, which explains why an ancient but largely ruined manor house stood in the park near where it was planned to build the palace. This, along with the swamp that surrounded it, could have presented problems, but Vanbrugh took a pragmatic, indeed inspired, view of these circumstances. He resolved to transform the old house into a beautiful and evocative ruin, and to turn the swamp into a lake, thus creating an opportunity to design a noble bridge.

This ingenious 'grand plan' led to the start of Vanbrugh's trouble with the thrifty and suspicious duchess. She soon made it clear that she wanted the ruined manor cleared away as so much dross, with its materials reused in construction works on the estate. And as for Vanbrugh's designs for the bridge – she thought them extravagant in the extreme. Neither would give way and thus started years of fencing around these two issues.

The First Week of Building

The foundation ceremony was clearly a joyful affair, but just five days later the local Woodstock quarries failed and Vanbrugh had to meet his first major problem – lack of stone. Supplies would have to be purchased and carted across rough country from as far as 20 miles (32 kilometres) away. And then the quarrymen 'grumbled very much because they had not more wages' and the local farmers providing the carts for the stone were 'disattisfyed, having a great occasion for there mony, it being Harvest time'. All of this would obviously incur vast extra costs not included in Wren's original estimate. Thus, within little over a week of starting work, the initial building estimate was looking wildly optimistic and the pattern was established for the financial and operational roller coaster that would vex the Blenheim construction site for the next 20 years.

Not one element of Vanbrugh's great plans was to run smoothly. From lack of money and materials to 'Raine without Intermition', from petty vandalism to 'the fflying of the Stone in the ffrost', not to mention the intrigues and feuding that would eventually lead to the duke's fall from favour well before his 'monument of gratitude' was completed, everything conspired against the project. And all this was set to the tune of Sarah's constant antagonism and meddling, which caused much of the house to be built not once, but twice over.

By August 1705 the number of workmen on site had risen to nearly 1500, and this figure rose again the following summer when the site comptrollers had to recruit a 'second army' of stone carters, a further 136 men. Some of the building materials, including marble, slates, gravel, lime, bricks, lead and timber, came by barge, but most came by road. Most of the roads were steep and narrow, and their weak surfaces were quickly rutted by the constant flow of carts carrying heavy building materials. It was said to take 21 horses to drag the largest blocks up the worst of the inclines, so bringing in stone was virtually impossible after rain, and completely abandoned by midwinter. The local population must have held very mixed views about the construction process. It offered much local

employment, but the farmers, who needed the roads to carry their produce, must soon have loathed the upstart Marlboroughs and their high and mighty palace.

The craftsmen working on site were the best of their day, many having gained valuable experience working for Wren on St Paul's Cathedral and the City churches. Vanbrugh explained his system of hiring men thus: 'I sent to great variety of Workmen of the same Trade (in different Countrys [counties], and quite unacquainted with one another) for their Proposals. And when by that means I had at last brought the Prices to be moderate Instead of throwing so great a Work into the hands of a few Undertakers, I divided it amongst many, three, or

four, or five, of each Trade... This I did, partly to raise an Emulation amongst them, and so have better Work done.'[7]

The chief masons were the Edward Strongs, father and son, who were responsible for the important stonework in the main building. Vanbrugh was extremely fortunate to secure the services of these masters of their trade, particularly since the Strong family also owned the quarries that were supplying stone. Sadly, it is unlikely that the Strongs felt equally fortunate in their choice of client for they were eventually to become among the main litigants in the battle to

Above: The old manor house of Woodstock, which Vanbrugh fought to save but the duchess finally destroyed.

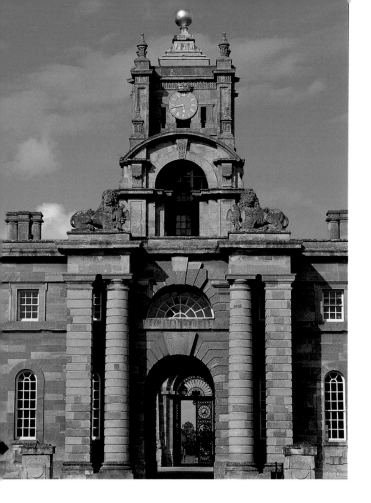

extract payment for work executed at Blenheim. Also employed were John Townsend, who probably worked on the clock tower and died in 1728, and his son William, whose contributions included the Woodstock Gate (1722–3) and the Column of Victory (1727–30).[8] At Blenheim he worked alongside Bartholomew Peisley, an Oxford master mason, whose family became one of the principal contractors on the site. It was Bartholomew Peisley II who built the Great Bridge. Another master mason employed at Blenheim was Henry Banks, who worked on the colonnades of the Great Court.

Grinling Gibbons, the virtuoso carver discovered and nurtured by Wren, supplied the ornamental stonework, such as the Corinthian capitals in the hall, and the external sculpture and statues, including the British lions savaging the cocks of France that loll on the Clock and Stable Towers. The top painters Sir James Thornhill and

Louis Laguerre were commissioned to paint ceilings and walls.

All these men were experienced, professional and proud, so the unfolding events at Blenheim were to bring them anguish on many levels.

Progress on the Palace

The dry summer in 1705 meant that, after the first upsets, work progressed well. Less than two months after the foundation stone was laid the foundations of the main house were complete.

But clouds were continuing to gather. One problem, which would grow more expensive as work progressed, was Vanbrugh's working method. He was quite happy to amend the design of the building once work was under way. Rather as he would have directed a play, Vanbrugh seems to have constantly re-evaluated the initial plan in response to changing conditions, 'players' and

intended audience. In fact, he admitted as much in a letter to the duke dated 22 June 1705, four days *after* the laying of the foundation stone: 'The drawings I sent yr. Grace were not (nor could not be) perfect in little perticulars wch at leisure have since been more thoroughly Consider'd.'[9] These 'little perticulars' might even have included the addition of a mighty north portico.

Given Vanbrugh's willingness to amend the plan as work progressed, it is hardly surprising that others felt at liberty to do the same. In July Godolphin and Lord Carlisle visited the site and suggested that the position of the chapel, kitchen and colonnades be altered from that suggested in early correspondence.[10] Vanbrugh, rather than being affronted, agreed to the 'appointed' change, and in a letter to the duke even took some credit for the amendment: 'There is Considerable alteration in the placing of the Chappell and Kitchen but it Appear'd to my

Lord Treasurer [Godolphin] so clear for the best that he thought there was no need of delaying the Work while your Graces Opinion might be knowing. And so we have gone on as I propos'd it to him.'[11]

Worse than this belated fiddling with the 'final' plan, and a terrible indication of things to come, was that, even during this relatively trouble-free phase, the flow of cash from the Treasury was sporadic.

As well as the promise of financial and constructional problems to come there were indications of a battle of another kind – this one regarding taste. In the early days, Marlborough showed his Blenheim plans secretly to the exiled Earl of Ailesbury, who disliked them and wrote to

Opposite: The clock tower, ornamented by British lions savaging French cocks.
Above: The north entrance front, with the central main block framed by lower subsidiary buildings – a sublime composition.

a friend: 'I understand but little or nothing of this matter, but enough to affirm (by the plan I saw) that the house is like one mass of stone without taste or relish.'[12]

Lord Ailesbury was only the first of many to dismiss Blenheim out of hand, and much of the aesthetic criticism was politically inspired. Woodstock was predominantly Whig in affiliation (due partly to the arrival of the Marlboroughs), but nearby Oxford was firmly Tory, and those who belittled Blenheim because they saw it as part of a Whig campaign kept a sharp eye on the palace, hoping for problems. The gleeful observations that the Oxford Jacobite Thomas Hearne made in his diary offer good examples of the venom of the circling vultures: ''Tis said that the stones with which they build the Duke of Marlborough's House at Woodstock are extreme bad and that they crack by the Frost; so that in all probability they must begin ye Foundation again.

'Tis looked upon as a bad Omen.' This was an exaggeration, but Vanbrugh was starting to have problems with his choice of stone.

Building operations were suspended over the winter of 1705, and work did not recommence until the following spring. All went well initially, but there were incidents of vandalism, which tend to suggest that there was antagonism on site. Whatever the motive, 'some ill person unknown' is recorded as breaking the moulded bases of some pilasters.

At this time Vanbrugh started to design the bridge over the Glyme valley, which was to form the northern entry of the palace. This seems to have been one of his favourite structures in the making of the Blenheim estate, as the dogged manner in which he was to defend his bridge

Above: The Grand Bridge, Vanbrugh's pride and joy, was compromised by the duchess.

design from the duchess reveals. But his first skirmish was with Wren, who had also made a design for the bridge – no doubt more sensible and less costly than Vanbrugh's. The man with control over the money, Lord Treasurer Godolphin, had to decide between the two, and on 19 April he chose Vanbrugh's design. This must have been, for Vanbrugh, a most encouraging triumph of art and youth over age and economy.

By May 1706 the main house had been raised to principal floor level, and by November the east wing and the kitchen wing had been roofed. But by June building costs were beginning seriously to outstrip Treasury payments. The root problem with the cash flow was the imprecise arrangement, seemingly dreamed up by Queen Anne, by which the construction of the palace was to be financed. Parliament had approved the project without voting any specific amount of money for construction. This loose arrangement, in which the Marlboroughs seemed to have been slipped a purpose-built palace as well as an estate, must have seemed like very clever work at the time. But it depended, due to its informality, on one crucial ingredient remaining constant: royal favour and support. When this support started to evaporate, the money supply not only dwindled but, by 1712, had ceased altogether.[13]

In the spring of 1706 this catastrophe was still inconceivable. In May Marlborough and his allies won the Battle of Ramillies, and in June he was fully occupied with the conquest of Belgium. He nonetheless had time to think of Blenheim, and on 3 June 1706 he wrote to Sarah: 'I am so persuaded that this campaign will bring us a good

peace that I beg of you to do all you can that the house at Woodstock may be carried up as much as possible, that I may have a prospect of living in it.' This was the cue for Sarah to begin to involve herself in earnest in the building works. She chivvied Vanbrugh, she harried the builders and wrote almost daily to the duke to advise him of the results. The complaining tone of Sarah's letters is revealed by Marlborough's replies. In October 1706 he wrote to his wife: 'I hope Mr Hawksmore will be able to mend those faults you find in the house, but the great fault I find is that I shall never live to see it finished; for I had flattered myself that if the war should happily have ended this next year, I might the next after have lived in it.'

In December 1706 the duke himself travelled to Woodstock to inspect the works. Given his long absence and Sarah's volume of critical letters, it must have been an anxious moment for the building team. But Marlborough, ever the gentleman and realist, approved the works. What else could he do?

But in the larger and corrupt world of political and court intrigue, of which the Woodstock extravaganza is such a typical expression, the first signs of discomfiture for the Marlboroughs were starting to appear. Sarah continued to vigorously advise – bully might be a better term – her increasingly exasperated old friend, Anne. The queen, under pressure, appointed Sarah's son-in-law, Charles Spencer, Earl of Sunderland, as secretary of state for the Southern Department. This appeared to be a very useful move for the Marlborough faction, but in the fickle, treacherous and small world of early eighteenth-century politics, successes had an awful habit of backfiring, or being turned to aid the interests of wily foes. Indeed, the stage was being set for just such a dramatic reversal of fortune: as Sunderland came into office, the Marlboroughs' bitter rival, the 45-year-old Tory Robert Harley, was gaining favour with the queen. And if Harley had the queen's ear, then Sarah was sure to lose it.

Harley is the quintessential creature of eighteenth-century politics, when personal connections were all-important and intrigue was virtually a mechanism of state. Harley entered Parliament in 1689 and was then associated with the Whigs. This was natural enough for a shrewd and ambitious politician, for the Whigs were then the power in the land, having orchestrated the Glorious Revolution of the previous year, which had brought William and Mary to the throne. His sympathies soon shifted, however, and by the time of Queen Anne's accession in 1702, he was a leader of the Tories. He was made secretary of state for the north in 1704, but because of his intrigues against the largely Whig government he was forced out of office by the Duke of Marlborough – hence the feud between the two men. But despite this reverse, Harley's influence on the queen continued through his kinswoman Abigail Masham, who, due to the good offices of her cousin the Duchess of Marlborough, had in 1704 been made the queen's lady of the bedchamber. There was an ironic twist in this piece of patronage on Sarah's part because Mrs Masham both promoted Harley (until they fell out in 1714) and gradually supplanted Sarah in the queen's affections.

Largely as a result of manoeuvrings in the queen's chambers and whispering campaigns against the Marlboroughs, the Treasury had allowed the Blenheim debt to rise to £20,000 by the spring of 1707. This was a colossal figure in eighteenth-century terms, when the construction of an average London terraced house cost no more than £300–£400, and an ordinary working man in England's towns and cities would earn between £40 and £50 per year. Clearly, an awful lot of tradesmen in Woodstock and the surrounding area were owed money for wages and materials, and, even worse, it was not clear who was responsible for payment – Vanbrugh, the Marlboroughs, the Crown or the government. Somebody was living on credit and, as was so often the case, it was the tradesmen who had to suffer.

As if the mounting chaos and uncertainty brought about by cash-flow problems was not enough to contend with, Vanbrugh added his own very particular contribution to the dangerous mix of rising construction costs and increasing debts. Some time in the early months of 1707, soon after the duke's site visit, Vanbrugh decided to change the main order on the palace from simple Doric to far more ornate and expensive Corinthian.[14] Presumably this decision was made following a discussion with the duke, and the fact that the main building had already risen to a height of 27 feet (8 metres) seems not to have greatly bothered either man. The Strongs' account for April 1707 records what happened: 'In pulling down the two sixty-foot stretches on ye south front joining to ye south-east and south west pavilions, the former being 27ft high... the latter 13ft... Also pulling down the 37 ft stretches

on the east side the south portico etc.'

In May, further alterations to the building were made, 'being my lord Duke's order', and for good measure the duchess ordered the west bow window – the one intended to serve the Long Library, and which had already been built to a height of 13 feet (4 metres) – be taken down and rebuilt to a design that would admit more light.

These continuing alterations to the fabric no doubt improved, or at least ennobled, the design, but it was a crazy way to run any building site, especially one already in debt to the tune of £20,000. The workforce, especially the seasoned masons accustomed to Wren's eminently professional methods, must have been amazed, appalled and then – considering their unpaid bills – disgusted.

The fragile edifice that was the Blenheim project started to unravel in earnest in the summer of 1707 when Sarah absented herself from court on account of Queen Anne's preference for Mrs Masham. Sarah's failure to manage the queen was a failure to manage the finances for the completion of Blenheim. Things now started to go to pieces with alarming speed. Treasury money to pay long-outstanding bills simply could not be obtained. Vanbrugh wrote: 'There is So much money requir'd for Publick good this Year that My Ld Treasurer can't Afford us at Blenheim half what we want' and by November Boulter was having a great deal of trouble persuading the carters to fetch stone as without money 'theyr wants are very Greate, wee having paid them noe mony for this year's service'.

In February 1708 Marlborough and Godolphin absented themselves from the cabinet council, making the conduct of business impossible, but they agreed to reattend after they had obtained their goal – Harley's resignation. Anne was further alienated by this cynical act of political gamesmanship, which showed no respect for her feelings or dignity. The relationship between the Marlboroughs and the queen

Above: Corinthian capitals in the entrance hall, carved by Grinling Gibbons.

worsened in May. The Whigs triumphed in the general election, but Anne was enraged by the conduct of the Marlboroughs' relative Lord Sunderland, who entered into an intrigue with the Jacobites to influence the Scottish elections in the summer of 1708.

In July 1708 Marlborough won the Battle of Oudenarde. This could have been expected to restore him to royal favour, at least publicly, and perhaps it would have if it had not been for Sarah's conduct. In August the queen and duchess went to St Paul's to give thanks for Marlborough's conquests, but argued in the newly completed west portico. There, to the mortification of all onlookers, the tempestuous Sarah commanded Anne to silence when the queen tried to speak to her. Henceforth the queen's 'sincere and tender passion' for Sarah and the duke was lost, and full favour bestowed on Mrs Masham and Harley, who made a quick political comeback. From this dramatic moment it became clear that the queen could not be counted upon for support in any Marlborough enterprise, and that, with the Blenheim adventure, the duke and duchess could well be on their own.

While Sarah started to realize the full extent of their fall from grace, the duke wrote to her: 'I can't entirely agree with your opinion of the queen; I must own I have a tenderness for her, and I would willingly believe that all which is amiss proceeds from the ambition and ill-judgment of Mrs. Masham and the knavery and artfulness of Mr. Harley.' But this attempt to reconcile Sarah to the queen was missing the essential point. Anne wanted nothing more to do with Sarah. The duchess seems to have realized

this painful possibility before her husband, and from August 1708 planned to build herself a house in London, prompted no doubt by the fear that she would soon lose her grace and favour apartment in St James's Palace. The house, to be built on a plot of land adjoining the palace and overlooking St James's Park (a gift from the queen in better days), was to be paid for by the Marlboroughs. So while hundreds of builders and their families suffered in Woodstock because bills and wages were not being paid, Sarah was preparing to spend lavish sums on a London palace. The duke initially opposed the scheme but not, it seems, because of expense: 'As for myself, I am so desirous of living at Woodstock that I should not much care to do anything but what is necessary anywhere else.' However, the duchess reported that he gave her 'leave to make this house precisely as I liked to have it and to employ who I pleased, upon which I sent for Sr. C. Wren and told him I hoped it would bee no great trouble to him to look after the building I was going to begin…but that he must promise me two things. First that hee would make the contracts reasonable and not as crown work… The other article was that hee must make my house strong, plain and convenient and that he must give me his word that this building should not have the least resemblance of any thing in that called Blenheim which I had never liked but could not prevail against Sr. John.'[15]

By building a home for herself next to St James's Palace Sarah would keep herself close to the queen. Even if not inclined to attend court, where she risked mortifying royal slights, her proximity made a reconciliation more feasible, and this, Sarah realized, was essential for her interests.

The immediate effect on Blenheim of Sarah's fall from grace was that she had more time to spend in Woodstock. Now she had the opportunity to take meddling to extremes. Although prepared to spend huge amounts of money on the duke and herself, she was resolved that everyone else should get as little as possible. In June she refused the quarry teams' requested penny a foot extra for fetching large blocks from distant quarries, and in December she had Marlborough's apartment altered to admit more light – a piece of construction that the masons had to execute twice without being paid once. She appears to have seen herself as the soul of prudent reason: 'I made Mr Vanbrugh my enemy by the constant disputes I had with him to prevent his extravagance.' The bickering between the two of them never ceased. Why, asked Sarah, should the bridge have so many rooms, and why should the kitchen court be provided with expensive covered walkways since it was only going to be used by servants?

Then, in 1708, Boulter (the comptroller whom Vanbrugh had called the duchess's 'creature') died and the duchess refused to transfer his salary (£350 per annum) to Vanbrugh, who was now obliged to undertake extra work. The relationship between the pair descended to as yet unplumbed levels of bitterness, but things must have improved a little when, in September, one Tileman Bobart was appointed by Godolphin to replace Boulter and relieve Vanbrugh of a little of his workload.

The year 1708 had been very bad for Blenheim, not least because of the 'execrable' weather. The following year, everyone seemed to agree, was a time to turn over a new leaf in the proceedings. Vanbrugh wrote a 25-page memorandum of 'the directions for Blenheim', which was (miraculously) endorsed by both the duke and the duchess. But this new spirit did not last long. In May the duke returned to The Hague and the duchess began to instigate her husband's wishes as she interpreted them. In June 1709 she wrote to Bobart: 'I have examined the Directions the Duke of Marlborough left at his going away and find them as follows: that the first worke to be finish'd is the Hall and Saloon: To compleat the Steps up to the North Portico being in number fourteen: to Pave the Hall and Corridores with Portland and black marble… the Stair cases on each side to be compleated… No Iron worke to be bespoke till I have seen the Pattern. The Bow-Window Room all boarded plaine without Parquetry.' Clearly the duke wanted the living quarters of the house finished first so that he could move in.

Then the argument began in earnest over the fate of the old manor house, a rambling building that was thought to date back to the reign of Henry I. For Sarah it spoiled the northern view from the palace, and to spend time and money on preserving it would be ludicrous. Vanbrugh thought otherwise, and on 11 June 1709 he wrote to the duchess to explain why, articulating many of the principles and convictions of the current conservation movement: 'There is perhaps no one thing, which the most Polite part of Mankind have more universally agreed in; than the Vallue they have ever set upon the Remains of distant Times…

On the Persons who have Inhabited them; On the remarkable things which have been transacted in them, Or the extraordinary Occasions of Erecting them.'

While the duchess was considering this plea for the old manor house, Vanbrugh took it upon himself to 'secure ye Old building from Tumbling downe withoutside and make it Inside a little dessent by plaister and floors and cover the Roofe with Lead and repair the Smiths house and build a boundary outwall', all of which cost about £1000. This was a drop in the ocean of Blenheim, but enough to enrage the duke and duchess. They resolved that the manor house had to go, and secured Godolphin's support for this sad act of vandalism.

But Vanbrugh was a man of spirit and was far from crushed by this rejection of his heartfelt plea for the power of history. His cunning first move was to pretend to accept defeat and to draw attention away from the ruins. He ordered demolition, but ensured that only roofless outbuildings were dismantled, and then only whenever the duchess or her supporters were sighted. Meanwhile, inside the manor house, the buttressing and rebuilding went on. This was plainly a declaration of war on the philistine duchess.

The subterfuge worked – at least at first. The duchess was satisfied that she had got her way, and in June 1709 wrote to Bobart instructing him to use the materials salvaged from the manor to help build the bridge. But four years passed and the manor still stood and had even found a new tenant – Vanbrugh. Quite how this trick was sustained for so long remains a mystery.

Presumably, Sarah conducted most of her meddling at long distance.

The Park

The job of creating the park itself fell to Henry Wise (1653–1738), gardener to William III and Queen Anne. Wise and his team were involved from the outset, clearing the ground and digging the foundations of the house before any garden work even started. In his report of 22 June 1705, Vanbrugh provided the duke with a hopelessly optimistic estimate of the time the landscaping would take: '…the Whole Gardens will be form'd and planted in a year from their beginning.'

In reality, by 1708 the formally planned gardens, covering 2000 acres (800 hectares), were only just taking shape. Two years later the men were still gravelling and turfing, and in November 1711 fruit trees and hedging were still arriving on the estate. To complicate matters, the 55-year-old duke, afraid that he would die before the garden was finished, asked Wise to speed things up. 'Accordingly Mr. Wise transplanted thither full grown trees in baskets, which he buried in the earth, which look and thrive the same as if they had stood there thirty or forty years.'[16]

The gardens, even more than the palace, were the duke's passion, and his confidence in Vanbrugh and Wise was well placed: even his enemies were impressed by the gardens.[17] On 9 March 1706 Hearne recorded in his diary that the gardens 'seem to be very extraordinary and to exceed anything of that nature in England'.

The Fall and Rise of the Marlboroughs

After the battle of Malplaquet in September 1709, Marlborough became aware of rumours that he was prolonging the war for his own greater gain and glory. He must have sensed that his enemies were closing in. He needed the queen's protection but feared that he would not enjoy it unless she and his wife were reconciled. He wrote to the queen and received a reply that was bafflingly ambiguous: 'I desire nothing but that she would leave off teasing and tormenting me and behave herself with the decency she ought both to her friend and Queen.' But what Sarah was later to refer to as 'the Great Change' had already taken place and was irrevocable. In the spring of 1710 Sarah contrived an interview at Kensington Palace, during which the queen coldly told her former friend that 'whatever you have to say, you may put it in writing'. They never met again.

And things got worse. In June 1710 Sarah's son-in-law, Lord Sunderland, was dismissed by the queen from his position as secretary of state. The rapid and very public decline of the Marlboroughs may have may been met with glee among people around Blenheim but it also provoked near panic. On 24 June Vanbrugh wrote to the duchess: 'Your Grace will not wonder that some of the People at Blenheim, who trust the works with very great sums (some of them more than they are really worth in the world) should be a little frightened with the news of my Lord Sutherland, and other things they daily hear. And this apprehension I find is like to

prove a great hindrance to the very hopeful progress this summer, unless something be done to encourage 'em; which I believe a Letter from your Grace would do…'[18]

Sarah responded in characteristic manner. Rather than offering any payment, she stopped the works and laid off the men 'till the crown should direct Money'. This did not happen until October, so there was no work on site for over three good building months.[19]

A second blow fell on 7 August 1710, when Queen Anne dismissed the Marlboroughs' friend Lord Godolphin after 30 years' service and put their enemy, Robert Harley, in his place. Again, panic hit Woodstock and the surrounding region – this time among merchants who, because of the Marlboroughs' status and good connections, had been supplying the works on credit and were owed large sums. Joynes wrote to the Treasury official Travers on 13 August: 'The ill news of my Lord Treasurer being out causes a Mighty Talk here and I am Afraid will make people in ye Country not give such Creditt as ye worke will require if we continue going on as we have without theirs such Supplys to Convince them that ye Building is in all likelihood to proceed as it has done for ye time past.' Travers responded: 'By this Change, the Duke of Marlborough will be fonder than ever of hastening to live at Blenheim…and nobody can think he will suffer the Work to be discontinued for want of the usual Supplys now 'tis so near an end.' But Travers was wrong in this assessment of the duke's mood for at this time Marlborough wrote to Sarah: 'Whilst Lord Godolphin was in and I had the Queen's favour I was very earnest to have it [Blenheim] finished; but as it is, I am grown very indifferent. For as things are now, I do not see how I can have any pleasure in living in a country where I have so few friends.'

In October 1710 Sarah sent orders to Joynes and Bobart that all works at Blenheim were to be stopped immediately until the Treasury issued money or the duke returned. The masons and workmen were unceremoniously turned off without payment. After five years the whole Blenheim project was within an ace of a most spectacular collapse. The palace would, it seemed, be a monument, but not of the sort that any had originally envisaged: it would be a ruin, standing beside the decayed manor house, commemorating the utter collapse of the Marlboroughs' ambition and power.

This mood of defeat and despair was picked up by the workforce which, unpaid and now unemployed, started to turn nasty. Joynes feared the consequences of '…turning off Such a body of poor Necessitous people without paying them' and noted that '…they have begun their pranks already in breaking Some Capitalls of ye Columns for Mr Banck's Colonade'.[20] Besides all this, an election at Woodstock was imminent, which meant more trouble, including riots that the Tories from Oxford would do their best to direct against Blenheim and the Marlboroughs. In an attempt to calm and appease 'the most clamorous' workers, the clearly conscientious Travers distributed £300 out of his own pocket.

Vanbrugh had his own solution to the problem. At the Treasury he approached Harley, now the power in the land and head of an entirely Tory ministry, and applied for money on the grounds that Blenheim was properly to be seen as a monument to the queen's glory rather than a palatial home for Harley's arch-enemy. This was a nicely reasoned argument but was insufficient in itself. The clinching inducement to Harley to release funds was the threat of the duke resigning his military obligations and returning home to make trouble. Consequently, in November 1710, Harley released £7000 for the works to tide things over. Essentially, this was a bribe to keep Marlborough away.

The duchess wrote bitterly in December 1710 that she could not care less what happened to Blenheim – it could stay as it was. As far as she could see, it would never be finished and so 'it could never be any advantage or pleasure to my Lord Marlborough or his Family, but might remain as a Monument of Ingratitude, instead of what was once intended'. A month later Joynes estimated the Blenheim debt at a massive £35,000.

The duke returned to England that same month to be told by the queen that Sarah had to remove herself entirely from court life. For the duke this was 'much greater mortification than any other personal thing', yet he could not in conscience resign his military role. 'I call God to witness that I love the Queen and my country with devotion, and it is from this motive that I have made so much effort to keep my post.' Sadly, the following month he returned to duty and to The Hague.

But, against all the odds, this was not the end for Blenheim. Somehow the duke recovered his tranquillity, presumably because he still regarded the palace as a national rather than a personal monument, which it was his duty to complete. In

June he went to talk to Robert Harley, the orchestrator of his downfall, about funds for the project. In June, Harley (now created Lord Oxford) requested an estimate for the completion of the works (Vanbrugh quoted £87,000), and obtained the queen's approval to release £20,000, with more to follow.

But Sarah's vindictive and foolish final action to spite the queen undid much of her husband's good work with Harley. When, in May, Sarah was ordered to leave her apartment in St James's Palace she stripped the rooms, taking even brass locks. (She was narrowly prevented by the duke from ripping out the marble fire surrounds.) The queen was so angry when she found out what had happened that she swore never to complete a house for the Duke of Marlborough when the duchess had pulled hers to pieces.

Despite this petulant last tantrum by Sarah, the promised £20,000 did make its way from the Treasury to Blenheim – but it was much too little to put the books in order. All Vanbrugh could do was to urge the workmen to continue and 'trust the building' despite their debts, which amounted to about £9000 for the Strongs alone. Then, when all were still reeling from the string of catastrophes, came the biggest of all. On New Year's Eve 1711 Queen Anne dismissed Marlborough from all his employments, both civil and military, on the grounds that information against him had been brought before Parliament on charges of embezzlement. At Blenheim people were 'amazed' and 'doubtful of ever being paid'.

But incredibly, as if this huge project had somehow acquired a life of its own, building work limped on through the spring of 1712. This was fuelled by the payment of £1000 a week from the Treasury – a sum used to cover only current expenses and not to pay arrears.

In the summer the duke, the fallen hero who was eventually to clear himself of the embezzlement charges, resolved to go abroad, so he visited Blenheim in August, perhaps for the last time. Joynes, as the senior resident clerk, was put in charge. His statement, repeated in subsequent lawsuits, claimed that the duke told him: 'I… determine to put the care of this Building into your hands, that if any damage comes to it you are the person I shall call to account… Do you take it into your possession and attend the same till you hear from me to the contrary.'

Years afterwards it was agreed in the courts, during actions to secure payment for long-overdue wages and bills, that work officially stopped on 1 June 1712, but nobody seemed to have realized it at the time. Money did indeed cease to come through from the Treasury, but that was nothing new, and no order to stop work was issued by either the queen or the Marlboroughs. But there was a limit as to how long building operations could continue without funds, and the work gradually petered out.

In July 1712 the outstanding debt for the Blenheim works was £44,947 14s 5d, with the Treasury having by then paid £233,000.

In January 1713 Vanbrugh suffered an unexpected blow as a result of his Blenheim activities. He wrote to the mayor of Woodstock, replying on the duke's behalf to a request for funds to help with the paving of the town. This letter reveals that there was bad blood between the palace and the people of Woodstock, no doubt a result of the many debts owed to local tradesmen. Vanbrugh suggested that the duke would already have paid for the paving scheme 'but for the continual plague and bitter persecution he has most barbarously been followed with for two years past'. This letter miscarried, going to a major in the town rather than the mayor, and eventually found its way into the hands of Harley. The indiscretions of the letter were enough for Harley to get poor, blustering Vanbrugh dismissed from his post at the Board of Works and to lose him his promotion at the College of Arms. Sarah, rather than feeling sorry for Vanbrugh's suffering on behalf of her family, merely remarked cattily that it was all due to the fellow's dreadful spelling.[21]

In February 1713 the duke and duchess quietly left the country, almost like debtors fleeing their creditors. Blenheim was now left to vegetate. Travers of the Treasury had no money to send and simply advised that, in his opinion, the best that could be done was to attempt to preserve the construction site 'from running to ruine'.

In November the first legal action was launched for recovery. Mr Barker, a joiner, decided that his best target was Marlborough rather than the Treasury (and by implication the queen) and sued the duke in his absence for £350. The action was settled out of court, presumably without Marlborough accepting liability for the debt.

This paved the way for other actions, one of which was launched by the master mason Edward Strong, who then retracted.

But then fate took a hand. In early August 1714 Queen Anne died, and within a day of her death the Marlboroughs were back in England. The Whigs brokered the establishment of the Hanoverians on the throne and Marlborough, long associated with the Whig party, was restored to his former position by George I. As an expression of his obligations to his architect, he promptly secured a knighthood for John Vanbrugh. The following month King George had Harley committed to the Tower and impeached for his conduct of the peace negotiations of 1713 and for his dealings with the Jacobites. He was eventually acquitted but his power was broken.

Basking in the glory of his newly regained status and high place at court, Marlborough announced that he was resolved to finish Blenheim, even at his own cost, once he had been 'discharged from the claim of the Workmen for the Debt in the Queens time' which he would not take responsibility for. In September 1716 the debt was acknowledged and adjusted: only £16,000 would be paid against the £45,000 owed. In December Blenheim creditors claiming £10 or less were paid in full by the Crown. The rest received approximately one-third of what was owed to them.

It was too much to expect those who had downed tools in 1712 to take them up again in 1716 with two-thirds of their debts unpaid. What was to be done? Vanbrugh came up with a ruthless solution that preyed on human frailty. If the master tradesmen and craftsmen could not be paid or persuaded to return to site, why not offer a chance to their foremen? These men, argued

Opposite: The ceiling in the saloon, painted by Laguerre, shows Marlborough in military triumph.

Vanbrugh, would leap at the chance to establish themselves and would be cheaper and nearly as skilled as their masters. The scheme worked, as is revealed by the four carved marble Doric door frames in the saloon. Almost certainly designed by Hawksmoor, only one was completed by Grinling Gibbons by the time works were halted in 1712. The others were carved by foreman masons after 1716 – and there was no discernible loss of quality.

But the roller-coaster ride was far from over. Just as things at Blenheim were once again starting to look rosy, the duke suffered a stroke and Sarah was, once more, in charge. Relations between her and Vanbrugh quickly returned to their old, strained footing.

The main source of conflict was the bridge. Sarah had always thought it too large and expensive, and in a fit of irritation she sent Vanbrugh's friend Brigadier Richards a 30-page diatribe listing the faults and inadequacies of her architect. This, finally, was more than Vanbrugh could take. He wrote to the duchess on 8 November 1716 and sacked her as his client before she could sack him as her architect. Referring to the letter she had sent to Richards, he said: 'These Papers Madam are so full of

Far-fetched, Labour'd Accusations, Mistaken Facts, Wrong Inferences, Groundless Jealousies and strain'd Constructions: That I shou'd put a very great affront upon your understanding if I suppos'd it possible you cou'd mean anything in earnest by them; but to put a Stop to my troubling you any more. You have your end Madam, for I will never trouble you more Unless the Duke of Marlborough recovers so far, to shelter me from such intolerable treatment.'

Blenheim no longer had an architect. Hawksmoor and the master builders had all gone or were going, and even the faithful comptroller

Above: The saloon, showing two of the four magnificent Doric door surrounds.

Joynes had had enough. Bobart, however, stayed on, and Sarah asked him to prepare a report and plan showing what remained to be done. This exercise highlighted the many unfinished areas, including the fact that 'there was not one of ye Stair cases finish'd in the whole House'. Years later, Sarah owned that in 1716 thousands described the house as a 'Chaos, and [said] that no body but God Almighty could finish it'.

James Moore, the man Sarah engaged to make Blenheim habitable, was as unlikely an architect as Vanbrugh, being a cabinet-maker who specialized in mirrors or pier glasses. Sarah called Moore her 'oracle, of very good sense… very honest and understanding of many trades…', and from 1717 until 1724 he weakly obeyed her orders. This, of course, involved clearing away what remained of the old manor house, and by 1719 work had advanced far enough on the main building for Sarah and the ailing duke to move in. This happened without fanfare or celebration and the couple had only two summers to enjoy their palace together. In 1722 the duke died, his life no doubt shortened by the worries and woes that had surrounded this monument to his glorious military feats – which by 1722 many had forgotten and some even repudiated. What had been intended as a great display of public gratitude had become a private nightmare. Sarah was left to deal with the avalanche of lawsuits.

Legal Battles

The Strongs, owed £12,526 10s 3d for Blenheim, had filed an action in the Court of Exchequer against the duke in 1718, which they won in

1721.[22] Vanbrugh, who gave evidence in the case, stressed that, as far as he was concerned, it was the Marlboroughs who were responsible for the Blenheim debt, not the Crown. This was to prove a damning interpretation of the situation for Sarah. Vanbrugh insisted that Marlborough had chosen him for Blenheim, and that the workmen's contracts were all in the duke's name: they had always looked upon the duke as their paymaster. Vanbrugh admitted that 'the Queen had in reality engag'd her honour to build the House of Blenheim at her own Expence', but she had not made it clear how much she meant to pay for it if it should exceed the original estimate. He supported this by referring to the warrant appointing him surveyor: this made it clear that he acted 'at the request and desire of the Duke of Marlborough', making no mention of the Crown at all.

Sarah protested that if Godolphin had signed such a warrant, he must have been tricked into it, and the duke should not be bound by a document he knew nothing about. In fact, Godolphin had named the duke in the warrants to ensure that the workmen charged lower rates than for Crown work, a move that backfired spectacularly.

After the Strongs won their case, the floodgates opened. The duchess took the stance generally adopted by an unprincipled client locked in a financial dispute: she would not pay because the tradesmen had not done the work well or as instructed, or because they were overcharging for what they had done. Her counter-petition and self-serving indignation aroused fury in the litigants. There was a great desire among them to 'spare no cost to pull downe ye Divel's Grandmother'.

The duchess's case was heard before Lord Chancellor Macclesfield on 4 July 1721. In it she named 401 people, who had 'combined and confederated together to load the Duke of Marlborough with ye payment of the debts due on account of ye Building before her late Majesty putt a Stop thereto' having charged 'excessive and unreasonable rates and prices for the same'.

Macclesfield (who was shortly afterwards fined £30,000 for bribery and embezzlement in the discharge of his judicial duties), took the duchess's side. He prevented Vanbrugh from suing the duke for the £1660 still owing to him, Joynes was to give a strict account of all the money he had received from Blenheim, and the others were to have their work remeasured and their cases restated, which would take two years, at which point further deliberation would ensue.

During this sordid dispute the duke died – almost 17 years to the day after the foundation stone was laid at Blenheim.

The bitter and unresolved legal battles, the exchange of accusations and the unpaid bills did not stop Sarah building at Blenheim, and nor, extraordinarily, did this recent history prevent her employing men who must have been tainted through association with her enemies.

In 1722 she employed Hawksmoor to design and Townsend and Peisley to build the Woodstock Gate, a triumphal arch that would act both as a memorial to the duke and a fitting entrance to the park from Woodstock. But even this enterprise soon ran into difficulties. A gardener in Woodstock refused to move from his cottage, which stood on the site Sarah required

for her arch. The duchess was forced to choose a less appealing site that would mean her guests approaching Blenheim via a circuitous route through the streets of Woodstock. This also met with opposition from the townspeople, who were clearly fed up with the Marlboroughs and their unpaid debts. This time Sarah won, and in October 1722 she dismissed local opinion with the haughty remark that 'no Body of that Town has Merit enough to put me to any inconvenience upon Their account'.

The gate, a handsome enough creation, is out of keeping with the tone of Blenheim, for Sarah used it to glorify her husband. She seems never to have understood the real meaning of Blenheim – a monument to England and military triumph. She saw it as a personal shrine rather than a national one.

The inscription she placed on the gate says it all: 'This gate was built the year after the death of the most illustrious John Duke of Marlborough by order of Sarah his most beloved wife, to whom

he left the sole direction of the many things that remained unfinished of this fabrick. The services of this great man to his country the pillar will tell you which the Duchess has erected for a lasting monument of his glory and her affection to him.'

The pillar referred to in the inscription had, in fact, not yet been started. Work began on the designs in 1725, but its erection was delayed due to confusion of purpose and uncertainty of siting.

Vanbrugh had envisaged some kind of plain column in his plans for Blenheim, and Hawksmoor drew endless plans for an 'obelisk'. But, wilful as ever, Sarah suddenly chose to reject the baroque architecture that had given Blenheim its distinct character and instead chose an orthodox classical design produced by two leading lights of the new Palladian movement, both outspoken critics of Vanbrugh and Hawksmoor. The Earl of

Above left: The Woodstock Gate, designed by Hawksmoor in 1722–3, is the main formal entry to the Blenheim estate.
Above right: The Column of Victory, completed in 1731.

Pembroke and Roger Morris, inspired by antique prototypes, offered the duchess a giant Doric column sitting on a pedestal.

As work commenced, Sarah began to think about the wording for the inscription on the column. She had a mind 'to expose the ingratitude even of those that reaped the advantages of these successes', but a friend wisely cautioned her that ''tis not worth going to the Tower for it'.

Ironically, the chosen inscription was supplied by Sarah's arch-enemy, Lord Bolingbroke, who had once fought side by side with the duke but then conspired to bring him down. The words he produced reflected his 'just and sincere Regard for the memory of the Duke of Marlborough' and Sarah 'thought it the finest thing that was possible for any man to write': 'The Battle was Bloody: the Event decisive. The Woods were pierced: the Fortifications trampled down. The Enemy fled. The Town was taken…'

The Battle Over

The column was in place by 1731 and Blenheim Palace itself was completed to the duchess's satisfaction by 1735.

Sarah considered that she had done her duty to the duke, but told her grand-daughter, Lady Diana Spencer, that one more job remained. She intended to erect a fine statue of Queen Anne '…in the bow window room at Blenheim with a proper inscription… I have a satisfaction in showing this respect to her, because her kindness to me was real. And what happened afterwards was compassed by the contrivance of such as are in power now.'

The 'proper inscription', penned by Sarah herself, is hardly warm: 'Queen Anne was very Graceful & Majestic in her Person… she always meant well… She had no Vanity in Her Expenses, nor bought any one Jewel in the whole Time of her Reign… as to her Robes, it will appear by the Records in the Exchequer that in Nine Years she spent only Thirty two Thousands and Fifty Pounds including of Coronation expense… her behaviour to all that approached Her was decent and full of Dignity, and shew'd Condescention, without Art or Meanness.'

The statue still stands in the 'bow window room' but now bears a more modest inscription: 'To The Memory of Queen Anne Under Whose Auspices John Duke of Marlborough Conquered And to Whose Munificence He and His Posterity with Gratitude Owe the Possession of Blenheim.'

Sarah seldom lived at Blenheim, but she was protective of it. In her will she stipulated that the house was not to be stripped, and it remained unaltered for 15 years after her death in 1744.

However, her great-grandson, George, who succeeded to the dukedom in 1758, wanted to 'embellish' Blenheim and bring it up to date. Little could be done to alter the imposing façade of the building, so George concentrated on the grounds. Lancelot (Capability) Brown was brought in and he advocated a more 'natural' approach to the landscape. Brown uprooted much of the formal garden to create swathes of grass, then daringly replaced the narrow canal that flowed beneath Vanbrugh's heroic bridge with a vast and meandering lake. This meant flooding the lower rooms in the bridge and putting over 100 acres (40 hectares) under water,

but it was worth it. Vanbrugh's monumental yet romantic architecture was given a setting that fully realized the heroic and sublime nature of the original concept.

From a monstrous process of creation – a maelstrom that plumbed the depths of human nature – a masterpiece had been born. Vanbrugh's very personal architecture will always divide opinion: it is far too provocative and idiosyncratic to please everyone, but it must be admitted that the palace in its park is one of the most memorable and moving architectural ensembles in the world. It is a monument to power both personal and national. It is also a reminder that beauty can be born out of chaos and that poisonous intentions can lead to poetry.

Sarah gave herself the last word. In 1730 she commissioned a magnificent tomb for her husband and herself. Designed by William Kent and executed by John Michael Rysbrack, it cost £2200 – the value of a couple of large West End houses at the time. It shows the duke standing in the garb of a Roman emperor while Sarah looks up at him admiringly. Below are representations of History and Fame, while a sarcophagus crushes not death, 'the last enemy of all', but through death destroys the evil dragon of envy.

The duke, a colossus on the battlefield and in world affairs, had been humbled, as Sarah saw it, by the envy of lesser men. But with his death, and through the splendid realization of Blenheim, the canker of envy was killed and the glory of Marlborough finally and fully revealed to posterity.

Opposite: The north front showing the entrance portico and, in the foreground, a pavilion topped by a military trophy.
Below left: The statue of Queen Anne in the library.
Below right: The tomb of the duke and duchess in the chapel.

Cardiff Castle

Cardiff Castle has a very unlikely setting for a great and ancient fortress. It stands among the swirl of a modern city, with roads encircling its walls, and nineteenth- and twentieth-century commercial buildings peering over its battlements. This strange setting is appropriate, for much about the castle is bizarre. The most striking features are the Clock Tower and an authentically medieval-looking, galleried wall walk. Are these remarkable survivals or are they spirited revivals of the Middle Ages? A glance inside the building reveals all.

Cardiff Castle enjoys a history stretching back nearly 2000 years, and the shell keep astride its mound is genuine twelfth century, but all the things that really matter here date from the later nineteenth century. The place is an overwhelmingly powerful evocation of the Middle Ages, at once quirky and individual, but also scholarly and archaeological. And among all the medieval paraphernalia and details is something else – a clear obsession with Creation. The great artistic inspiration is natural history – the worlds of plants, insects, animals – geology

and mineralogy, and the planets and the heavens. This fusion of authentic and revived Gothic, of medieval motifs and forms with those of natural history is designed and executed with such skill that these interiors are among the greatest and most personal architectural creations of nineteenth-century Britain. But what does it all mean?

This is more difficult to answer than it should be for such a recent and significant building. The architect for the works, William Burges, and his client, the Marquis

of Bute, did not document the reasons that underpinned this extraordinary artistic collaboration. All that can now be done is to look at the building in detail and try to explain the castle by placing it in the cultural and scientific context of its age.

Darwin and His Theories

In many ways, the story starts with a meeting of the British Association for the Advancement of Science that took place in the Oxford University Museum in 1860. This was the first key debate between modern men of science and theologians. Progressive science in the 1860s championed the work of Charles Darwin, who, in 1859, published his epoch-making analysis of life, *On the Origin of Species*. Darwin's theories challenged the biblical account of Creation, thus undermining the very foundations on which orthodox Christianity was based. Consequently, the Church of England felt obliged to belittle Darwin and his work. Darwin, who never intended to challenge Christianity, and was more horrified than anyone by the implications of his work, was too ill through nervous exhaustion to appear at the debate. Putting his case was his enthusiastic supporter Thomas Henry Huxley. Putting the case for the Church was the Bishop of Oxford.

The bishop, with the full weight of convention behind him, scented an easy victory over these myopic scientists. During the debate he asked condescendingly and, as he thought, crushingly

Previous page: The towered romance of Cardiff Castle looking east from the garden.
Opposite: Aerial view of Cardiff Castle in its city-centre context.

whether it was through his grandmother or grandfather that Huxley claimed descent from an ape. Huxley, whispering 'The Lord hath delivered him into mine hands,' rose to the challenge and told the bishop: 'I would rather have a miserable ape for a grandfather than a man highly endowed by nature and possessed of great means and influence and yet who employs these faculties for the mere purpose of introducing ridicule into a grave scientific discussion.'[1]

In the context of the time and place, this constituted a witty and humiliating rebuff to the bishop, and meant that the debate ended in a manner few had anticipated. Science was seen to have won the argument. The biblical account of Creation in Genesis was no more than a myth, with the reality, outlined by Darwin, being a more convincing account of the creation and evolution of life on Earth.

The Church, and the disconcerted bishop, realized they had a genuine fight on their hands – a fight for the survival of their particular interpretation of Christian belief and for the proposition that the Bible is the word of God and must be taken literally.

Darwin had not intended to produce a controversial book. He was a meticulous researcher who had compiled and objectively analyzed much material gathered from the far corners of the globe over many years. During this work he had made a number of observations, which, linked together and developed, led him to a conclusion that was inevitable but which he trembled to express. Man was not, as stated in the Bible, a divine creature made by God in his image, but a mere animal that, like other animals,

had evolved over millennia by a random and arbitrary process of natural selection, which meant that some life forms flourished while others perished.

Darwin had drawn much of his inspiration from methods used by animal and plant breeders to produce modifications in domestic species. These techniques of 'artificial selection' inspired Darwin to call the equivalent process in nature 'natural selection'. What most alarmed him about the conclusions he was reaching was that the

selection process appeared so random – so unpredictable. It implied that God worked without a plan or direction. The essence of Darwinian theory lay in the concept of trial and error – the trial being provided by variations, and the error being expressed by extinct species. The variations that flourished in the 'struggle for life' Darwin called the 'favoured races', but it was not then apparent to him that those species that survived were necessarily better suited to their environment than those that perished. Indeed, if suitability for habitat was the prerequisite for survival, then, as Darwin later confided to a friend, the Siberian mammoth would be alive to this day. The concept of the 'survival of the fittest' – the process of natural selection by which 'superior' organisms, their forms continually adapting and adjusting to their environment, win the competition for the limited resources needed for survival – was to be grafted on to Darwin's work at a later date by another pioneering naturalist, the sociologist and philosopher Herbert Spencer.

A fundamental requirement for Darwin's theory to work is time. Evolution, as explained in *Origin of Species*, was slow, reforming rather than revolutionary, demanding long periods of time over which the evolutionary process can take its course.

The orthodox Christian view in the 1850s, based on the analysis of biblical texts, was that the world was around 6000 years old. This was not nearly long enough for Darwin's theory to work in practice, so it not only undermined Christian notions about the origin of life and man's divine nature, but also challenged the Christian concept of the age of the Earth.

But on this latter point at least Darwin was not alone.

Geological Evidence

The erosion of orthodox Christian views and the Victorian fascination with natural history were not sparked off by the ideas of Darwin. His writings were the culmination of 50 years of intense scientific speculation and exploration into all

aspects of creation, living and extinct, active and inert, for an answer to a number of big questions. How was life created? Why and how did life evolve? What is the relationship between all living things? Where did man come from?

These new insights were stimulated by imperial expansion, which revealed startling new life forms, and by massive engineering projects, such as the excavation of canals, railway cuttings and deep coal mines, which exposed the Earth's geological and fossil secrets. Suddenly animals, birds, fishes, beetles, plants, the Earth's crust were seen to hold the great secret of life and of the origin of man.

Since the late eighteenth century, botanists, philosophers and geologists had been making discoveries that suggested the world had developed over an incredibly long period, and that species had apparently evolved and become extinct. It was clear to many that Christianity had to accommodate rather than reject new, objective, scientific revelations about the age of the planet and about the nature of life. For example, in 1802 the Reverend Paley argued that all the recent excavation discoveries supported rather than challenged the presence of God. They indicated, he said, that a profound and divine plan was in operation, and all its complex, evolving and adapting parts were, as in a mighty watch, working together for a great purpose, often not apparent to the limited vision of man. God was the great watchmaker! Quite simply, since nature was the work of God, all things that were the product of natural forces were also, ultimately and arguably, the works of God.[2]

The first coherent and scientific analysis of

geological evidence was compiled by Charles Lyell and published as *Principles of Geology* in three volumes between 1830 and 1833. Lyell concluded that the world was of extreme age and had been created gradually by forces, such as erosion, earthquakes and volcanoes, that are still at work. This challenged earlier theories, such as that of Georges Cuvier, the father of French natural history, that the world and life were the consequences of extraordinary catastrophes or unrepeated phenomena such as biblical creation.

Lyell's convincing argument for the great antiquity of the Earth and for gradual change provided a firm foundation for Darwin's theory of evolution through slow biological change. Lyell's exploration and explanation of the fossil record, the nature of the construction of the Earth, the dates of stones and clays, the evidence of ancient changes in the nature of the Earth did question the literal truth of the Bible's account of a six-day act of Creation. As Lyell explained, one of his reasons for compiling *Principles of Geology* was 'to sink the diluvianists'. But he did not want specifically to challenge God's role in the creation of Earth, and in fact his investigations revealed only that different strata of the Earth contained different types of fossils and that, through the centuries, these fossil creatures transformed and became gradually more complex. This implied a sense of progress and suggested that all was being developed in accordance with a divine plan.

To many Christians, however, even relatively modest discoveries had potentially disturbing implications. If the biblical account of Creation was acknowledged to be wrong or, put more charitably, was accepted not as literal truth but as myth, then what else in the Bible would also be revealed as wrong or mythical? This heralded a crisis of faith like nothing in the last 1500 years of Christianity. In question was not how to worship, but whether to worship at all. God himself, or at least the Christian perception of God as portrayed in the Bible, was under attack.

John Ruskin, the devout architectural pundit, had a reaction that was typical. In the early 1850s, to understand and interpret the apparently anti-biblical information about Creation latent in geology and fossils, Ruskin indulged in amateur geological activity. He found the experience deeply disturbing. The sound of geologists' hammers took on a terrible meaning – they were knocking away the foundations of his faith. 'If only the geologists would leave me alone, I could do very well, but those dreadful hammers! I hear the clink of them at the very end of every cadence of the Bible verse.'[3]

The theological problems that Ruskin and other Christians had to deal with were formidable. New geological insights made it clear that the planet was far older than the 6000 years implied by biblical texts, and new fossil discoveries, including dinosaurs, made the orthodox Christian view – that fossils were either evidence of animals still alive yet secreted in unexplored parts of the Earth, or were of species that had been killed off in the flood – increasingly untenable. To concede, as mounting scientific evidence suggested, that fossil remains belonged to extinct species that had died out millions of years ago was tantamount to admitting that God had made a mistake in his scheme of Creation and that the Bible account of Creation was wrong.

This challenge to the Bible concentrated the minds of churchmen and Christian scientists alike, and an accommodation to the geological discoveries of Lyell proved possible. The key to this accommodation was that scientific findings could be interpreted to suggest that transformations and evolution had been in accordance with a great plan drawn up by God, with man as the final and supreme act of creation.

William Buckland, geologist, canon at Christ Church, Oxford, dean of Westminster and, in 1848, the first naturalist to be a trustee of the British Museum, consolidated and expressed the new view on the relationship between Christianity and the recent discoveries of natural history. God, as all conceded, works in wondrous ways, and it was now clear that the whole world had been purposely prepared by God for its habitation by man.[4] And what was more, the Earth's crust, with its mineral resources, had apparently been specifically designed to sustain life in the nineteenth century. Deposits of coal, iron and limestone were all divinely intended to make Britain the most powerful and richest nation on Earth. Geology and natural history seemed to provide an ethical basis which allowed the technologically most advanced branch of mankind, the Europeans, to exploit less advanced peoples and remain true to Christian principles. If it were God's will to make Europeans more powerful, then it must be God's will that they use that power. This gave moral stature to the theory of 'manifest destiny' by which Europeans, or peoples of European extraction, such as the Americans, colonized and exploited the majority of the globe. Soon the new discoveries of geology

were not a threat because everything was the work of God. Stones, fossils, all works of nature began to assume a newly sacred significance.

This new, questioning way of viewing the familiar world of nature was a source of inspiration for artists. The seventeenth-century religious philosopher Sir Thomas Browne had observed that 'Nature is the art of God',[5] and quite suddenly this pleasing phrase embodied a startling new truth, which fired the imagination and led to a fresh appreciation of nature. It also had a very direct influence on the architecture of the 1850s and 1860s. For one thing, it made it legitimate to reveal materials and forms of construction – a useful liberation, given the urgent requirement of the railway age for mighty iron and glass engine sheds built quickly by industrial methods (see The Midland Grand Hotel, St Pancras, p. 176). A fascination with organic growth also paved the way for an organic architecture and, incidentally, made the structural engineer – the scientific member of the building team who better understood the complexities, implications and potential of natural growth – of greater importance. William Burges himself admitted that 'the Civil Engineer is the real nineteenth-century architect'.[6]

The most spectacular example of these changing attitudes was the Crystal Palace, designed by Joseph Paxton, significantly a gardener and designer of greenhouses rather than an architect, for the 1851 Great Exhibition. Made of iron and glass, its exposed roof structure was inspired by the *Victoria amazonica* waterlily. First discovered in the Amazon in 1837, the lily was remarkable for the huge size of its leaves, up to

7 feet (2 metres) in diameter. Clearly something this large needed a powerful structure to keep it in working order. Paxton acquired a specimen in 1848 and was deeply impressed by its immensely strong, lattice-like leaves with their network of many small ribs – a structure strong enough to carry the weight of Paxton's small daughter as she walked across the foliage. As medieval masons were inspired by sacred geometry (see Durham Cathedral, p. 40), so mid-Victorian architects and engineers were inspired by God's work as revealed through natural history.

A key building of the 1850s attempted in its fabric to represent and reflect the accommodation recently reached between science and Christianity. The Oxford University Museum, where the memorable confrontation between Huxley and the Bishop of Oxford took place, was designed by Dublin architects Deane & Woodward, but the driving forces behind its creation were Dr Henry Acland – the instigator and promoter of the museum – and John Ruskin. The museum, vaguely Venetian Gothic in manner with a central court covered by a pioneering roof structure of iron and glass, was described by Acland and Ruskin in *The Oxford Museum* (1859). This is a remarkable document for it says much about the spiritual struggles of the age, reveals how the compromise between science and religion was reached and is very explicit about the new sacred and inspirational status of natural history. 'All the building', they wrote, 'was intended to teach some great lesson, not only in art and architecture, but also in illustrations afforded' showing the relationship between art, science

Above: The iron and glass roof covering the inner court of the 1850s Oxford University Museum.

and faith. 'The very pillars around the corridors would teach geology; the iron foliage of the spandrels of the roof would teach botany... the capitals and corbels...would...exhibit a complete series of our flora and fauna.' In total the museum was to reveal the 'knowledge of the great material design of which the Supreme Master-Worker has made us a constituent part'.

Acland explained the relationship, as he saw it, between the Christian faith and natural history in a very concise manner that, in all likelihood, had a direct influence on the design of Cardiff Castle over 10 years later. 'There are two books from which I collect my divinity,' wrote Acland, 'besides that one of God, another of his servant, Nature – that universal and public manuscript that lies expansed to the eyes of all.' The museum was, in its design, decoration and materials of construction, to expose and explain God's 'Book of Nature', and by so doing 'use His natural works to explain His wonder'.

Ruskin emphasized the powerful connection between the Gothic Revival, of which he was a champion, and the appreciation of natural history. 'The great principle of the Gothic Revivalists is that all art employed in decoration should be informative, conveying truthful statements about natural facts – if it represents organic forms...it will give that form [truthfully]... I hold it simply and entirely...that ornamentation is always...most valuable and beautiful when it is founded on the most extended knowledge of natural forms.'

William Burges was, like most of his generation, a serious student of Ruskin's writings, and this passage gives a clue to Burges's intentions when he wove natural history and Gothic together

in such a startling way at Cardiff Castle.

As Acland and Ruskin wrote cosily, complacently and, as it turned out, prematurely in their museum book: '...all the phenomena of nature which were intended by the Creator to enforce His eternal laws of love and judgment... remain [until now] unread, or...read backwards... How strange it seems that physical science should ever have been thought adverse to religion...'

The happy compromise between Christianity and science that had been reached by the late 1850s explains the violent reaction of most churchmen and the majority of natural historians and scientists to Darwin's theories. Just when they believed that the threat of science had been dealt with, a new and more powerful argument arose to challenge the Bible.

As far as Darwin could see, natural selection was a random process that did not appear to reflect any divine or omnipotent plan, purpose, or sense of progress. And, more provocative still, he saw no distinction between the evolution of man and of other life forms. Man could be just the arbitrary consequence of random natural selection – the product of the vagaries of nature was just another animal, seemingly intimately related to apes.

But if Darwin was right and there was no divine plan to Creation, then nature was just a vast, amoral, savage and unfathomable free-for-all in which the strong and ruthless prospered at the expense of the weak and vulnerable. Many found this view of nature – careless of life and brutally selfish – profoundly disturbing. A nature that was, as Tennyson had prophetically described in 1833, 'red in tooth and claw'.[7]

Horror that the facts he had so diligently

amassed could be interpreted in this way plunged Darwin into an abyss of uncertainty that prostrated him for the remainder of his life. Publishing his finds was, he admitted to a friend, 'like confessing to a murder'.

The Nightmare

The possibility that man might not be a divine creation but a mere chemical 'automation' (reaction) created by a random process of natural selection settled like a dark cloud upon mid-Victorian Britain. Even Huxley, the champion of scientific agnosticism, acknowledged that 'the consciousness of this great truth weighs like a nightmare, I believe, upon many of the best minds of these days'.

The key question raised by Darwin – were people merely evolved animals or were they of a fundamentally different nature, created in the image of God – meant that the differences and similarities between humans and other animals, particularly apes, became critical. Darwin addressed this subject in his *Descent of Man* (1871), in which he clearly expressed his theory that man was no more than an evolved ape. Two camps now ranged against each other. On one side were the evolutionists with their commitment to random natural selection, and on the other were those committed to a view of Creation that was essentially reconcilable with the Bible – and dividing the two was the ape. Was he man's ancestor or merely a ferocious animal?

Once again, churchmen were uncomfortable that Darwin's theory suggested no overall divine plan or direction. A compromise had to be found, and this time it took the form of 'the survival of the fittest', a phrase, coined by the 'scientific functionalist' Herbert Spencer, which implied a satisfactory sense of progress. It had a ringing moral tone that appealed to the muscular, evangelical Christianity of the Victorians. It suggested that survival was not random, but based on excellence – moral, spiritual, intellectual and physical.

Spencer's redefining of Darwin's theory made natural selection broadly acceptable to Christian opinion. So successful was this transformation that by the mid-1870s progressive clergymen, such as the novelist Charles Kingsley, were able to become believers in Darwinism and argue most happily that it was in accord with basic Christian theology.

Apes and Architecture

It was within the context of this intellectual and spiritual turmoil that Bute and Burges created Cardiff Castle. It is only by understanding the times that it is possible to unravel the meaning of the extraordinary and enigmatic world these two men forged – a world that sometimes seems an ironic parody of the great natural history debate, but that also hints at something darker.

The characters of the two men are as strange as their creation, and their partnership, considering their disparate natures, was surprisingly successful. The Third Marquis of Bute, allegedly the richest man in Britain in the mid-nineteenth century, owned vast tracts of land in England, Scotland and Wales, including fabulously profitable coal mines and most of

like many of his generation, to Gothic art and to a romantic evocation of the Middle Ages. This passion, along with his charming eccentricities and wide personal experience of the architecture of Europe, must have been what attracted Bute to Burges.

A particularly evocative vignette of Burges was noted by the zoologist Edmund Gosse: 'He used to give the quaintest little tea parties in his bare bachelor chambers, all very dowdy, but the meal served in beaten gold, the cream poured out of a single onyx, and the tea structured in its descent on account of real rubies in the pot… His work was really more jewel-like than architecture.'[8]

Burges had turned his artistic temperament to practical means by studying engineering and then by working in a number of leading architectural offices. In 1851, just as the natural history revolution was starting to polarize opinion, he set up in practice as an architect. The passionate debate seemed to impinge little upon him: fortified by opium and alcohol, he was enthusiastically setting about the recreation of his particular vision of the medieval world.

In 1855 he won a competition to design Lille Cathedral, and in 1856 won another to design a Crimea Memorial Church. Both of these came to nothing, and it was not until 1863 that he secured his first major commission – to design St Finbar's Cathedral in Cork. It was three years later that Bute asked for his help.

The Cardiff Castle that the third marquis inherited was a sorry affair. The twelfth- and thirteenth-century castle had been enlarged in the early fifteenth century by the Earl of Warwick,

Cardiff. This material wealth he determined to use to further his passion for history, art, archaeology – and for the liturgy and ritual of religion which led him, at the age of 21, to convert to Roman Catholicism. This, in mid-Victorian Britain, was still a highly controversial action, especially when taken by a member of a rich and powerful aristocratic family. In addition, reading the clues offered by Cardiff Castle, the third marquis was fascinated by magic, the occult and mythology, and was especially interested in natural history and all its topical ramifications.

William Burges was an extravagant, inventive artist of independent means, who was devoted,

Above: William Burges, in merry mood, dressed as a medieval court jester.

who added a comfortable residential range (domestic quarters) against the west wall. This range was extended in the late sixteenth century to make the castle a luxurious and fashionable abode. But then the swirl of fashion moved away from Cardiff, and it was not until 1774, after generations of neglect, that the First Marquis of Bute employed Lancelot 'Capability' Brown and architect Henry Holland to remodel the grounds and reconstruct and extend the fifteenth- and sixteenth-century residential range. Work went slowly, was abandoned in 1794 and eventually completed only in 1817. To the third marquis the place was a mess: the alterations and additions made by Brown and Holland were archaeologically incorrect and certainly not medieval in character. They were an affront to the historically minded young Bute, with his fashionable fantasies about the arts and architecture of the Middle Ages. And, to make matters worse, the new works were still hardly habitable. Contemplating the castle, Bute realized to his dismay that he had inherited a partly ruinous, dubiously detailed 'picturesque seat'.[9] The solution he hit upon was to hire Burges to return the authentic spirit of the Middle Ages to the mutilated castle.

In 1866 Burges produced a report on the castle for the Bute trustees. It recommended three possible approaches: 1) 'Strictly conservative', only justifiable 'were the remains of high interest in the history of architecture or precious on account of their art'; 2) 'Antiquarian', leading to 'the replacement of everything that a study of archaeology would lead us to suppose was lost'; 3) 'Modern', a more radical approach, and clearly what both Bute and Burges wanted.

It was, wrote Burges, 'a conservative [method] as far as the preservation of old work is concerned, but it would involve sundry additions which are to a certain degree demanded by the fact of the castle being used as a nobleman's residence'. It was most important to remember, he concluded, 'that Cardiff Castle is not an antiquarian ruin but the seat of the Marquis of Bute'.[10]

Unsurprisingly, the 'modern' approach was chosen by the trustees, and when Bute came of age in 1868 work started straight away. In composition, the 'modern' nobleman's seat was to be a miniature city of towers inspired by medieval fantasies and by his experience, direct or through books, of the towered towns of Italy, such as San Gimignano, the campaniles of Florence and Siena, and the spiky profiles of Nuremberg and Avignon. So, utilizing the existing fifteenth- to eighteenth-century structures along the west side of the castle wall, Burges designed a long, asymmetrical range bristling with towers of different shapes and heights. As his biographer, J.M. Crook, puts it: 'Seen from its Western side, reflected in water and framed by foliage [the] silhouette is unforgettable: five towers in profile… an explosion of archaeology and romanticism.'[11]

The greatest of the towers is the Clock Tower, standing at the south end of the west range. But before the construction of this tower started in March 1869, Bute and Burges had together enjoyed the gentle fantasy of recreating a medieval garden on the site of the old moat outside the west wall of the castle. Inspired by medieval manuscripts, the garden (for the use of the public) was to contain vines and be surrounded by a high stone wall, and on top of the wall were to be

stone-carved beasts. Burges produced a sketch showing the sort of thing he wanted, then moved on to the greater challenge of the castle itself. Unfortunately, in 1881, he died before the animals could be carved, but Bute continued the project in the original spirit, ensuring that the animals were not stylized or heraldic but naturalistic. They were to be monuments to themselves, to the variety and wonder of God's creation, to the power of natural history. The animals that Burges and Bute chose are telling. Predictably they include a pair of lions (which contrive to look lifelike despite an obligation to clutch shields emblazoned with the Bute arms), a lioness, a lynx, a bear, a sea lion, a wolf, a hyena and, of course, a pair of apes. Inspired by medieval precedent or by a desire to make the animals look as realistic as possible, all were painted in natural colours and furnished with sparkling glass eyes.

The Clock Tower itself had one dominant theme – time, as represented by the movements of the heavenly bodies and temporal divisions. And time was an essential ingredient in the debate about the workability of Darwin's theory. Natural selection, according to Darwin, was gradual, so time, like apes, was a hot topic in the 1860s. Outside, the tower is furnished with a huge clock, flanked by statues representing the seven planets standing on their respective signs of the zodiac.

The tower was to provide bachelor apartments for the young marquis. They are exotically

Opposite: The Clock Tower, started in 1869, with decorations inspired by the theme of time.
Right: A lioness − one of the beasts lolling on Burges's high stone animal wall.

medieval in their decoration but also well heated and comfortable, revealing that, even for Bute and Burges, the evocation of the Middle Ages had its limits. The Winter Smoking Room, where in languid luxury Bute could puff away on his cigars in a dense smog of tobacco smoke (a Victorian room use that had absolutely nothing to do with the genuine Middle Ages), shows the worldly cycle of time and astrology. The grimacing demonic face above the entrance is, presumably, a nicotine devil warning those uninitiated in the pleasures of tobacco to keep out. Within the room the ceiling vault is painted with the signs of the zodiac, the four seasons appear in pictorial

OMNIA VINCIT AMOR ET NOS CEDAMVS AMORI

form on the walls, the six stained-glass windows show the Norse gods after whom the Saxons named the days of the week, and in the corners of the room are corbels representing the times of the day. One pair shows the sun god (also, of course, representing the seventh day of the week) depicting sunrise and noon; opposite, the moon goddess represents dusk and night. Bubbling through this major theme of time is Burges's passion for natural history. In this room, as in most in the castle, beasts abound, mostly naturalistic, sometimes grotesque, as with the marquetry monkeys that inhabit the walnut panelling and china cupboard, and the birds on the corbels.

The Bachelor Bedroom, created before Bute married in 1872, takes the wonders and wealth of the mineral and living world as its theme – a highly appropriate study for Bute since much of his fortune was won from the Earth in the form of coal. The chimney overmantel, conceived as a miniature mountain, is dotted with examples of minerals found on Bute estates; the walls are decorated with paintings showing legends from classical literature about the pursuit of precious stones, metals, pearls and coral; and above the fireplace is a homage to alchemy in the image of Hermes Trismegistus, who sought to turn base metal into gold. The 12 signs of the zodiac are represented by their respective precious stones, and the stained-glass windows depict allegories of six precious jewels – ruby, topaz, diamond,

emerald, sapphire and pearl. Looking down on this are portraits of great goldsmiths and jewellers, including Cellini and Ghiberti. Again, modern standards of comfort are followed, and adjoining the bedroom is a bathroom complete with a massive marble bath brought from Rome, and walls lined with pink 'Penarth' alabaster from the Bute estate. Burges's little creatures also make an appearance here inside the bath, which is inlaid with naturalistic metal renderings of aquatic life forms that shimmer and come to life when seen through water.

Opposite: The Winter Smoking Room invokes the worldly cycle of time and astrology.
Right: A corbel showing noon, represented by the sun god holding the sun aloft.

The climax of the Clock Tower is the Summer Smoking Room. Double-height and galleried, it occupies the upper storey and roof, and offers spectacular views over the gardens, city and surrounding country. This room, constructed between 1871 and 1874, was understandably Bute's favourite: its views, its rich and complex decorative scheme organized around the power of nature, and the summer breezes that wafted across its tile-clad floor and walls made it a wonderful retreat. The floor shows the Earth at the centre of the cosmos, a medieval view in accord with the Ptolemaic system, which postulated that the universe revolved around the

Earth. Also shown are the five continents and the life cycles of the birds and beasts of the Earth. The walls show legends associated with each sign of the zodiac (painted by Frederick Smallfield, who, with Frederick Weekes, executed much of the interior decoration). These feature extraordinary, indeed unlikely, juxtapositions of faithfully detailed creatures with romantic and emblematic figures. For example, a gigantic crab, pink, as if freshly boiled, battles a medieval warrior, while on another panel a ferocious stag

Above: Wall painting and vault in the Bachelor Bedroom showing coral and pearls being won from the sea
Opposite: The galleried Summer Smoking Room.

beetle shows its warlike mettle. The chimneypiece is embellished with the amusements of summer, including lovemaking which leads, most respectably, to courtship and matrimony. (Bute himself was married while this room was being constructed.)

In the four corners of the room are stone corbels supporting the gallery, each representing almost life-size personifications of the eight winds of classical antiquity. Looking up into the clerestory space above the gallery is to look into the heavens. The dome is painted with the constellations together with personifications of the four elements of earth, fire, air and water, all painted by Weekes. Looking down from the spandrels of the dome are portraits of astronomers, including Kepler, Herschel, La Place, Copernicus and Newton. Suspended from the dome is a gilded bronze chandelier in the form of the sun god standing upon his chariot wheel. And everywhere naturalistically painted or carved creatures abound: by the door to the stair, a small mouse emerges from the surface of the wall.

The Clock Tower was complete by 1873, and Bute, now a married man expecting a family, had to contemplate the next move. But before work could start he was hit by a crisis – the richest man

Above: In the Summer Smoking Room, painted alabaster figures representing two of the eight winds of classical antiquity.
Opposite left: A small mouse scurries along a root while a butterfly flits around a tree.
Opposite right: A large and life-like crab attacking a medieval warrior.

in Britain was in financial trouble. In 1871 and 1873 there had been major coal strikes; now the capital value of agricultural land was falling, and with it the scale of rentals, and much of Bute's capital was tied up in dock development in Cardiff. Suddenly his medieval fantasies looked rather like grotesque and inappropriate extravagance. Certainly Bute's trustees thought so. From now on the completion of Cardiff Castle and Bute's other pet project – the restoration by Burges of the thirteenth-century ruins of Castell Coch as a summer retreat – had to be paid for by the marquis from his personal income. To his credit, this did not diminish the scale of his vision, but it did delay it. Work staggered on through early 1873, and in March the foundation stone of the Bute Tower was laid. Work

commenced on the Small Dining Room within the tower, but by November 1874 Burges recorded that works at Cardiff 'had very nearly stopped'. In the spring of 1875 Bute wrote to his wife that 'Affairs are, I must say, looking as black as night… I hardly know what to say or do… If the money can't be raised, the workmen…will have to be paid off… We shall have to consider living abroad.' But money was borrowed so that works started in 1873 could be fully completed as originally conceived.

The Small Dining Room confirms that none of the vigour, richness or symbolism of the Clock Tower interior had been lost or diluted. But there is a new major theme that is continued through all the rooms in the Bute Tower. Astrology, alchemy, magic, pagan myths and gods are

replaced by biblical imagery. The story selected for the Small Dining Room comes from the book of Genesis, the key Bible text of the time, for it outlined Creation; so it seems that Burges and Bute had something more to contribute, in a most private manner, to the great evolution debate. Quite what they are saying is hard to determine with certainty. The story chosen is the life of Abraham, with scenes from Genesis in the stained-glass windows and on the overmantel above the chimneypiece. The latter illustrates the episode when Abraham and Sarah were visited by three disguised angels, who foretold the birth of a son – an unlikely event since Sarah was in her nineties and Abraham a hundred years old. The Bible describes Sarah laughing when she heard the prophecy, so she is shown laughing behind her hand. It is tempting to see this as Bute's and Burges's response to the whole earnest debate over Creation that was causing Christian scientists such agony. A comment made by Sarah after she duly gave birth to Isaac does indeed suggest that this eccentric duo saw the funny side of it all: 'God hath made me to laugh, so that all that hear me will laugh with me.' (Genesis 21:6). Perhaps, calmed by the interpretation of Spencer, who presented evolution as part of a divine plan, Bute and Burges are reflecting a new sense of optimism, even humour, about the whole trying issue.

But, despite this move towards biblical inspiration, the theme of natural history is continued. The vegetable world is venerated by carved oak trees, the leaves and roots of which – complete with life-size snail – protrude in a strange manner through holes in the overmantel. Naturalistic painted butterflies and birds fly around and above the doors, and a mischievous howler monkey, miniature but perfectly formed, lurks beside the door to the library with a nut in his mouth which, when pushed, would ring a bell to summon the castle steward.

Above the dining room in the Bute Tower Burges created the marquis's sitting room, bedroom and roof garden. The interiors are remarkable. The sitting room, which in fact incorporates some late eighteenth-century fabric, continues the Christian theme, with a frieze showing scenes from the life of St Blane, a sixth-century saint associated with the Isle of Bute. The chimneypiece, made in 1873, is another monument to natural history, this time represented by a writhing group of beavers, industrious animals much admired by Bute and introduced into the castle grounds in 1874.

Lord Bute's bedroom is of intense interest. It is dedicated to the Book of Revelation, a prophetic biblical text that always appeals to romantics and mystics such as Bute. Above the fireplace stands a statue (designed by Burges) of the author of Revelation, St John the Evangelist. The stained-glass windows illustrate the seven churches of Asia described in Revelation, and the ceiling, formed by nearly 200 bevelled-glass mirrors, reflects the name John (written in Greek on beams just below the ceiling) in both true and mirror image. The riddle is, as with life, to tell what is real and what is illusory. And again, as always, homage is played to the natural world, the wealth of minerals being represented by 36 different types of marble on the walls and on columns as in the Oxford University Museum. There are also realistic paintings of birds, notably

a fine partridge, and running as a frieze around the room is a very museum of naturally carved creatures, including beetles, frogs, turtles and sea horses. To complete the picture, a stained-glass window in the attached bathroom is embellished with a picture of a very lifelike parrot.

The staircase in the Bute Tower now rises to the roof garden, a colonnaded room completed by 1876, which is open to the sky and inspired by a Roman peristyle that Burges saw at Pompeii. But before this room is reached there is a sudden explosion of nature. The stone dome over the staircase appears to spring from carved roots that dangle below its base, and the staircase itself terminates with an extraordinary panel containing a frisking fox and beaver, while another fox sits on top of the panel. The roof garden has tiled walls telling stories from the Book of Kings and a bronze fountain of 1876, swarming with creatures, including fish, beavers and lions. Most unexpectedly, a bronze door to an adjoining room incorporates a large and very three-dimensional incarcerated otter.

The theme of natural history is echoed in other rooms. The Nursery (of 1879) in the Guest Tower has a fireplace with a fox frieze. The magnificent 'stalactite' ceiling in the Arab Room (Burges's last work before his death) is gilded and painted with animals and birds, and the Great Hall (essentially a fifteenth- and sixteenth-century structure) abounds with painted monkeys and animals, including a boar, a wolf and a fox carved

Top to bottom: In the Small Dining Room, detail of the fireplace showing Sarah laughing behind her hand, and oak leaves and roots; birds and butterflies embellish a doorway; a monkey bell-push.

on corbels, while a huge and very lifelike salmon bursts from the wall.

Below the Great Hall is the Library, and these two rooms are connected by a newel winding staircase created by Burges within the fifteenth-century octagonal Beauchamp Tower. This was not intended to be the main staircase of the castle, but became so when Burges's magnificent Grand Staircase, never completed, was demolished in 1927 and replaced by the existing modest entrance hall. Burges's newel staircase, originally to be used only by the family and guests, is a repository of natural history images that are bizarre, perhaps sinister, and certainly the product of an overheated imagination. The walls heave with images of foxes, birds and insects, mostly inspired by Aesop's fables. A corbel at the base of the stairs is supported by a particularly bloodthirsty-looking bat, while at the top of the stairs a small naked boy lies on the handrail, a ravenous crocodile perching on the newel above.

At the foot of the staircase are three doors each surmounted by an emblem revealing the different worlds to which they lead. An angel shows the way to the chapel, children point to the family rooms, and the door to the library is marked by a beaver gnawing at the Tree of Knowledge. This clearly reveals Bute's unconventional attitude to learning.

The decoration of the library, created between 1873 and 1880, has the theme of literature, language and learning, but the immediate and overwhelming impression is of nature run riot.

The bookcases and desks are embellished with a fantastic range of life forms, all carved as if they were museum specimens, including ants, stag beetles, dragonflies, parrots and even a duck-billed platypus. Around the door to the staircase are chameleons, changing colour as they scurry on their way. Amazingly, and revealingly, the most important doors of the room are decorated not with images of saints or kings, as they might be in genuine medieval work, but with carvings of monkeys. There is a tree, presumably intended as the Tree of Knowledge, full of monkeys holding apples. Some monkeys climb up the tree while others, having taken a bite of their apples and thus lost their innocence, appear to be on the way down. There is also a pair of monkeys peering into an open book – perhaps Dr Acland's 'Book of Nature', for Bute was at Oxford in the 1860s and would have been aware of the symbolism of the University Museum and the debate that surrounded its decoration. Other monkeys are concealing a book – are they ignoring the truth?

Opposite: Lord Bute's Bedroom, inspired by Revelation. A statue of St John the Evangelist stands above the fireplace.
Right: Detail from Lord Bute's Bedroom showing a Connemara marble column with a ring decorated with frogs.

All must now be speculation for the meaning of this enigmatic monkey puzzle was not recorded. But what is surely certain is that it is a comment on the times, when the hapless monkey seemed set to undo man's arrogant pride in himself, in his certainty of his superiority – of his divinity. And if this is indeed the case, Bute's and Burges's response seems to have been refreshingly witty and ironic. As with the Small Dining Room, they seem to be poking fun at issues that many at the time found crippling. If Cardiff Castle is a critique of one of the greatest debates to confront Western man for 1500 years, then it was delivered with an almost irreligious sense of mischief. But if subtle and sophisticated fun is being poked at the great

debate – at the discomfiture being suffered by orthodox Christians as the Book of Genesis was questioned and by those objective scientists obliged to put the question – then one thing seems to be taken seriously. There is veneration for natural history, for it is in rocks, plants and animals that the sacred lies – in Acland's divine and ever-open 'Book of Nature'.

Above: The Great Hall, created within an authentic medieval fabric, is packed with images of natural history.
Opposite top left: A salmon bursts from a wall in the Library.
Opposite top right: Monkeys cavort around the main doors of the Library, perhaps peering into the 'Book of Nature'.
Opposite centre: A giant frog acts as a corbel.
Opposite: Natural history runs riot in the Library.

6

The Midland Grand Hotel, St Pancras

The Midland Grand Hotel at St Pancras Station, London, is among the most evocative and controversial revived Gothic buildings completed in Britain during the nineteenth century. It is erudite and inventively eclectic in its use of diverse sources, and is a monument to the nineteenth-century architectural conviction that all buildings – even novel types, such as railway station hotels – demanded the pedigree of historic precedent.

The design of the hotel is based on medieval prototypes, but in aspects of its construction and servicing it is pioneeringly modern. In addition, it has a complex organization in which the new technologies of heating and ventilation were integrated with ornament, and in which various potentially conflicting uses and circulation systems were elegantly reconciled. All this was achieved by the architect George Gilbert Scott, despite increasing conflict with the client over costs and dramatic changes in the brief.

The hotel was designed in 1865 and construction work began in earnest in 1868. It was completed in 1876, while the adjoining St Pancras station shed, designed by engineer William Henry Barlow, was in service eight years earlier. Despite the hotel's historical importance, it remains something of a mystery. Very few of Scott's original drawings survive,[1] building accounts have disappeared and the exact relationship between Barlow's sublime station shed and Scott's more studied hotel has, as a result, been confused.

Building History

The basic building history of St Pancras is as follows: The Midland Railway Company obtained an Act of Parliament on 22 June 1863 for extending its line into London and for the construction of a terminus. This terminus was designed by the company's consulting engineer, W.H. Barlow, whose plans were accepted in the spring of 1865, and the construction of the main feature of the station – the iron-built train shed – got under way in November 1867. This shed was pioneering: its width of 245 feet (75 metres) made it the widest single-span structure in the world (at 105 feet/30 metres high it is still the tallest), and it covered the tracks in one bound to allow maximum operational flexibility.

Unlike its predecessors, such as Isambard Kingdom Brunel's Paddington station shed started in 1851, the St Pancras shed has a pointed apex. Although very much in the Gothic spirit of the age, this pointed form was chosen for practical rather than aesthetic reasons. As Barlow explained, it provided the greatest possible protection against lateral wind pressure. Also novel was his decision to make the curved ribs forming the roof trusses spring from ground level. This meant that the iron girders tying the ends of the trusses together could be concealed below platform level, and therefore also act as the floor structure for the platforms and tracks.

The Midland Railway Company, learning from

Previous page: The hotel with the clock tower in the foreground.
Left: Engineering meets architecture: the trusses of the iron roof abut the Gothic windows of Scott's station buildings.

the mistakes made at the earlier and neighbouring King's Cross station, decided to bring its line into London by crossing above rather than below the Regent's Canal. This meant that trains did not have to toil along a steep gradient to reach their terminus, as was the case at King's Cross. But it also meant that the platforms at St Pancras had to be set at high level, about 15 feet (4.5 metres) above the Euston Road. Poised on a strong and extensive substructure, they were reached from Euston and Pancras Roads by a winding ramp for vehicles and stairs for pedestrians.

Construction of the vaults and related works started in the spring of 1866. The ribs of the roof trusses are made of wrought-iron sheets riveted together, a relatively new development in the 1860s. Cast iron was used for structural iron-work until about 1850 because it was cheap to manufacture, but wrought iron had greater tensile strength and quickly became the standard material for ribs and beams. The fabrication and erection of the iron for the shed roof, undertaken by the Butterley Company of Derby, was contracted to start in November 1866, but the schedule slipped and the first bay was not raised until a year later.

The Hotel

The Midland Railway Company had always intended that its London terminus should include a hotel to place it 'upon a par with the Great Northern, the London & North Western, and the Great Western [which] received a large accession of traffic from the construction of their hotels',[2] and Barlow had allocated a plot of land for a

hotel in his station plan. As with the Great Western Hotel at Paddington of 1851–3, but unlike the Great Northern Hotel at King's Cross of 1854, the hotel at St Pancras was to be built transversely across the southern end of the shed. The advantage of this arrangement was that the two elements could be unified to create a more coherent station with easy and direct access from platforms to hotel. Also, the area between hotel and station could be used as a covered concourse on which passengers could gather and shelter.

Barlow accepted that the prestigious hotel should be designed by an architect rather than an engineer, and at the company's Construction Committee meeting on 3 May 1865 it was decided that a limited competition should be held among a small number of architects for the design of the hotel and a certain number of station buildings.[3] The hotel was to include office accommodation, to allow the Midland Railway Company to move its headquarters from Derby to London, a move that was eventually abandoned because the company ran into financial difficulties and had to cut back on its building operations.

The competition was won in January 1866 by Scott and construction of the hotel started in March 1868. The station shed, the platform buildings forming the abutments for the shed trusses, and the raised station forecourt to Euston Road were completed in September 1868 and the station was in use from 1 October. The first phase of the hotel opened on 5 May 1873, and was finally completed in 1876.

What the few surviving contemporary documents do not make clear is the extent of

Scott's involvement in the station design. The chronology suggests that the platform buildings, which appear to act as abutments for Barlow's shed, were designed before Scott came on the scene in early 1866. In fact, Scott's competition drawings show these platform buildings much as they were eventually built, and the known delay in starting construction of the shed means that he was on the St Pancras team around 20 months before any building work began. It seems likely, then, that Scott was responsible for the platform buildings and this is supported by a few construction drawings, dated November 1867 and signed by Scott, that show both platform buildings and the hotel. From the time construction of the platform buildings started, Scott's office was clearly in charge of design and detailing.

Despite first appearances, the platform buildings do not act as buttresses to help withstand the outward thrust of the roof arches. Roof and buildings are structurally independent, and even a quick inspection reveals that the platform buildings are much too flimsy to function as abutments. The roof trusses are restrained from spreading solely by the tie-beams below the platforms and tracks. The platform buildings may help to brace the roof structure, and photographs of the shed under construction in early 1868 show the construction process very clearly.[4] The bottom members of each truss were set into the ground and these stood independently until they were linked vertically by the upper

Above: The station shed under construction. Iron components of each truss are being assembled off the timber scaffold.

ironwork to form a truss and horizontally by the brick-built platform buildings.

The Site

As Jack Simmons observes in his perceptive book *St Pancras Station* (1968),[5] the directors of the company could hardly have chosen a more difficult site for their London terminus. 'It was occupied by a canal, a gasworks, an ancient parish church with a large crowded graveyard, and some of the most atrocious slums in London; and through it all ran the Fleet River.' The way in which the company and Barlow, faced up to the incredible difficulties presented by the site created some of the stranger legends of London history. Particularly trying was the task of pushing the line through St Pancras churchyard immediately north of the proposed station. By the time Scott came on the scene, most of the worst site problems had been solved. The graveyard had been tunnelled through (with some distressing consequences) and the Fleet River, really no more than a large enclosed sewer, had, with ingenuity, been left undisturbed. The gasworks had been neatly skirted (although the funnelling of the tracks and the short platforms that were necessary to achieve this were to prove an operational headache for generations of station managers). The slums had been cleared and a connection had been achieved with the world's first underground line – the Metropolitan Railway – which ran immediately beneath the station forecourt. All that was missing from this breathtakingly grandiose project was the hotel.

The competition for the hotel, held in May

1865, invited 11 architects to submit plans. This group, which was soon expanded to 14, included G.H Stokes, E.M. Barry, Edward I'Anson, Somers Clarke, F.P. Cockerell, H.A. Darbishire and Owen Jones, as well as Scott. The competitors' work was submitted in the autumn, exhibited in Derby, and Scott was announced the victor in January 1866. The winning scheme was chosen by the Midland Railway Company's directors, chaired by the general manager, James Allport, with no professional assessors to guide them.

Scott's winning design was very different from the design that eventually began to rise on site in March 1868. For reasons that are now obscure, Scott chose to design a building that was substantially larger than asked for. The estimated cost of his competition design was £316,000, some £50,000 more than the next most expensive scheme. The board held an informal inquiry to discover how a scheme that expanded on the accommodation asked for in the brief, and was so expensive, had won. But after questioning their general manager, the dynamic Allport, the board decided that he had 'acted both honourably and impartially through the whole proceedings'.[6]

How did Scott and Allport get away with disregarding the conditions of the competition? The answer is probably straightforward. The directors wanted a terminus that would trumpet the arrival of the Midland Railway Company in London and eclipse the station's rivals – the nearby King's Cross and Euston stations. Central to this ambition was the design of the hotel which would, in many ways, be the public face of the company, especially as it planned to have its headquarters there. Scott's design was a powerful piece of bravura architecture that rose above the mere functional or commercial. It was an architectural statement that promised to tower both physically and aspirationally above the neighbouring and utilitarian King's Cross. The hotel was a magnificent sales pitch that would, if all went well, put the company on the map by generating confidence in its activities and profits. No wonder Allport and his directors were sold on Scott's bold design. At a stroke he gave the Midland a major metropolitan image and identity.

The evolution of Scott's competition-winning design can now only be surmised, for little is recorded of the theory that underpins the appearance of the building. The only explanation by Scott about the architectural style of the hotel comes from his *Personal and Professional Recollections*, published in 1879: 'I made my designs while detained for several weeks with Mrs Scott by the severe illness of our son Alwyne, at a small seaside hotel at Hayling in September and October, 1865. I completely worked out the whole design then, and made elevations to a large scale with details. It was in the same style which I had almost originated several years earlier, for the Government offices, but divested of the Italian element.'

The government building to which Scott referred is the Foreign Office in Whitehall, the commission for which he eventually won in 1858 after much political manoeuvring and lobbying. Scott's initial design was Gothic, which provoked an extraordinary reaction from Lord Palmerston when he regained power as prime minister in

May 1859. No sooner was he in office than he decreed that the new government offices should not be in the Gothic style as proposed by Scott, but in the Italianate manner. Scott had a painful decision to make. Should he refuse and hand the commission to a Palmerstonian candidate, thus losing money but preserving his artistic integrity, or should he bow to the prime minister's direction and classicize his design? Scott chose the latter course, but not before attempting a compromise with an Italio-Byzantine scheme that he felt more consistent 'with my antecedents' but which Palmerston also rejected as 'neither one thing nor t'other – a regular mongrel'. Scott swallowed this further insult, 'bought some costly books on Italian architecture, and set vigorously to work'. His classical design was approved in 1861 and built between 1863 and 1875.

This painful and very public about-face at the height of the 'battle of the styles' was potentially disastrous for Scott. He was a leading Goth, and this was a crucial time for the Gothic Revival. Scott's colleagues were striving to establish Gothic as a credible alternative to classical architecture and as a morally superior style (more rational in its constructional logic and Christian in its origins) suitable for all types of modern building. And then came this betrayal. But Scott's abandonment of his principles did not do his career any damage: perhaps potential clients found his preference for employment and money over artistic integrity rather reassuring. Scott, however, felt deeply humiliated: his principles, and more importantly his pride, had been hurt. Clearly, the Midland Grand Hotel project offered Scott an opportunity to vindicate himself and show the British public just what it had been denied by Palmerston's high-handed interference.

Despite their many differences, the initial designs for the Foreign Office and the Midland Grand Hotel are, as Scott admitted, united by the style of their architecture – and it is a very odd style indeed. In common with other leading mid-nineteenth-century Goths, such as William Burges and Alfred Waterhouse, Scott sought to create a modern Gothic architecture that was a fusion of the style's best design and structural traditions while also reflecting and satisfying the aspirations of the modern age. This meant an architecture that was capable of realizing the potential offered by current building technology, with modern ideas of comfort and convenience, but which was also true to the decorative and craft traditions of the Gothic movement. Scott described his quest for an authentic modern Gothic style based on an interpretation of the best historic precedents in *Secular and Domestic Architecture*. This was published in 1857, nearly 10 years before he embarked on the design of the Midland Grand Hotel, but the description of his thinking behind the Gothic design for the Foreign Office is relevant given the strong connection between the two projects. As Scott explained: 'I did not aim at making my style "Italian Gothic"; my ideas ran much more upon the French… I did, however, aim at gathering a few hints from Italy [and] I also aimed at another thing which people consider Italian – I mean a certain squareness and horizontality of outline. This I consider pre-eminently suited to the street front of a public

building. I combined this, however, with gables, high pitched roofs, and dormers.'

Scott's fusion of sources was rich indeed, as is demonstrated by his design for the Midland Grand Hotel. The Venetian domestic Gothic favoured and promoted by John Ruskin during the 1850s as the most suitable historic style to emulate was combined with French ecclesiastical detail, mostly of thirteenth-century type, along with Flemish and English Gothic. But stranger than the amalgamation of so many sources is the fact that all this Gothic detail is cast upon a frame that is, in many respects, classical. The most obvious evidence of this is Scott's decision to tame the natural verticality of Gothic architecture in favour of the classical preference for a horizontal emphasis in the composition. On the main south and east elevations of the hotel the grouping of the windows follows strictly classical principles of hierarchy, despite the wonderfully varied Gothic detailing of their design. Ground-floor windows are rich and the first-floor *piano nobile* windows are richer still, with a distinct simplification as the storeys get higher. This is a sensible reflection of the relative importance of the different floor levels in the hotel, but is also a fenestration pattern much like that of a Georgian classical terrace. It can be argued that this is the type of regularity aspired to, and often achieved, in large authentic Gothic buildings, such as Salisbury Cathedral. But the Midland Grand Hotel possesses a mechanical, almost ruthless, order in the disposition of its parts and the laying

Opposite: The hotel from the south-west showing the main entrance within the loggia.

of its bricks that is characteristic of classical design but hardly ever found in authentic medieval buildings.

These criticisms apply equally to the elevations and details of the hotel as designed by Scott in 1865, and to the design that actually got under way in 1869. But what did change dramatically between these two dates was the scale of the building. The competition design envisaged a five-storey building set back on the raised courtyard facing the Euston Road (which meant a six-storey elevation to the St Pancras Road), with two floors within a deep pitched roof. At the east end was to be a clock tower, at the west end a quadrant that brought the elevation forward to the very edge of the Euston Road. This quadrant was separated visually from the main body of the hotel by a tower that was to rise above a tall arch spanning the carriageway for use by passengers arriving at the station. A corresponding arch, set further east, was for use by passengers leaving the station. The internal organization of the hotel was generally straightforward. The main public rooms, including a spectacular staircase, were to be set within the west quadrant-shaped wing that would contain the main entry to the hotel. Principal hotel suites and the company offices were to be set behind the lower storeys of the Euston Road frontage, with servants' rooms at the higher levels.

Although the directors of the Midland showed extraordinary, perhaps reckless, courage in selecting Scott's large and expensive scheme, they soon began to display more predictable, commercially conscious behaviour. The summer of 1866 proved to be a difficult time for many companies, including the Midland, which decided to cut expenditure by abandoning the idea of moving its headquarters from Derby to London. This had an immediate and profound influence upon Scott's design for the hotel. Omitting the offices and some bedrooms meant that the building could be a storey lower and significantly cheaper to build.

In December 1866 Scott was invited to a meeting of the Midland board to present revised drawings and costings arising from the changes. He estimated that elimination of the upper floors would reduce expenditure by £20,000 in capital costs, but he was asked to make further savings 'wherever it was practicable to do so'.[7] Thus started a long battle between architect and directors. Scott was determined to maintain a high standard in materials and finish, and to protect his design from gradual mutilation by the increasingly anxious directors.

Construction work on the hotel made a tentative start in January 1867, but by May the directors had already decided to slow down operations, and thus expenditure, by ordering that only those parts of the building essential for the operation of the station should go ahead. It took another year before they could nerve themselves to make a real start on the hotel, but this was not before Scott had been instructed to make yet more savings. He had already been told to reduce the cost of decoration and abandon the use of granite columns wherever possible, and now he had to agree to replace Ketton stone with cheaper Ancaster, and to a further general reduction in ornament. Scott now estimated that phase one of the building works would cost £38,000. A tender for £37,580 was secured from

Messrs Jackson & Shaw on 31 March 1868 and construction work proper finally started.

To everyone's dismay work progressed in fits and starts. In July the supply of bricks ground to a temporary halt. In November there were delays in the delivery of stone. While Scott was wrestling with these problems, he was also engaged in making additional designs for the station. Early in 1869 the booking hall was completed – three months behind schedule, but users of the station at last had a proper place in which to buy their tickets.

In the same year the construction of the clock tower on St Pancras Road got under way, but the western tower over the great entrance arch was not started until 1870. This slow progress must have been frustrating for Scott, but worse still was the Construction Committee's increasing reluctance to give him a free hand in the interior detailing of the hotel, and its constant demands for the cheapest solutions to every challenge or problem. But in 1872 Scott's position was suddenly strengthened by the appointment of an experienced and able hotel manager, Mr R.

Etzenberger, who insisted that Scott's design be completed forthwith and as planned.

The Evolution of the Hotel

But what kind of hotel did Etzenberger get? In the 1860s the hotel was a relatively new building type, which had evolved from the medieval inn. Large, purpose-built hotels, such as the Sydney Hotel in Bath, first appeared in Britain in the late eighteenth century. But the architectural image to which these early hotels aspired was that of the country house or town mansion crossed with an assembly room, and incorporating something of the coffee house or the newly fashionable Parisian restaurant. These hotels were an architectural hybrid, and in Britain it was not until the early railway hotels appeared that a distinct building type began to coalesce. This took place not just because these hotels were of greater scale, with the now familiar balance between different types

Above: Scott's original five-storey design for the south elevation of the hotel.

of bedrooms and a mixture of public rooms, but because they achieved an unprecedented scale of convenience, even luxury. Not much mention is made of bathrooms and lavatories in the early British hotels but these comforts became important at an early date in North American hotels and were expected by American visitors to Britain, who were an important source of income by the mid-nineteenth century. Constant hot water also became essential, as did forms of heating beyond the traditional smelly and dirty coal fire.

By the time the Midland Grand Hotel was under way, the more sophisticated guest also expected the new North American invention, the 'ascending room', or, as it was vulgarly called, the lift. In the 1860s, therefore, the hotel was an emergent building type, kept in a state of constant flux by innovations and technological developments.

Above: St Pancras station booking office. The panelled screen is original but the flat ceiling is recent.

Exactly what Scott offered in the way of an up-to-date hotel is now surprisingly difficult to determine. This is partly because most of the original documents, including the final building plans, have been destroyed or lost, but also because the business of the hotel was conducted with obsessive secrecy. Running a great London hotel was a cut-throat operation, and to have knowledge of the business methods of competitors was a great advantage. There are only a few surviving drawings of Scott's competition-winning design, but these indicate the uses of the rooms. Such is the interest and importance of the building and its crucial position in the development of the hotel as a building type, that it is worth attempting to reconstruct Scott's internal organization in some detail.

The problem facing Scott was how to integrate a series of complementary, though sometimes conflicting, uses. There were communal rooms for the guests, and communal rooms that might also be used by the public. As the hotel catered for various classes of guest, each had to be provided with suitable (and perhaps segregated) private and communal rooms. This meant that Scott had to provide a wide spectrum of accommodation, ranging from modest single rooms overlooking the station roof to majestic suites of rooms enjoying an airy prospect over the then-pleasant Euston Road. In addition, there was an army of staff to be housed, and, in line with the moral thinking of the time, male and female staff had to be segregated, provided with separate bathrooms and lavatories, and even have independent staircases to the bedroom floors. To make things more complicated still, the servants

of guests had to be accommodated in a manner that reflected the status of their employers, and kept apart from hotel staff.

Food had to be stored, prepared and cooked for all these people in a series of subterranean rooms, and then dispatched, along with drink from the vast cellars, around the hotel at maximum speed by means of service stairs and hand-operated goods lifts. Finally, guests and the public had to have quick and easy access to appropriate parts of the hotel, which meant including a series of different entrances and staircases. For example, there was a secondary entrance to the hotel directly from the station platform so that guests arriving by train did not have to walk around to the main front entrance. Once inside the hotel, the public and guests were funnelled through centrally placed corridors towards the main internal ornament of the hotel – the stunning grand staircase – and the main rooms of the hotel, particularly the Coffee Room and the Dining Room. These rooms were located next to the grand staircase on the ground and first floors of the curving wing. Guests or their visitors who wished to reach higher levels with minimum exertion could use one of the novelties of the hotel – the hydraulically operated 'ascending room' located next to the grand staircase. Supplied and installed by Sir William Armstrong, probably acting under licence from the Elisha Otis Company of New York, the lift in the Midland Grand Hotel was, it seems, the first in London. In 1874 Armstrong installed a second set of lifts, reached at ground floor just north of the Coffee Room, this time piston-operated because of a mishap with the hydraulic lift. The Midland

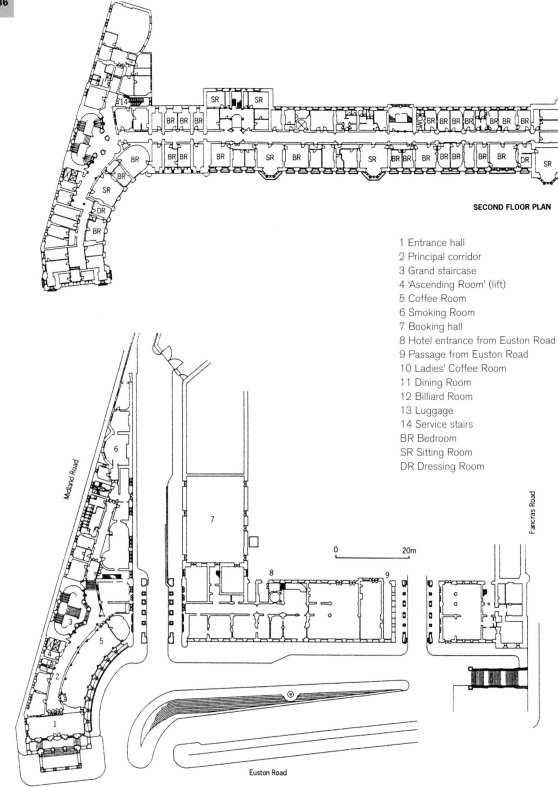

SECOND FLOOR PLAN

1 Entrance hall
2 Principal corridor
3 Grand staircase
4 'Ascending Room' (lift)
5 Coffee Room
6 Smoking Room
7 Booking hall
8 Hotel entrance from Euston Road
9 Passage from Euston Road
10 Ladies' Coffee Room
11 Dining Room
12 Billiard Room
13 Luggage
14 Service stairs
BR Bedroom
SR Sitting Room
DR Dressing Room

Midland Road

Pancras Road

0   20m

Euston Road

GROUND FLOOR PLAN

Above: Ground- and second-floor plans showing the original room uses.

Grand Hotel also pioneered the use of electric bells so that guests could summon servants more efficiently and from more distant parts than was possible with the old wire-operated system.

How the Hotel Operated

The plans and perspectives of the hotel lodged at the Royal Institute of British Architects (RIBA) are tantalizing. They are undated, although some are signed by Scott. They appear to be the competition drawings of 1865 and certainly show the hotel in its initial, larger, form, incorporating an extensive suite of offices to be used by the directors and staff of the Midland Railway Company. Despite the fact that the upper floors and the company offices were eventually omitted, these plans appear to show the general disposition and uses of rooms as built, and correspond closely to a partial description of the hotel published in the *Building News* in 1874.[8] In addition to the competition drawings, there are a few working drawings at the RIBA dated late in 1867 and a large plan of the ground floor, which looks very much like a preliminary sketch and could well be Scott's final sketch plan produced at Hayling in 1865 before he started work on the drawings for the competition. It bears a simple pencil inscription: 'Sir G.G. Scott's sketches of plan'.

Another, more detailed, plan shows not just the ground floor of the hotel but also the station and track layout and the platform buildings. The plan is, alas, undated, but if it is one of the competition drawings it is yet further evidence that Scott was involved with, or at least consulted about, the design of the platform buildings from

the start of his involvement with St Pancras in late 1865. This plan is packed with fascinating information that echoes and enlarges on the room uses scribbled on Scott's sketch plan.

The hotel's main entrance hall leads to a corridor with the Coffee Room on its east side, while a series of small rooms to the west of the corridor are denominated as Bar, Inner Bar, Manager's Office, 'Ascending Room' and Smoking Room. The last of these, an almost detached octagonal building never saw the light of day in that form. It was instead built as an oblong with a faceted bay to the west. The *Building News* confirms this use and, indeed, the use of the northern part of the west wing in general: 'The rear of this wing is appropriated to casual visitors, and comprises billiard and smoking rooms, lavatories, and other offices'. The rooms on the west side of the corridor leading to the octagonal smoking room are labelled Luggage Room, Still Room and Boardroom. The rooms on the east side, overlooking the 'covered road' separating the hotel from the station, are dominated by an odd double-apsed room designated as Restaurant. This was presumably intended as the main dining room since at this stage Scott did not envisage the splendid curved first-floor dining room that was eventually built. Clearly, it was soon felt that this ground-floor room was too mean, obscure, dark and noisy for first-class guests, but the space was built as shown in the competition design. If it was used as a restaurant, it must have been for humble guests or solely for travellers. Another restaurant was constructed approximately above this one at second-floor level. Its clientele remain something

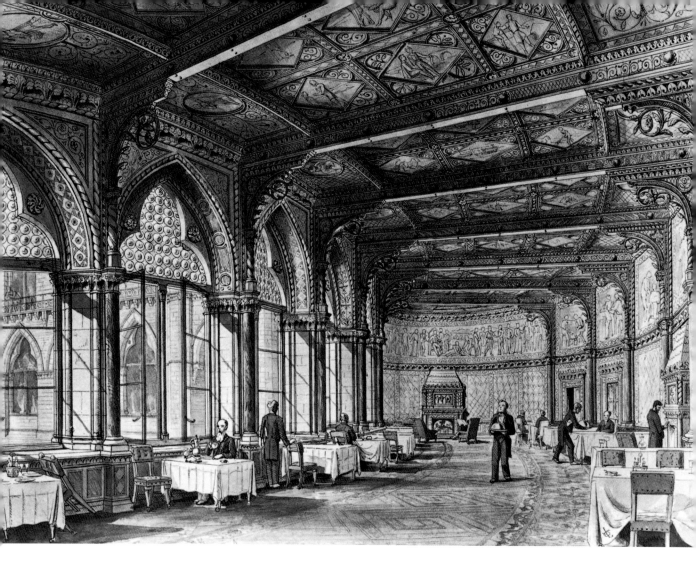

of a mystery: perhaps it was for parties, or for the modest denizens of the upper regions of the hotel.

The ground floor of the main hotel building, forming the southern end of the station, was to be given over largely to station uses. From west to east were offices, with the Directors' Staircase leading to those on the first floor, a Refreshment Room, a Waiting Room, an Excursion Booking Office, a stair and luggage lift leading directly to the hotel, a Ladies' Waiting Room, a Left Luggage Office, a Telegraph Room and a Parcels Office. The *Building News* description confirms all this, but suggests that the eventual loss of accommodation on the floors above pushed some uses down to the ground floor, for as well as various station offices and a refreshment room

there was a 'suite of rooms for private letting'.

The first-floor plan on this set of drawings was greatly altered in execution. The Ladies' Coffee Room above the entrance hall was built as shown and is one of the most fascinating of the hotel interiors to survive. With its stone internal arcade and full-height French windows, it was conceived as a semi-external space that could be used as an open loggia in the summer. But the final location of Scott's memorable curved Dining Room (echoing the Coffee Room below) is at this stage occupied by a Library and Reading Room (a pleasant utility that the guests did not finally

Above: The first-floor Dining Room as originally conceived. The iron girders of the ceiling structure were exposed.
Opposite: The Dining Room today has been much altered but the original fireplace survives.

receive), a Communal Sitting Room, a staircase and a bedroom. The northern half of the west wing was, with the exception of the octagon (at this level to be a Billiard Room), generally built as shown. It was to contain individual bedrooms of modest size. The main block of the hotel to the east was to contain a grand Directors' Staircase and landing, a Boardroom and offices (all abandoned in 1866), a Dining Room for Parties overlooking the station shed, and a couple of large suites with bedrooms, sitting rooms and private WCs located in mezzanines above dressing rooms. This highly convenient arrangement was soon abandoned as part of an early cost-cutting exercise.

The second floor is given over to the serious business of packing in bedrooms of a wide variety of classes, with only one public guest room, a

Dining Room for Parties (never actually built), placed above the entrance hall overlooking the Euston Road. The Manager's Private Apartments ranged behind the north-west elevation of the west wing. In the main block we begin to see one of the fatal flaws in Scott's vision of the modern hotel – the absence of adequate plumbing. The main hotel building, set between the station shed and the Euston Road forecourt, was to contain 24 bedrooms of various sizes, six dressing rooms, four sitting rooms and one drawing room. Some of the suites overlooking the Euston Road were extremely large (one was to include a dining room and a drawing room, as well as three bedrooms and a dressing room) and were clearly intended for the grandest of guests. But for all these rooms Scott provided only six WCs and two bathrooms. Admittedly, three suites did have

their own WCs and one had its own bath, but the other guests – no matter how grand – had to make do with three communal WCs and one bathroom. And as for servants, no immediate provision was made and they would have had to drag themselves across the entire length and depth of the hotel before they could find relief in the servants' lavatories in the basement beneath the entrance hall. Mornings in the Midland Grand Hotel must have presented an interesting sight, with lines of gowned grandees with pinched faces queuing down the corridors. Or perhaps, in the manner of the eighteenth century, guests were expected to wash in hip baths dragged before the fire and filled by hand, and to have 'swilled out' in the morning by emptying their chamber pots down the nearest WC. If this was the case, then a night at the Midland Grand must have been a shocking experience for many a genteel and cosseted North American nurtured on luxury and the most modern of conveniences.

The proposal for the third floor is grimmer still. It was to contain 54 bedrooms, six dressing rooms and four sitting rooms, but only 10 WCs and one bathroom. The suites were, as on the lower levels, arranged along the Euston Road frontage. They had entrance vestibules along the central spine corridor, and their sitting rooms had generous oriel windows. On this plan is written 'same plan will apply to fourth floor should it be adopted'.

The fifth floor would have been the domain of commercial travellers or less affluent guests, and perhaps have included some servant bedrooms. The plan shows 74 small bedrooms, no sitting rooms or dressing rooms, and only 10 WCs and

one bathroom. On this level Scott placed a pair of service staircases leading to servants' bedrooms on the floor above: one in the north-west corner of the main block was for men, and another in the south-east corner was for women. Additional insight into sex segregation within the Victorian hotel is revealed by a note written on the plan: 'The upper attic will be devoted to bedrooms for servants which will be divided into four classes and the rooms approached by distinct staircases. 1. Male visitors' servants; 2. Female visitors' servants; 3. Male hotel servants; 4. Female hotel servants.' The bedrooms were presumably categorized along the same lines. Clearly, the management wanted to ensure that guests' servants were not in a position to lead their staff astray.

Among the RIBA drawings is also a plan of the basement and the mezzanine level in the west wing. These areas were, of course, the realm of the servant, and give a good idea of the way in which the comfort of hotel guests and visitors was to be achieved. In the west wing, set below the grand staircase, was the main double-height kitchen flanked by storage and food-preparation rooms. Beneath the entrance hall were four WCs and bathrooms for male servants.

The basement mezzanine level, through which the double-height kitchen was to rise, was organized along the lines of the servants' quarters in a country house or town mansion. There was to be secure storage space for valuable items, such as the hotel plate, candlesticks and linen, a room for 'receiving and weighing' goods, the laundry and the dairy, all to be presided over by the hotel housekeeper, who had her quarters in this area. The female servants' WCs and bathrooms were also on this level, as were the servants' hall and social rooms. These comprised a sitting room for maids, dining rooms for hotel servants and for guests' servants, and that most convivial of servant amenities, the hotel tap (bar).

The Hotel Today

A close inspection of the hotel building as it survives today, forlorn and long abandoned, adds a little extra information about the way it was originally used. The main alterations from the competition design have already been pointed out, and most of these were the result of reducing the size of the building rather than arising from a radical change of mind about the suitability of Scott's initial design.

The basement rooms now stand dark, dirty and mostly derelict, but with a lot of original detail still in place: easy-to-wash tiles cover the walls, hooks still hang from the ceiling of the meat store and ancient machines, such as belt-driven spits, are still to be found in the kitchen.

On the first floor everyday details such as doors, locks, escutcheons, hinges and coloured glass in fanlights are remarkably well preserved, and it has recently been established that much of the original stencil decoration survives on the walls. The intricate hierarchy and variety of the architectural embellishment in major and secondary rooms is still legible, and clearly shows Scott's combination of classical and Gothic traditions. On this floor, as in those above, is a rich array of Gothic-detailed fire surrounds,

designed to reflect the importance of the rooms they serve, with plaster cornices and timber door surrounds formed with abstracted classical and Gothic details. WCs were probably located as shown on the competition designs, and those that survive in the north-east corner of the west wing seem to be original.

The second floor confirms clearly that the bedroom strategy of the competition design was put into practice. Small bedrooms were placed to the north overlooking the noisy and smoky station shed, while an array of grander suites overlooked the relatively quiet and attractive Euston Road. The planning of these suites appears to be more flexible than envisaged in the competition design, with interconnecting doors making it possible to compose suites of various sizes as required. Entrance vestibules led to suites that were capable of incorporating up to 10 rooms if all interconnecting doors were unlocked.

The second floor also appears to have incorporated the much-reduced suite of company offices. The long corridor in the main hotel block contains, towards its east end, a pair of arches decorated with heraldic beasts – wyverns and griffins – that formed part of the arms of the Midland Railway Company. Immediately to the north-west of the arches is a spacious staircase up which the directors would have ascended with appropriate dignity. At the far south-east corner of the floor is a room that is assumed to have been the Boardroom. It is served by an oriel window and retains a fine painted ceiling, but the most convincing proof of its original use is the fact that it looks down upon the neighbouring King's Cross station, which, from this vantage

point, appears to sprawl at the feet of St Pancras.

The third floor is packed with bedrooms, both in the spirit of the competition design and to compensate for the fact that cost-cutting had led to the loss of hotel accommodation. From this level, it seems, certain of the numerous service stairs would have been nominated for male and female servants. That this system of sexual segregation found its way into the hotel is confirmed by an article published in the *Engineer* in 1867, which observed of the servants' rooms in the attic that 'the male and female departments having no communication with each other…are approached by different staircases'.[9] An additional staircase at this level, located in the north-west corner of the west wing, may have been for the exclusive use of servants' guests.

The Structure

The fourth floor is a barracks of servants' rooms, with many being of immense and strange architectural character, such as polygonal corner rooms in the west wing. Much original detailing, such as panelled doors and Gothic fire surrounds, survives. These rooms also reveal some fascinating facts about Scott's structure. The building is essentially of traditional load-bearing brick construction, having floors formed with shallow brick arches where great strength combined with fire protection was needed. A good example of this is the roof over the main kitchen, which supports the grand staircase above. This was a conventional solution in the 1860s, but recent repair works have revealed that Scott also used pioneering techniques to achieve fire protection between floors in the main hotel building.

Here he developed a system he had used at the Foreign Office. It consists of I-section iron girders between which are spans of lattice-beams with gently curved top sections. Over these beams are sheets of corrugated iron that conform to the curved top section of the beams to gain extra strength. Above the corrugated sheeting is a layer of coarse concrete on which sit timber joists supporting wooden floors. The underside of the structure is concealed by suspended plaster ceilings hung from a lower series of timber joists.

But not all structural ironwork was concealed.

Above: The Ladies' Coffee Room soon after the hotel opened. The exposed iron ceiling girders are visible on the right.
Opposite: The fireproof floor and ceiling structure revealed, showing iron girders and beams.

The honest expression of structure, like the expression of the nature and true colours of different building materials, became a key concern for mid-nineteenth-century Goths. In the Foreign Office Scott had stuck to a number of his Gothic principles and exposed iron girders embossed with rivets in even the most important interiors. He attempted something similar in the Midland Grand Hotel, where, it seems, floors were universally supported on I-section iron girders spanning between brick walls.

A little of this structure can be seen above the south window of the Ladies' Coffee Room. More daring, however, is Scott's decision to expose iron girders in the elegant sitting rooms embellished with oriel windows, now seen best at second-floor level. In a domestic setting, among conventional decorative details, these would have shocked the average, genteel Victorian guest. Also, much structural ironwork of bold, almost utilitarian design is exposed on the various service and secondary staircases.

At fourth- and fifth-floor levels, where the roof structure and some partitions are now exposed, it becomes apparent that Scott married this use of wrought iron and cast iron to heavy carpentry construction of a truly medieval-cathedral character. The technology crossover is at times bizarre: some joints in the massive timber roof trusses are pegged in traditional manner, while others are reinforced with iron straps.

This fusion of pioneeringly modern and traditional materials and means of construction reaches heroic proportions in the west tower. Its top stage contains the general manager's suite, a splendid eyrie that gave physical expression to the manager's dominant position in the hotel hierarchy. Above his office is the towering roof structure, which can be entered through a trap-door. The structure is phenomenal, with iron and timber construction intimately entwined. Deep-section iron lattice-girders act as supports for large-section, timber-braced trusses, while iron trusses of minimal section act as supports for suspended ceilings. Here are ancient and modern construction combined as never before.

Scott's feel for the potential of honestly expressed structure is also revealed in the fifth-floor corridor. This is a wonderful space. It cuts through the mighty roof trusses so that the collars of the trusses are exposed and run across the corridor just above head height. This revealed structure is embellished in the most delightful way by the addition of small-scale castellations to the collars. In addition, cross-walls are pierced with large round openings so that the vista and light are not obscured. Just what these cross-walls are doing in the corridor is hard to explain. They are clearly not firebreaks or main structural walls

natural light into the bowels of the building. These options were not available, or would produce inadequate results, on the upper floors, so here Scott top-lit the fifth-floor corridor by means of roof lanterns and then cut wells into the corridor floor to flood light into the fourth-floor corridor. This was a very bold, sculptural and effective solution.

Services

The way in which Scott organized the services in the hotel remains somewhat obscure. It is clear that the plumbing was not extensive, with water run to only a very limited number of WCs and bathrooms. The hotel was lit by a combination of gas (with elaborate fittings made by F.A. Skidmore of Coventry to Scott's designs) and candle. Electricity was introduced between 1888 and 1902.

Heating and ventilation were probably more complex and in the absence of building accounts Scott's solutions can only be surmised from a few surviving documents and by examination of the hotel itself. All the public rooms, all the bedrooms and rooms in the guest suites, and virtually all the staff rooms are provided with fireplaces, so it must be assumed that coal fires were not so much ornamental as the prime source of heating. The hotel seems to have had some steam-based central heating from the time it opened. The Midland's Construction Committee's

because they do not continue through the adjoining rooms to meet the outer walls. Perhaps Scott intended them to help brace the roof structure.

Getting light into the potentially gloomy corridors at all levels was an inherent problem as they were placed centrally. At lower levels Scott attempted to solve this by placing large windows at the eastern end of the long, straight corridor in the main block, by borrowing light from the rooms on each side of the corridor by means of large fanlights placed above the doors, and by opening top-lit service stairs to the corridors. Working as light wells, these stairs brought some

Above: The fifth-floor corridor showing a cross-wall and ingenious light wells.
Opposite left: An early hot-water radiator.
Opposite right: A cornice pierced for the extraction of stale air.

minutes record that in 1867 and in September 1870 Scott consulted 'the eminent warming engineer' Mr Haden about heating the hotel, and that Haden's tenders for the installation of heating were eventually accepted.[10] Two massive and ancient Lemont high-pressure hot-water boilers survive in the hotel basement and could well have been the source of heat for the radiators. To judge by surviving, seemingly original, radiators only the public circulation routes were centrally heated, but the system could have been installed at a later stage because radiators are placed against skirting and it is still clear that newly laid floors were damaged by the installation of pipes.

Given technological developments in the mid-nineteenth century, it would be expected that Scott supplemented coal fires in the large public rooms, such as the Coffee Room and Dining Room, with a supplementary system of piped and pumped hot air. But it seems clear that he did not. If planned, such a system may have been an early victim of the economies imposed by the directors. Perhaps even more surprising is Scott's inadequate approach to ventilation. Gasoliers produced noxious fumes and, before the invention of mantels, released an uncomfortable

amount of unburnt gas through their burners. It was essential that these fumes, along with other disagreeable smells, be expelled from the building as quickly as possible. The ceiling cornices in the Coffee and Dining Rooms are perforated, which suggests that Scott used a limited system of ventilation: stale air was sucked through the perforations via pipes attached to, and heated by, the chimney stacks, then expelled at roof level. If the heating and ventilation of the hotel was as limited as it seems, then it must have been, at certain times and seasons, an extremely unpleasant place to inhabit. This is certainly suggested by the stack of ducts that runs within the hall of the grand staircase. These ducts are clearly not original but, with their Tudor-style panelled covers, are obviously very early introductions. They may well be evidence of a more efficient mechanical ventilation system, perhaps utilizing the perforated cornices in the Coffee and Dining Rooms, introduced during the 1880s.

Decoration

Scott's scheme of decoration for the hotel is still not fully understood. Recent investigations have

revealed that the wall surfaces in all the main public rooms and circulation spaces were richly coloured and incorporated complex stencil patterns, with the grand staircase – the primary focus of Scott's scheme – being one of the great set pieces of nineteenth-century interior design. In its eclectic mixture of sources and structural sleights of hand it is a fitting monument to its age.

The staircase was conceived as an essentially classical design – a variant of the grand imperial staircases beloved by late eighteenth-century neo-classical architects. Typically of the type, Scott's staircase has a single flight leading from ground level to a half-landing, where the stair divides in two and rises on each side to reach the first floor. As well as being the great showpiece of the hotel, the staircase is also one of its great structural and philosophical puzzles. The treads and landings are made of stone, and the landings and the lower flights of the staircase appear to be supported by delicately detailed Tudor-Gothic-style beams and

brackets. But all is illusory and far removed from the principles of the honest expression of materials and means of construction that were supposed to underpin the architecture of the Gothic Revival. The decorated beams are made of plaster, painted to look like wood, and most of the beams and all the brackets apparently supporting the landings are structurally super-fluous. In fact, the staircase is a sophisticated combination of several structural systems. The landings are supported by iron girders that are concealed within a few of the plaster beams. The treads are partly cantilevered and partly locked together between the landings by means of grooves cut into the bottom of each tread. This 'pressure-bearing' type of construction, in which the bottom of each stone tread locks into the top of the tread or surface from which it rises, was used in England from the early seventeenth century, and Scott would have seen this as a traditional solution. Interestingly, the true structural principle of the construction is revealed in the top flights, where the ornamental but structurally pointless supporting beams are dispensed with. Why Scott decided to conceal the iron structure and indulge in a riot of dishonest decoration is now impossible to tell. Perhaps he or the directors felt that public taste was not ready for a grand staircase visibly supported on industrial-looking iron girders. Or perhaps Scott was showing in plaster what he would have

Left: One of the bold secondary staircases in which the iron structure is exposed.
Opposite: The grand staircase. Curving girders appear to support lower flights of stairs but upper flights are ostentatiously unsupported.

STRICTLY
NO
ADMITTANCE!

achieved in cast iron if he had been allowed the budget to indulge in delicate but expensive castings. Whatever the reason, old-fashioned beauty triumphed over modern and ruthless honesty.

Above the staircase is perched a spectacular polychromatic rib vault, while the ground-floor lobby, over which the stair seems to hover in a state of miraculous poise, is clad with beautiful Minton tiles. The walls were originally stencilled with rich patterns. (The existing fleur-de-lis scheme is twentieth century.) The paint decoration and wall colours were probably not the work of Scott but the responsibility of A.B. Donaldson, the chief decorator of Gillows, the company that executed the interiors. Scott commissioned schemes and details from other designers and decorators, but the main contract for the interior decoration of the hotel was won in November 1872 by F. Sang, one of the leading decorators of the day, who, at the Midland Grand Hotel, generally worked to designs produced by Scott's office. A partial description of the interior, written in 1882 by an American guest called M.D. Conway, offers a tantalizing vignette: '…it has been decorated by Robert [sic] Sang and furnished by Gillow, in the most expensive style and certainly presents rich interiors. The reading room [Conway means the Ladies' Coffee Room] has green cloth wallpaper [it was in fact stencilled, and areas survive], and a ceiling gay with huge leaf frescoes. It is divided by a double arch with gilded architraves. The mantlepieces are dark maple [this must be a printer's mistake for marble] with two small piers of yellow set on either side. The coffee room has a general tone of drab with touches of gold in the paper, and a sort of sarcophagus chimney piece surmounted by an antique mirror of beveled glass. The sitting room has a floral paper and an imitation mosaic ceiling. One of the bedrooms has deep green wallpaper with gold lines and spots, and bed curtains somewhat similar. The halls and corridors have a dado of fine dark brown tile and bright fleur-de-lisle paper above.'[11]

When the hotel opened on 5 March 1873 it was well, if quietly, received. It had, perhaps, been too long under construction and had already become a too-familiar London sight for its final completion to raise great excitement. The *Railway News*, for example, merely observed that 'the apartments are reported to be magnificent and the charges moderate'.[12]

The hotel appears to have proved a commercial success. In 1878 the chairman of the Midland Railway Company announced that the hotel had started to bring in 'a very handsome net revenue'.[13] The previous year he had revealed the cost of the hotel to be £438,000. This broke down into roughly £49,000 for decoration and fittings, £84,000 for furnishings and £304,000 for the fabric. Scott's initial estimate in 1865 for his original large plan had been £316,000, reduced to around £296,000 for the smaller version that was built. Considering that the project had been dragged out over 10 years, Scott's estimate for the fabric, and his cost control, were admirable and amazingly accurate.

But the success of the hotel did not ease the final completion of the project. If anything, the

Opposite: The decoration of the vault above the grand staircase is to the original design.
Right: A section of recently revealed original wall stencilling.

success encouraged the directors to attempt to maximize profits by cutting out what they saw as superfluous decoration. The façade of the hotel, for example, incorporated a number of ornate niches that were to be filled with sculptures, but when Scott asked for funds to do this the Construction Committee refused. In the end, a solitary statue of Britannia was erected to peer down in triumphant isolation over King's Cross station.

Scott's final accounts were settled on 5 September 1876 and he withdrew from what had, in many ways, been his greatest single challenge and is, arguably, his greatest building. But not all thought so at the time. As early as April 1872, when the hotel was only just emerging from its scaffold, a journalist called J.T. Emmett wrote a devastating yet perceptive attack in the *Quarterly Review*. Emmett believed the design too pretentious, too grand for a mere railway hotel, and it clearly offended his sense of architectural propriety. His main targets were the architecturally ignorant directors who chose Scott's design, and the architectural profession and tastes of the time that made such a design possible. As for the design itself, Emmett argued that 'the noble art of building has been treated as a mere trade advertisement, showy and expensive'. It represented, he continued, 'a complete travesty of noble associations, and not the slightest care to save these from sordid contact. An elaboration that might be suitable for a Chapter-house, or a Cathedral choir, is used as an "advertising medium" for bagmen's bedrooms and the costly comforts of a terminus hotel, and the architect is thus a mere expensive rival to the company's head cook, in catering for the low enjoyments of

the travelling crowd.' To be consistent, observed Emmett, the directors should order their porters 'to be dressed as javelin men, their guards as beefeaters, and their station-masters don the picturesque attire of Garter-king-at-arms'.

All Scott had to say of the hotel is recorded in his *Personal and Professional Recollections*, which he started in 1864 but completed only in 1872, no doubt partly as a means of responding to the article in the *Quarterly Review*. The Midland Grand Hotel, wrote Scott, 'has been spoken of by one of the revilers of my profession with abject contempt. I have to set off against this, the too excessive praise of it which I receive from other quarters.' And Scott conceded, in a curious echo of one of Emmett's criticisms, that 'it is often spoken of to me as the finest building in London [but] my own belief is that it is possibly *too good* for its purpose'. Scott could have said much more. Clearly, the hotel was the final built expression of many of the ideas that Scott had explored in his 1857 book, *Remarks on Secular and Domestic Architecture, Present and Future*, about the glories of Gothic architecture and its appropriateness for the realization of a wide range of modern buildings. In this book Scott revealed that he wanted to show that Gothic was 'pre-eminently free, comprehensive, and practical: ready to adapt itself to every change in the habits of society, to embrace every new material or system, and to adopt implicitly and naturally, and with hearty good will, every invention or improvement, whether artistic,

Opposite: The hotel in c. 1927, eight years before it was converted to offices.

constructional, or directed to the increase of comfort and convenience'. Much, observed Scott, had been done recently in applying the potential of Gothic to church architecture, but 'our civil architecture is as yet unrevolutionized'. The Midland Grand Hotel was Scott's chance to put this revolution into effect. It also stands as a demonstration of his thinking about the suitability of Gothic for the design of a modern building. He clearly believed that the hotel was a great, if qualified, success. His erudite use of historical details combined with his bold and modern solutions to functional and structural challenges produced a building that has vigour and originality, and which is no mere pastiche of past styles.

Both station and hotel worked well for the first 60 years. Indeed, the station still works although there are currently massive plans to adapt it to the demands of twenty-first-century international rail travel. By the 1930s the hotel

was deemed to be unviable and it was closed. There was truth in this, and Scott must bear some of the blame because of his failure to produce a plan that allowed adequate space for lavatories and bathrooms. Massive reconstruction would have been an answer, but the ever-increasing traffic noise and pollution of the St Pancras area suggested that this was no longer a suitable location for a grand hotel. So in 1935 a new use was found – railway offices.

The subsequent adaptations were ad hoc rather than radical, and although much internal detail was damaged or destroyed, a remarkable amount survives, certainly far more than would have survived a 1930s' hotel revamp. Now this powerful building, which epitomizes the artistic aspirations and commercial vision of mid-Victorian Britain and which only just escaped demolition in the 1960s, is to be repaired, restored, and to serve again as a grand hotel.

7

Tower Bridge

Ever since Tower Bridge first opened to the public on 30 June 1894, it has fascinated Londoners and visitors alike. Its design is both audacious and contradictory, historical yet modern. Here is one of the great, pioneering building types of the nineteenth century – a steel-framed bridge that used state-of-the-art technology to raise its bascules (literally 'see-saws') to allow vessels to pass through it. Yet these utilitarian bascules are treated as a medieval drawbridge, and the steel frame of the bridge is disguised to look like an overscaled Tudor Gothic or baronial, gatehouse.

Unlikely as it may seem, Tower Bridge was both a reflection of changes that were transforming London during the second half of the nineteenth century and an agent for that change. London's population was expanding rapidly, as was the built-up area: the City of London was being dragged into the modern world, and traditional trades and patterns of commerce – particularly water-borne ones – were in dramatic and rapid transition. Tower Bridge was a product of all this, and during the 30 years of its gestation and construction it

presided over the making of the modern metropolis. In an uncannily accurate way its fancy dress and scientifically engineered structure and lifting machinery mirrored both the old world and the new. For these reasons it is an evocative, haunting monument.

Tower Bridge spans the Thames between Little Tower Hill on the north bank and Horselydown Old Stairs on the south bank. Until the Queen Elizabeth II Bridge was built at Dartford in 1997, it represented the most easterly point that traffic could cross the Thames.

Bridge-building Across the Thames

Until the middle of the eighteenth century, there were no permanent crossings at all between Kingston, Surrey, and London Bridge itself (a distance of 20 miles/32 kilometres). Therefore, to fully understand the significance of plans to construct a permanent crossing below London Bridge, it is necessary to investigate the evolution of the City's relationship with the river.

Probably since Roman times, and certainly since the Saxon era (fifth century AD), there has been a permanent crossing over the Thames on the site of London Bridge. The first bridge was built of wood, and records show that it was replaced several times between 1000 and 1150 as a result of Viking attacks, storms and fire. The last wooden bridge, built in 1163, owed its construction to expertise gleaned from a group of White Friars, the Frères Pontifes (literally 'bridge brothers'), who were leading exponents in what was still considered a holy task. It fell to Peter, chaplain of St Mary Colechurch, to oversee the construction work, and he was also responsible for the first stone bridge on the site, built between 1176 and 1209. The foundation of this structure remained intact until it was demolished in 1831–2.

Previous page: Tower Bridge – when opened in 1894 it formed the maritime gateway to the commercial heart of the capital.
Above: Old London Bridge, from the south bank of the Thames, in the mid-seventeenth century.

Peter's stone bridge contained 19 Gothic arches, the seventeenth of these incorporating a wooden drawbridge that was raised to allow shipping to pass up the Thames. To emphasize the religious connection, a chapel was constructed towards the middle of the bridge. This survived a serious fire in 1209 and partial collapse in 1384, only to be turned into a grocer's shop on the orders of Henry VIII. Funding for the bridge was partially gained from landed estates donated by the Crown and private patrons. These lands were to provide finance for future repairs and the construction of subsequent bridges across the Thames for centuries to come. In addition, taxes were periodically granted, but another source of income was tolls, controlled by gates on either end of the bridge.

The heads of so-called traitors, such as William Wallace, Jack Cade and Sir Thomas More, were mounted on spikes and displayed on the drawbridge tower and the gates. Houses and shops gradually lined the bridge, their frontages crowding in on either side of the central carriage-way, while the main structures jutted over the sides of the bridge, supported by myriad poles, stakes and rubble. The consequence of this debris was to hold the water back, so the level on the west side was often several feet higher than on the east, and the flow between the openings was transformed into a raging torrent that was highly dangerous to pass.

The removal of the drawbridge in 1577 turned the bridge into a physical barrier to shipping, and thus marked the boundary beyond which large vessels could not pass. Upstream, a string of licensed ferries and numerous watermen would ship passengers and goods across the water, while below the bridge the Pool of London became a major commercial centre where ships would unload their wares on to ancient wharves. The growth of commerce and shipping in the seventeenth and early eighteenth centuries led inevitably to the growth of London. Although it had always been far larger than most other urban centres throughout the medieval period, its emerging financial markets and distribution networks for its nascent companies led to rapid expansion of the City and its surrounding residential areas. To cope with increased demand, pressure grew for further crossings between Kingston and London Bridge to be considered.

Concerns were initially voiced over London Bridge's ability to cope with an increasing flow of traffic. Plans were mooted in 1722 to clear the bridge of the houses and shops on it, but these were not put into effect until 1756. Within a couple of years, emergency repairs were required for the Great Arch, and the tolls were raised to help cover the expense. By the time they were abolished in 1781 they accounted for nearly £3000 a year, and their curtailment brought widespread condemnation: congestion increased dramatically, and a committee was established in 1800 to review the situation. It was decided that the bridge itself was a hindrance to the smooth flow of traffic, so the entire structure was replaced. In 1831 John Rennie's new design was completed alongside, and the medieval bridge, after six centuries of use, was demolished.

In the meantime, other bridges had sprung up across the Thames, financed by investors who obtained private Acts of Parliament that gave them authority to build. The first new bridge to appear was Putney (1730), followed by Westminster (1750), Battersea (formerly Chelsea, 1771), Richmond (1777) and Blackfriars (1796). Of greater consequence for the congestion problems gripping the City was the construction of bridges in quick succession at Vauxhall (1816), Waterloo (1817) and Southwark (1819), which changed the face of London and opened up new lines of communication. Between 1845 and 1873 a further 11 bridges were built, of which seven catered for the new railway networks. Despite these new rail links, which connected London with the rest of Britain, only the west of London was well served with bridges. The growth of the East End below London Bridge and of south-east London around the sprawling Surrey Docks, stimulated by commercial success, was left largely unresolved.

The Need for a Crossing

While ports such as Bristol, Southampton and Liverpool had evolved during the eighteenth century to handle a large proportion of Britain's commercial trade with its colonies in the West Indies and North America, London acquired a central role in handling trade with India and Africa. Goods were loaded and unloaded in the Pool of London either for re-export to the west of England, or for distribution around Britain via internal networks. At the heart of the process were the market traders, dealers, dockers and wharfingers who lived and worked to the east of London Bridge, where most medieval wharves and eighteenth-century warehouses were located.

With the coming of the railways, demand for products within Britain increased dramatically, as did the requirement to transfer goods across the Thames. Further pressure came from the nineteenth-century population expansion brought about by the knock-on effects of the Industrial Revolution. Between 1851 and 1901 the total number of Londoners increased from 2.5 million to 6.5 million, and nearly a third of this number lived to the east of the City. Existing capacity on

the roads on either side of the Thames had been saturated by the 1860s, resulting in traffic queues several miles long waiting to cross the river. Despite the clearance and widening of London Bridge, the redevelopment of the streets and thoroughfares leading to London's principal crossing, and the construction of other bridges, there was clearly a problem that was worsening with every passing year. For all these reasons there was a growing need to find an easier route across the Thames than by road to the bridges upstream from London Bridge.

Yet the traders, merchants and hauliers who sought easier access to the western parts of the city found themselves increasingly at odds with the dockers and wharfingers who relied upon unobstructed passage to the Pool of London,

Below: Wharves and warehouses on the north bank of the Thames west of London Bridge, in the mid-nineteenth century.

where, at the height of the season, sailing vessels would jostle for hours for prime position so that they could unload their cargoes. Many wharf owners had invested vast sums of money in building warehouses to receive the goods brought in from overseas, as well as in developing a network of docks and wharves to maximize the number of long-distance vessels that could be accommodated in a day. While they too appreciated better communications with the rest of London, their interests lay in protecting access to the Pool via the river rather than the roads. They therefore strongly resisted growing demands for a new road crossing east of the Pool.

As early as 1863 *The Times* printed an article on the need for a new crossing, urging the City authorities to take action. However, first to act was a private company seeking to remedy the situation with new technology. Capitalizing on the popularity of the Thames Tunnel (opened by Marc Brunel in 1824), the Tower Subway Company petitioned the House of Commons in 1868 and won permission to build a private toll-charge tunnel under the Thames at Tower Hill. Construction, utilizing a pioneering boring machine invented by William Barlow, began in 1869 and was completed a year later. Lifts were installed, which took fare-payers down to an underground railway run on a narrow-gauge track. A 14-seater carriage hauled by a 4 hp engine (operated by a system of pulleys and ropes) took passengers on a two-minute journey under the Thames at a cost of tuppence per ride. While the Tower Subway can be described as the forerunner of the modern underground system, the mechanism was prone to break down. Within

two months of opening the engine, tracks and lifts were withdrawn, and the entire route pedestrianized. The new subway nonetheless proved very popular, with over a million people a year paying the one penny toll to walk the gloomy and echoing tunnel. The subway continued as a viable option until Tower Bridge was opened in 1894, after which use quickly declined. It finally closed in 1897, and became a service shaft for numerous cables and pipes. The entrance can still be seen today near Tower Hill.

The Debate

Despite the initial success of the Tower Subway, the thorny question of commercial traffic from one side of the Thames to the other still remained. The burden of responsibility initially fell on the Corporation of London, an organization that had its roots in medieval times and oversaw the administration of the City of London within the Square Mile. It was also responsible for the Bridge House Estates – lands that had been granted during the medieval period for the maintenance of London Bridge – and by the 1870s this included London, Blackfriars and Southwark bridges too. Yet in 1855 the establishment of the Metropolitan Board of Works to oversee the regeneration and modernization of the capital created a rival organization with a vested interest in London's communications. Furthermore, the Metropolitan Board of Works had been granted huge parliamentary subsidies to carry out its work, and had the engineering talents of Sir Joseph Bazalgette at its disposal. Bazalgette was responsible for the network of sewers installed to combat London's appalling public health record, and for the embankment on the north side of the Thames, from Westminster to the City, that ingeniously combined underground railway, sewers and subterranean services with improved new roads. (Bazalgette was later to design Hammersmith Bridge.) While the Metropolitan Board of Works had been granted wide-reaching powers of co-ordination under the Metropolis Act of 1855, it could not influence the Corporation within the Square Mile, which had withdrawn its operations to within its geographical boundaries. Battle lines between the two rival bodies had already been drawn by the time the issue of a new crossing had reached a critical point.

Given the growing concerns of Londoners, the City's Court of Common Council, another medieval representative body responsible for administrative decisions, had requested a report into the various options for securing another crossing to the east of London Bridge. In response, the Corporation formed a Special Bridge or Subway Committee in 1876 to hear proposals and receive plans from architects interested in designing the crossing. One of the main adjudicators was Sir Horace Jones, the architect and surveyor to the City of London, and in the paid employment of the Corporation.

The site for the proposed bridge was fairly obvious, as even a brief scrutiny of a map of mid-Victorian London would reveal. The only site in the east of the City where a bridgehead and related approach road could be constructed without vast demolition and purchase of private property was on the land known as Little Tower Hill adjoining the east moat of the Tower of London. This was the only readily available site of adequate size running down to the Thames on the north bank. The south bank, where riverside land was less densely occupied and less expensive, could fall in with the north bank site relatively easily. For the loss of its land the Tower was to be compensated with storage vaults below the road leading up to the bridge. These, alarming as it now sounds, were eventually used to store ordnance.

Over 50 plans were put forward once the Committee had been publicly convened, of which the 10 most viable were assessed by Jones and taken forward in a report presented to the Court of Common Council at Mansion House in December 1876. These included Frederic Barnett's proposal for a low-level bridge, at the centre of which were two swing bridges on turntables, separated by a central pier, which permitted vehicular traffic to pass over the bridge yet also accommodated two waterways through which large vessels could pass when the swings were open. This was similar to John Pond Drake's plans for a swing bridge, which opened up whenever river traffic required to pass. G. Barclay Bruce Jr devised a roller bridge, whereby steam-operated sections rolled from one set of piers to another, thereby leaving spaces open to river traffic at all times, while conveying vehicles on the moving platforms. Thomas Chatfield Clark just ignored the requirements of river traffic and opted for a simple low-level bridge. The most popular design, however, was a high-level bridge, though access was a problem given the relatively

limited space on either bank to construct ramps of sufficient height. Sidingham Duer proposed hydraulic lifts at each end to convey vehicles to the height of the bridge. By contrast, T. Claxton Fidler suggested a high-level suspension bridge approached by spiral ramps at a gradient of 1:40. Edward Perrett, on the other hand, combined both ideas and suggested a combination of lifts and a level viaduct.

Alternative suggestions to bridges were also considered. John Keith drew up grand designs for a subway leading from Minories to Bermondsey New Road, complete with shops lining two carriageways. In a similar vein, C.T. Guthrie proposed a railway ford, with a double or single line of railway tracks running at a uniform level. Edmund Waller, managing director of the Thames Steam Ferry Company, suggested an extension of his existing service for the proposed site.

When the Court accepted the report and requested the Committee to look into funding the crossing, the race to build the bridge began in earnest. A second report was submitted by Jones in May 1877, which considered the merits of each type of crossing in turn. A high-level bridge posed problems of access as a survey of shipping showed that most vessels required a clearance of 82 feet (27 metres). The necessary gradient of 1:40 posed severe problems for horse-drawn carriages. By contrast, the low-level bridge removed these problems, but Stephen William Leach, engineer to an important pressure group, the Conservators of the River Thames, suggested that such an obstruction to navigation would outweigh the public benefits of the bridge.

Above: The Pool of London and Tower of London in 1805. The site of the future Tower Bridge is in the right foreground.

The subway encountered problems of access similar to those of the high-level bridge, and Jones was forced to conclude that, all things considered, a low-level bridge was the best option. Certainly, in terms of cost, it was the cheapest – £750,000 compared to £2 million for the high-level bridge and £1.5 million for the tunnel.

The slow process of report, assessment and revised report exhausted the patience of engineers and investors, who were being urged by commercial operators to speed up plans for a new crossing. In 1877 a Private Bill 'for making a bridge across the River Thames near the Tower of London' was introduced into the House of Commons by the Tower Bridge Company, which included entrepreneurs such as William Colley, Frederic Barnett and Robert Fauntleroy. They proposed raising 37,200 shares to create capital of £375,000 to finance building the bridge, and then

introducing tolls to recoup the expense. Although the Bill was later withdrawn, Henry Isaacs, chairman of the Special Bridge or Subway Committee, publicly disassociated the Corporation from the scheme, stating in June 1878 that '[the Corporation is] in no wise identified with, nor does it in any way countenance, the "Tower Bridge (No.1) Bill" therein described'. It also seems that the Corporation felt obliged to use the national press to defend the slow pace of progress, stating in the same year that they were 'thoroughly in earnest with the work in hand, though it may appear that we are making little progress, it is important to give it our full consideration'. Replying to criticisms from one of the original proposers, Le Fevre and Company, that a toll bridge was better than none at all, Isaacs wrote that 'this appears to be an attempt to delay the Corporation's work', and that although the site for the bridge had already been decided upon by the Corporation, the counterproposals were an attempt to 'make some profit out of the business'. Yet, as a shipping tycoon operating from the Upper Pool, Isaacs himself stood to lose out if trade moved downstream, and one wonders if the Special Committee's lack of decisiveness stems from Isaacs' unwillingness to jeopardize his own livelihood.

However, by late 1877 the initiative had already passed away from the Corporation. The Metropolitan Board of Works had asked Bazalgette to prepare a report on the Corporation's proposals, and Bazalgette was not slow to put pen to paper. His first step was to agree to meet Jones on 5 December 1877 to discuss the proposals outlined in May. It appears from separate accounts of the meeting that it was undertaken somewhat grudgingly, and that neither man was overtly keen to adopt a joint approach, although both agreed that the site for the new bridge had to be between the Tower and St Katharine's Dock. In March 1878, Bazalgette reported to the Board that Jones was unable to provide a final plan, but was working on a scheme of his own for 'a low-level bridge with an opening for passage of vessels through it, in accordance with the conclusions of the Special Bridge or Subway Committee… but that the City Architect did not wish these plans to be considered as his own matured and adopted views; but rather as forming part of his own thoughts in working out the subject'.

Bazalgette then presented the Board with his own plans, consisting of a single-span, high-level bridge 850 feet (257 metres) long, plus two variations for a three-span, high-level bridge. The first option, a highly ambitious proposal, was recommended for consideration at a cost of £1.25 million with approaches, which the Board accepted. Bazalgette's designs were then taken to Parliament as the 1879 Tower High-Level Bridge (Metropolis) Bill.

Jones was less reticent about the meeting, and indicates that Bazalgette had shown no intention of working with the Corporation. In a stinging critique of Bazalgette's plans in a report to the Special Committee, Jones stated: 'It is a matter of personal regret that I have not the pleasure of presenting a joint report with Sir Joseph Bazalgette, as I believe it was your Committee's intention that this should have been done, if we were fortunate enough to concur on some general

and feasible plan that would have been likely to meet with the approval of this Committee, the Court of Common Council and the Metropolitan Board of Works… whether there would have been any utility in holding a further interview I am not prepared to say, but I gathered reluctantly that Sir Joseph Bazalgette did not propose or desire to pursue the subject jointly with me.'

Jones then turned his attention to Bazalgette's report: 'A design which, however talented, ignores or shows a thorough disregard of all the evidence, views, wishes and interests of the wharfingers and of ship owners trading between the site of the proposed bridge and London Bridge.'

He attacked the scheme on grounds of cost, gradients of approach and obstruction to river traffic, concluding that Bazalgette had been influenced by 'the wharfingers below St Katharine's Docks, and has ignored the opinion of wharfingers to the west of that point, for the evidence of the wharfingers between the Tower and London Bridge, as given by the Deputation who attended before your Committee, is dramatically opposed to Sir Joseph Bazalgette's conclusion'.

Jones then put forward his own designs, clearly more sophisticated than those discussed at the ill-fated meeting. He proposed a low-level bridge with a simple 'drawbridge' opening mechanism – the bascule bridge. There would be two fixed spans, each 190 feet (58 metres) long, with a centre span of 300 feet (90 metres) bridged by two hinged platforms suspended by chains over barrels fixed in arches between the towers, which would hold steam or hydraulic hoisting equipment. The advantages were several: it was low level, therefore providing an easy gradient for land traffic; it offered an easy economy of construction on either bank; it occupied less river space than a swing bridge; there was less interference with the tideway and navigation; and the rapidity of working would not impair river traffic. In total, the scheme would cost in the region of £750,000. In addition, it was argued that the beauty of its form would make it the most picturesque bridge on the river. The image was of fantastic, fairy-tale Gothic. The towers, with tall pitched roofs and an array of turrets, appeared to have been plucked from the most romantic of French castles while the mechanism of the bridge gave the design the look of a mighty, medieval drawbridge. This was, indeed, to be a gate to London in full accord with the Gothic Revival spirit of the times.

This scheme was to be the basis for the eventual design, but Jones's moment had passed. Bazalgette and the Metropolitan Board of Works were pushing ahead with their plans, pre-empting the Special Committee's recommendation of the bascule bridge to the Court of Common Council in October 1878. Indeed, doubts about Jones's scheme were raised, mainly centred on practical concerns about how effectively and speedily the chain mechanism would operate. Having abandoned plans of its own, the Corporation threw all its resources into a desperate attempt to prevent the rival scheme from gaining parliamentary consent, and Jones aired his criticisms of Bazalgette's plans in the newspapers.

The debate turned into an ugly public wrangle for control of the project. Battle lines had been clearly drawn, with the Corporation standing for the ancient interests of the wharfingers and traders situated between the Tower and London Bridge, while the Board was seen to favour docks and wharves further downstream, plus the needs of landed traders on the south bank, who desired a more convenient route across the Thames. Lobbying was fierce. The Corporation organized local companies and wharf owners to present petitions in opposition to the bill: Joseph Barker and Co, the Courage brewing company, Chester's and Galley Quays stated that 'it was inexpedient for the Metropolitan Board of Works to start the Bill'; Beresford's and Co, wharfingers at Hartley's Wharf and St Olave's Wharf, complained that

Right: Portrait of Sir Horace Jones, 1886.

'the scheme costs too much'; Besley & Wilson of Nicholson's Wharf and Botulph Wharf cited 'damage to trade by inconvenience caused to high-mast ocean-going vessels'; the Tower Subway Company faced 'considerable loss of income' from a bridge opening only a quarter of a mile away; and the General Steam Navigation Society cited similar grounds.

In addition to providing strong economic and financial arguments, the agents of the Corporation were prepared to play dirty. An anonymous memorandum, bound up with papers and petitions relating to the 1879 Bill, states: 'The Board of Works are promoting this scheme in order to find themselves employment. That unless they occupy themselves with promoting works of this kind (having completed the sewers) their main functions are exhausted. The promotion of this scheme is undertaken to find them occupation. £5m unexpended now in the possession of the Board. £2m more for this bridge, total £7m.'

On the reverse of the memo is a note of these questions, raised before the Select Committee by Alderman Cotton. In the printed list of opposing petitions that accompanied the Bill, 'the Lord Mayor, Aldermen and Commons of the City of London in Common Council Assembled' appeared fourth on the list. Their stated reasons for challenging the Bill revealed the depth of rivalry with the Board: on grounds that the Bill was 'injurious to the City and its inhabitants', it stated that 'too many powers' had accrued to the

Top left: Sir Joseph Bazalgette's 1878 plan for a single-span, high-level bridge.
Left: Sir Horace Jones's initial design for Tower Bridge, dated 1884.

Metropolitan Board of Works. The Corporation found support from other interest groups violently opposed to the Board, including the Conservators of the River Thames, who objected that the Bill contradicted 'the powers granted to the petitioners'. Many of the individual wharfingers expressed similar concerns.

The battle for control of the process grew increasingly bitter. On 16 July 1879, the eve of the parliamentary decision, a report was published by a Select Committee on Privilege that lifted the lid on the unseen bargaining behind the Bill. Mr Hooker, the parliamentary agent acting on behalf of the wharfingers opposed to the Bill, claimed to have been approached by a third party, Mr Ward, acting for Mr Grissell, a Member of Parliament sitting on the Committee that would decide the fate of the Bill. Grissell claimed to be able to control the decision of the Committee and secure a rejection of the Bill in return for £2000. When the wharfingers made the alleged transaction public, Grissell was forced to apologize to the Committee, who promptly found him guilty of a breach of House of Commons privileges.

Back to the Drawing Board

The fierce opposition spearheaded by the Corporation of London won the day, and the Select Committee did not approve the Bill. Yet the debacle of the entire process left the problem unresolved and the two sides at loggerheads. Both had to reconsider the problem, virtually from first principles, and meanwhile the debate raged on. In 1881 the two rival authorities cautiously approached each other, holding a meeting in July to discuss the possibility of a joint approach, before agreeing three months later that neither side could force the City architect to talk to the Board's engineer. Debate rumbled on through 1882. A census on London Bridge showed that an estimated 22,000 vehicles and 110,000 pedestrians crossed every day, and that traffic would often be queued up on either side for hours, yet opponents to a new bridge could still be found. When plans were raised for a duplex bridge (basically two swing bridges on turntables), the Southwark and City Riverside Workmen's Committee petitioned the Lord Mayor in July 1882 to oppose the construction of any crossing below London Bridge.

The continued delays gave Jones another chance. In 1884 the engineer John Wolfe Barry was asked by the Bridge House Estates Committee to re-examine Jones's plans. This he did, remodelling the technical aspects of the design to provide greater reliability and far speedier lifting times by replacing the cumbersome chains proposed by Jones with hydraulically powered lifting mechanisms built into the towers. The Corporation embraced the amended plans, and in the face of further pressure from the Board (which unsuccessfully applied for its own Thames Crossings Bill in 1884) drafted a Bill outlining its proposals for a low-level opening bridge and presented it before Parliament for consideration.

Once again, the vested interest groups came out in force. When news broke that the Corporation was adopting a low-level bridge, an influential deputation of inhabitants and ratepayers met their alderman, none other than

Henry Isaacs, on 22 October 1884 and demanded reassurances about their livelihood. The residents feared that the erection of the bridge would drive the shipping miles away from the City, diverting the trade of Billingsgate to the proposed market of Shadwell. As reported in *The Times*, Isaacs concurred with the views expressed, suggesting that he would do everything in his power to ensure trade would continue at the Pool rather than at the docks further downstream, which would cause such a block as to drive shipping away from London altogether. He also proposed that a subway would answer every purpose, a far cry from the recommendations made to the Special Committee he had presided over 10 years earlier. Other former allies of the Corporation expressed their astonishment. Thomas Kelly, the General Secretary of the Amalgamated Society of Riverside Workmen and other bodies of the Trade Industries, representing many thousands of men, stated in July 1884 that 'the proposal to construct a low-level bridge out of the funds of the Corporation of the City has come like a thunderbolt and has created surprise and consternation amongst the vast body of working men dependent upon the navigation of the Upper Pool of the port… 3,000 would be ruinously affected, especially at a time when 30% of the labour force of the Port of London are unemployed'.

Various arguments were marshalled against the proposal, including evidence previously used to reject the Metropolitan Board of Works Crossing Bill from 1884. Sir Joseph Bazalgette stated that he had 'no doubt that such a bridge would be a very great impediment to the river and no use whatever to road traffic'; Sir Frederick Bramwell, civil engineer, thought that a similar suggestion to put an opening in London Bridge would be considered 'mad'; and Benjamin Barker, another civil engineer, referred to similar plans in Chicago, when two subways were found to be the best solution. Petitions from the usual suspects were heard, including the General Steam Navigation Company, the Conservators of the River Thames, the Tower Subway Company, the Steamship Owners' Association and the Traffic Committee of Billingsgate. Both John Wolfe Barry and Horace Jones were called before the House of Commons Select Committee in 1885 and received a grilling. Jones was cross-examined about the feasibility of a low-level bridge, and was also forced to answer questions about the vexed issue of compensation for those who would be disadvantaged by the proposal.

There were also rumblings from the highest in the land. The Public Record Office holds correspondence between General Sir H. Ponsonby, Private Secretary to Queen Victoria, and Lord Chelmsford, Lieutenant of the Tower, that reveals a deep distrust of the entire project.[1] This arose not just from the design of the proposed bridge, but because it could compromise the setting and defensive potential of the Tower.

On 20 December 1884 Ponsonby informed Chelmsford that 'the Queen is strongly opposed to [the] arrangement' as she understood it. On 15 January 1885 Ponsonby recommended to Chelmsford that he get Wolfe Barry 'to put his arguments on paper' so that they could decide whether to 'recommend the Queen to sanction them or not'. Wolfe Barry duly appeared to explain 'the mode of treating the works of the proposed Tower Bridge so as to make them harmonize with the architecture of the Tower and also meet the military questions'. The royal party was clearly unconvinced, for on 14 March Ponsonby wrote to Chelmsford in ironic strain, having heard 'that [the proposed bridge] will increase the defensive strength of the Tower… and improve the beauty and ancient associations of the place. The only answer I can give to all this is bosh!'

But it soon became clear that the debate was too heated – too political – for the queen to risk venturing her opinion publicly. On 31 March Ponsonby again wrote to Chelmsford: '…we have been told that this question is a very delicate one and that Her Majesty's name should not appear…as the poor people of London are clamouring for [the bridge] – which is nonsense (only those below the Tower are affected). However she has consented to be advised by the First Commissioner of Works on the subject.' The latter admitted to the Queen in May that he did not like any of the plans but it was 'impossible to resist the growing cry for a bridge and therefore it was better to secure the best plan we could'. In July Ponsonby threw in the towel, telling Chelmsford that since 'Government agree on this Tower Bridge scheme…it is useless trying to oppose it, though I believe it will be a serious disfigurement'.

The Bill was passed in August 1885, and the Corporation of London was empowered by Act of Parliament to build London's first-ever above-ground river crossing to the east of London Bridge. The Prince of Wales drove the first pile into the Thames with great ceremony in April 1886, and the project was expected to take four years to complete. In fact, it took twice as long, claiming the lives of 10 workers in the process. One further casualty was the architect himself. Sir Horace Jones, now knighted for his services to the City, did not live long enough to see his dream turned into a reality, and died in 1887.

Construction

The task of building the bridge was shared among seven contractors, each with responsibility for a different area of the work. The successful bidders were Sir John Jackson (piers, northern approaches and abutments); William Webster (southern approach); Sir W.G. Armstrong, Mitchell and Co. (hydraulic machinery); Sir William Arrol (steel superstructure); and Perry and Co. (masonry cladding). Wolfe Barry took advantage of his appointment as chief architect after Jones's death to personalize the designs for the stone cladding and ornamentation, and the final structure differed greatly from Jones's initial sketches drawn up in 1878. It is fortunate that working papers, blueprints, contracts and correspondence relating to the construction process survive at both the Corporation of London Record Office and in the Bridge Archives, permitting detailed knowledge not only of the building process but also of the hydraulic lifting technology installed inside the towers, which made the bridge the finest example of its type in the world.

The bridge is a combination of suspension and bascule, with two side spans, each 270 feet (82 metres) long, suspended on chains from abutment towers on the shore to the much higher main towers constructed on piers 185 feet (56 metres) long and 70 feet (21 metres) wide in the middle of the river. The third span between the piers consists of two high-level footways, over 140 feet (42 metres) above the level of the river, and a single low-level roadway 200 feet (60 metres) long made up by the two bascules.

Work first started on the central piers, but in response to the petition drawn up by the Conservators of the River Thames, one of the clauses in the Act stipulated that at all times there should be a clear passage through the Thames of 160 feet (49 metres). This meant that it was not possible to work on both piers simultaneously, which accounted for the slow progress of work in the early years. Wrought-iron caissons were used to secure the foundations, sunk to a depth of 21 feet (6 metres) into the river. The water was pumped out, permitting workmen to sink further sections of the caissons into the river bed. Once they were filled with concrete, the foundations had brickwork and masonry constructed on top, then the steel frames of the towers were built. These frames were also fabricated in sections, bolted into the foundations and then layered with smaller girders until the maximum height was reached. Cornish granite and Portland stone were used to clad the steel tower frames. These were intended to harmonize with the neighbouring Tower of London, and it was these that Wolfe Barry greatly altered.

Top: Portrait of Sir John Wolfe Barry.
Above: The design of Tower Bridge as envisaged when construction started in 1886.

It is now difficult to understand the thinking behind the change of design. Jones's romantic mock-Gothic towers had little enough to do with the gaunt Romanesque of the Tower of London, but Wolfe Barry's curiously bloodless and machine-made Tudor Gothic has even less. Since the objective behind this historicist posturing and the concealment of the honest steel structure within a skin of stone was to flatter the Tower, it is curious, to say the least, that Wolfe Barry chose to upstage the historic setting with his insensitive and showy design. Presumably, he believed that any mock history of a vaguely medieval sort would do the trick, and he happened to prefer the Tudor Gothic of the Houses of Parliament, which had been designed by his father, Charles Barry, and A.W.N. Pugin, to other types of camouflage.

Fabricating the massive bascules was the great technical challenge of the building process, partly because of the requirement to keep 160 feet (49 metres) of river clear at all times, which meant that large sections of each bascule had to be constructed on shore and then ferried out to the bridge. The counterweights were made of 290 tons (294 tonnes) of lead and 60 tons (61 tonnes) of iron, set in ballast boxes at the extreme end of the bascule girder and attached to a solid pivot, which itself weighed 25 tons (26 tonnes).

The process of construction proved to be a popular public spectacle for Londoners and

Above: A photograph showing Tower Bridge under construction in April 1892.
Opposite: One of the two mighty bascule chambers, into which the counter-weighted end of one of the 1200-ton (1219-tonne) bascules moves when the bridge is opened.

visitors alike. Their curiosity was matched by interest from the engineering community around the world. On completion, Wolfe Barry gave a lecture on the construction process entitled 'Description of the Tower Bridge, its Design and Construction' (published in 1894) in which he refers to the cladding as masking the true structural genius of the bridge: 'We may forget that the towers have skeletons as much concealed as that of the human body, of which we do not think when we contemplate examples of manly or feminine beauty.'

When first proposed, the scheme was meant to cost £750,000 but it eventually totalled over £1 million when the bridge was completed nearly eight years later in 1894 – and all this came from City funds, notably from the income of the Bridge House Estates. It was, and remains, remarkable that this great enterprise, which was to benefit London and the south-east of England as a whole, was funded not by government but by the City Corporation, and that this body required no return on its investment through tolls from pedestrians, vehicles or ships. This really was, despite the unseemly tussles that took place during the 1870s between Jones and Bazalgette, one of the great civic and public-spirited works of the nineteenth century.

The Bridge Comes to Life

The opening ceremony on 30 June 1894 was a grand affair. The streets surrounding the bridge were lined with cheering people anxious to catch a glimpse of the royal party. The Prince of Wales was the officiating dignitary, having driven the first pile into the Thames eight years previously. Once on the bridge, he set the lever in motion and watched as the bascules rose smoothly into the air, taking only 90 seconds to rise to the full open position. Contemporary accounts state that when the prince declared the bridge open by land as well as by water, there was a tumultuous roar from the crowd, guns were fired, and a procession of vessels made its way through the bridge.

Despite the years of argument, it appeared that the bridge was a success. During the first month of opening, the bascules were raised 655 times; and it took only five minutes for the bridge to open, the vessel pass through, and the bascules to close again. Indeed, it caused so little interruption to pedestrians that the high-level walkways, designed to allow pedestrians to cross the river while the bascules were raised, were used very little, except by sightseers who wished to gain a panoramic view of the capital, and by Whitechapel harlots who seem to have thought that the general sense of excitement surrounding the bridge could work to their advantage.

However, although a popular and practical success, Tower Bridge was not universally admired. *The Builder* magazine, the leading journal of the construction industry, published a long review of the bridge in June 1894. It was critical in the extreme. The romantic illusion of covering technology with a veneer of history might appeal to the public but not to the moral-minded building professional. Having acknowledged that the bridge 'in a purely engineering sense is one of the most important among modern structures', *The Builder* then attacked the architecture cladding the engineering: 'The towers are about as choice specimens of architectural gimcrack on a large scale as one could wish to see… What strikes one at present is that the whole structure is the most monstrous and preposterous architectural sham that we have ever known of, and is in that sense a discredit to the generation that has erected it. Far better would it have been to have built simply the naked steel-work, and let the construction show us what it really is; the effect, if somewhat bare-looking, would have been at least honest.'

Within four months of completion, Tower Bridge was involved in a bizarre and tragic accident that was to set a sad precedent. A local man, notorious for jumping off bridges, managed to gain access to the upper walkway and plunge into the Thames to his death. The fatality achieved wide media coverage, and was reported the next day in *The Times*: 'Yesterday morning, between 7 and 8 o'clock, [Benjamin Fuller] contrived, by skilfully disguising himself, to elude the vigilance of the police and to mount through a trap door to the roof of the high-level Tower Bridge, from which he dived. He was seen to rise once and wipe his face, but immediately afterwards he sunk and disappeared. He left on

the bridge a new blue serge suit, false whiskers and a moustache, and a wig.'

Fuller had been planning the stunt for some time, and had positioned an accomplice in a rowing boat ready to rescue him from the Thames. It appears that the force of hitting the water knocked the air from his lungs, and the strength of the current carried him away from his associate. Fuller's body was eventually washed up in St Katharine's Dock further downstream, and the coroner's inquest returned a verdict of death by misadventure. Thereafter the high-level walkways became a popular place for people to commit suicide, and in 1909 they were finally closed to the public.

A stipulation of the Act that permitted construction of the bridge was that compensation should be provided for aggrieved parties whose trade or livelihood had been adversely affected by

Below left: One of the steam engines used to build up the water pressure needed to raise the bridge's bascules.
Below right: A boiler created steam to power the engines.

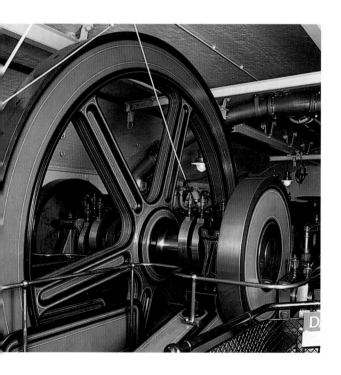

the new bridge. The main losers were, not surprisingly, the Tower Subway Company, whose business had virtually dried up within a few months of the bridge opening: they simply could not compete with a toll-free new bridge. Similarly, the Horseferry Steam Ferry Company received money for loss of trade, as did landowners whose property had been purchased and demolished so that the approaches to the bridge could be constructed. Yet other local landowners benefited from its presence, most notably the Bridge House Estates. Rents were to rise significantly in the following years as property values in the surrounding area, particularly south of the river, increased sharply with the improved communications.

Yet the arguments that had been put forward by the wharfingers of the Pool appear to have had the ring of truth about them, for statistics show that the frequency with which the bascules

Above: A control cabin from which one of the bascules could be operated.
Opposite: View along one of the high-level walkways, originally to be used by the public when the bascules were raised.

were opened began to drop away. Clearly, fewer ships were heading into the Pool. However, it would be unfair to lay the blame solely on the new bridge. A changing economic climate, and the development of deep-water docks further downstream, meant that by the time the bridge opened, the Upper Pool of London had seen its heyday pass by. Large ocean-going steamers had replaced the high-masted wooden vessels that the bridge had been designed to accommodate, and within a few decades the functional aspect of the bridge had all but disappeared. In terms of practical value, Tower Bridge had become a white elephant.

The Bridge Today

As its practical value as an opening bridge decreased so, ironically, Tower Bridge's symbolic and sentimental value increased. Consequently, when war broke out in 1939, there were fears

that the German air force would target the bridge, for it had become a symbol of national identity and its destruction would be a major propaganda triumph, as well as a military one. In fact, the bridge was only slightly damaged during the air raids of 1940, probably more by chance than by design. It was hit again in 1944 when a bomb bounced from the iron crest of the north tower, causing superficial damage to the face of the south tower.

Plans for repairing the bomb damage were first mooted in 1943, and the architect, W. F. C. Holden, submitted a remarkable scheme to encase the entire structure in glass. He intended to completely close the bridge to traffic and convert it to a 'state of the art' office block and shopping centre. Holden calculated that he could let 200,000 square feet (18,000 square metres) at about 5–10 shillings per square foot (£5.50–£11 per square metre), netting the Corporation between £50,000 to £100,000 per

annum. Holden also stressed that his novel design would 'fit in with the post-war planning of London, and possibly form a keynote focus for reconstruction in the vicinity'. Although the minutes of the Bridge House Estates Committee record that the plans were indeed put forward for discussion, there is no evidence that they were ever given serious consideration.

For many the most famous incident in the bridge's post-war history occurred on 30 December 1952, when it and that other symbol of London, the double-decker bus, came into near-fatal conflict. A number 78 found itself travelling across the bridge as the bascules were being raised. The driver was left with little choice but to race the bus across the widening gap, which he succeeded in doing. The bus dropped 3 feet (90 centimetres), injuring eight passengers along with the conductor and the driver. An inquiry blamed the bridge, or rather the acting head watchman, who had failed to operate the red warning light. He was duly demoted.

At the time of the accident over 70 men were employed on the bridge, an unnecessarily high number, it was thought, as demand to raise the bascules had declined. Staffing levels were reduced, and it was even debated whether the bridge should stop opening altogether. This last threat did not come about, and in 1974 the steam-powered hydraulic system was replaced with an electro-hydraulic drive, which now opens the bascules. The original equipment was preserved as a museum piece, and can still be seen on site.

Although just over a century old and despite being quickly overtaken by the changing nature of trade on the river and by technology, Tower Bridge is cherished as one of London's most characterful landmarks. Quite why it is hard to say – perhaps because of the charming absurdity of the whole enterprise? As a piece of functional and sophisticated engineering tricked out in baronial fancy dress, it encapsulates the topsy-turvy values of the late Victorian epoch. It is very much a structure of its age.

Opposite: Tower Bridge from the west in September 1940 with the docks burning following a German raid in the Blitz.
Below: Tower Bridge forms a gateway for land traffic travelling between east and south-east London.

Highpoint One

Highpoint One, a Modernist apartment block, stands on an elevated
site in Highgate, north London, commanding magnificent views over
the city. As London's first example of modern high-rise housing it was
intended to demonstrate not only the benefits of collective living but
also the progressive social and political philosophy of its designer,
Berthold Lubetkin. Highpoint One was to be the key building in
Lubetkin's cherished crusade to introduce the British to the social,
artistic and structural benefits of Modernist architecture.

Designed in 1934, Highpoint One was
the product of the artistic, political
and social turmoil that had rocked Europe
since the beginning of the twentieth century.
The architectural and urban consequences
of these traumatic decades, when people
were stunned by the horror of the First
World War in which technology had proved
itself the all-powerful master of men, was
first and most visibly expressed in prophetic
words and drawings. Antonio Sant'Elia's
Manifesto of Futurist Architecture (1914)
outlined the *citta nuova* in which history was

rejected and new technology and a new
social order embraced. Le Corbusier's *Vers
une Architecture* (*Towards a New Architecture*,
1923) rhapsodized about a wide variety of
inspirations – machines, Greek proportions,
technology, industrial and utilitarian
constructions, such as grain elevators, and
rational design. The book also launched
what Le Corbusier called 'a glittering
epithet which aroused the poet in us' – the
City of Towers. Two years later Le Corbusier's
Urbanisme (or *The City of Tomorrow and Its
Planning*, as it is called in English) developed

the theme of the high-rise city with towers soaring from a Cartesian plan and an architecture that realized the potential of contemporary technology and machine-like imagery. Ornament and references to past historical architectural styles were dead. The machine and new technology were the new inspiration – the new masters.

This new modern architecture was to be the expression of a new world order. Cities were to be rebuilt and the dark 'canyon street', formed by terraced houses and apartment blocks, swept away. As Le Corbusier put it in *Vers une Architecture*: 'It is time that we should repudiate the existing layout of our towns, in which the congestion of buildings grows greater, interlaced by narrow streets full of noise, petrol fumes…. dust [and] foul confusion.' Cramped and slum dwellings were to give way to tall, sculptural, well-lit and well-ventilated residential towers set in parkland, as illustrated by Le Corbusier in *Urbanisme*, with polemical designs for a 'contemporary city'. And the materials to realize this dream were, argued Le Corbusier, reinforced concrete, steel and glass. In this futuristic city, he claimed, it would be sufficient 'to bring together at certain points…the great density of our modern populations and to build at these points enormous constructions 60 storeys high' – an 'audacity' that could be achieved by concrete and steel alone.

Design was to be based on scientific principles, taking utilitarian structures and functional machines, such as the aeroplane and automobile, as the inspiration. Buildings were to be fit for their function, and all was to be governed by a sense of utility, social equality and purpose.

The architects behind this Modern Movement in architecture – christened the International Style in a 1932 New York exhibition organized by Henry Russell Hitchcock and Philip Johnson – were passionate in their determination to create a new world, healthy in mind and body. The artistic decadence of the nineteenth century, obsessed with reviving past historical styles, was to be replaced with an authentic architecture of the twentieth century. The forms taken by this socially enlightened architecture, honestly and logically expressing function and methods and materials of construction, would, argued its champions, create its own exciting new aesthetic. Modern Movement buildings would have a bold and honest sculptural beauty far superior to earlier buildings in which all was deceit, with purpose and construction usually concealed, confused or denied under layers of inappropriate ornament.

But in Britain in the 1920s modern architecture was viewed with deep suspicion. It was not only foreign but, worse still, seemingly German and French in origin – an unholy alliance indeed. And, furthermore, it embraced – even promoted – a socialist, or at least uncomfortably anti-hierarchical, classless society.

In addition, the arts in Britain had developed a distinctly national and rather idiosyncratic character based on the vigorous and creative revival of much-loved building traditions. The Queen Anne style had been revived, or rather reinvented, in the 1870s to realize a domestic

Previous page: Highpoint One from the garden.
Opposite: Kelling Hall in Norfolk, built to E.S. Prior's designs, fused tradition with modern construction techniques.

ideal, and the vernacular Gothic, the architecture of Christopher Wren and the English baroque of Nicholas Hawksmoor and John Vanbrugh were all being delved into and drawn on for inspiration in the early years of the twentieth century. This use of tradition was, unlikely as it may seem, being made to work well. Architects such as Sir Edwin Lutyens, Charles Voysey and E.S. Prior evolved a British architecture in which history and modernity, both in design and in use of materials, were fused in a gentle and often ingenious and witty manner to realize modern building types. For example, Prior's design for Kelling Hall in Norfolk (1904–6) combined local stone and tiles with mass concrete, and created a generous, well-lit and open interior while working within the tradition of the English medieval hall house. Buildings such as this entirely satisfied the tastes and aspirations of most English clients in the early decades of the twentieth century.

As a result, modern architecture was generally viewed in Britain as not only essentially foreign and artistically suspect, but also largely irrelevant and functionally inappropriate. Its flat roofs and extensive bands of glazing were seen as unwelcome in the damp and cold British climate, while its ruthlessly machine-like and industrial appearance was both ugly and – in the democracy of its design and detail – politically worrying.

There were few British clients who wanted to encourage this artistically and socially perturbing foreign growth, and those who did used this revolutionary aesthetic not to build healthy housing or factories for workers but to create their own amusingly 'modern' private houses. Typical is a private house called 'High and Over' in Buckinghamshire. Designed in 1928, and influenced by the work of Le Corbusier, it is about the earliest Modern Movement building in Britain. It was commissioned by a former director of the British School at Rome from young

Modernist architects Connell, Ward and Lucas.

It seemed, at the time, that the only way the British were going to accept Modernism was as an exotic foreign style, much as they had enjoyed Chinese and Greek styles in the eighteenth and early nineteenth centuries.

This state of affairs was transformed during the early 1930s with the arrival in Britain of a number of earnest and eager architectural émigrés – refugees from Hitler's Germany. Erich Mendelsohn arrived in 1933, Walter Gropius in 1934 and Marcel Breuer in 1935. These men, and their fellow architectural émigrés, displayed an

almost missionary zeal in applying their architectural principles to the British condition, come what may.

Among this first wave of Modernist pioneers was Berthold Lubetkin, who, virtually single-handedly, was to transform the fortunes of Modernism in Britain. Lubetkin had trained and worked as an architect in Moscow, Berlin, Warsaw and Paris, and arrived in London, aged 30, in 1931. By the following year he had formed an architectural practice called Tecton with a group of eager young Englishmen and set about the crusade to introduce the British to the serious benefits of Modernism. To Lubetkin this was a highly political activity that aimed at no less than a fundamental change in society and a massive improvement of the conditions in which the mass of ordinary people lived and worked. It was to be a battle with established powers and reactionary artistic tastes. For Lubetkin, architecture was the ideological means to a social end; buildings were three-dimensional, concrete philosophy. As he put it: 'in the same way as philosophy changes and illuminates various aspects of existence, so art and architecture in parallel reflect the same doubts, hopes and aspirations.' Paraphrasing Karl von Clausewitz, the early nineteenth-century German theorist of war, Lubetkin wrote that 'architecture is politics, only pursued by other means'.[1]

His first major job came in 1932, when he was asked to design, of all things, a gorilla house at London Zoo. So it was here that London got its

Above left: Berthold Lubetkin in 1948.
Opposite: The Gorilla House in London Zoo. When completed in 1933 it was Lubetkin's first English building.

initial glimpse of modern architecture, and here too that the first great twentieth-century experiment in modern living was conducted – on animals.

The Gorilla House

The research anatomist at the zoo was Solly Zuckerman, a cosmopolitan European to whom the 'scientific' aspirations of Modernism greatly appealed. In addition, Zuckerman was a friend of the engineer Godfrey Samuel, who had been one of those who had invited Lubetkin to England and who was also a partner in Tecton. The secretary of the zoo, Sir Peter Chalmers Mitchell, was also a God-given client for Lubetkin: he was socially progressive, preferring to be described as an anarchist rather than a communist,[2] and keen

to make the zoo less a research centre and more a popular attraction. Mitchell and Zuckerman, along with the pro-communist superintendent of the zoo, Geoffrey Vevers, were prepared to believe that Lubetkin had the architectural means to do this.

Lubetkin and Zuckerman hit it off from the start for both believed in the power of so-called objective research. Lubetkin declared that his architecture would be a response to the scientific analysis of the problem of housing animals, and his buildings were, in their way, to be laboratories for understanding animal, and therefore human, behaviour.

Lubetkin's Gorilla House is an extraordinary affair. It was claimed, when it opened in 1933, to be based on a close study of the needs of gorillas,

but there is little evidence that this was the case. Indeed, there is ample circumstantial evidence to suggest otherwise. From the start of his career in Britain, Lubetkin revealed a Stalinist tendency to manipulate facts to suit ideological ends.

The Gorilla House was given a simple geometrical form, essentially a drum split in two to provide winter and summer accommodation, with one half being entirely cage. This made a clear and memorable architectural statement: Modernism preferred bold, no-nonsense forms that in themselves implied a rational and scientific approach to design. The bold, clean-cut lines of the drum were just the sort of image that Modernism required to get it noticed and – to make the modern image even more pronounced – Lubetkin decided that the drum should be formed out of steel-reinforced concrete. This was to be poured *in situ* so that the grain marks of the timber boards forming the shuttering, or mould, would be left on the surface of the concrete when set. Board-marked concrete had become something of a trademark among radical Modernists, for it displayed, in all its ruthless and honest beauty, the industrial process by which the building had been fabricated. It was never entirely clear why Lubetkin and his clients believed a drum-form and this material specially suited gorillas, nor was it revealed exactly what research had been undertaken to arrive at the conclusion that this visually striking form was what gorillas craved for their homes. What is clear is that Lubetkin claimed to have undertaken research.

Quite obviously, the building makes no attempt to create a natural habitat for the gorillas,

and the only concession to providing the animals with some privacy was to install a shutter system that could reduce the size of the cage opening. Lubetkin admitted that he wanted to exhibit the gorillas as clearly as possible in order to give the ticket-purchasing public a good chance to view the animals at close quarters. His defence for this approach, which ran counter to current advanced ideas among zoologists that a simulated natural habit was preferable, was that it prevented shy animals from hiding themselves indefinitely, and gave those with a taste for display a chance to indulge it to the best advantage. For Lubetkin the zoo was not to be a man-made jungle, but a theatre in which animals were permitted or coaxed to display their most distinctive characteristics. In pursuing this approach with the Gorilla House, Lubetkin was evidently imposing a theory – an ideology – rather than responding to objective and scientific research into what type of habitat the animals would actually prefer.

The Gorilla House was well received by the professional and popular press when it opened in 1933. *The Times* informed its readers on 29 April that the 'Fellows of the Zoological Society...saw the new house for the first time and expressed themselves highly satisfied with its appearance and amenities', while the gorillas 'galloped around in an excess of high spirits and swung from rope to rope and swing to swing'. On the same day the *Daily Sketch* wrote humorously about the gorillas' house-warming party given in 'the apes' luxury flat'.

In fact, the gorillas started to pine in their drum, where they had little escape from the public gaze, and by 1939 the zoo finally accepted that the building was unsuitable in form and scale for large animals such as gorillas. It was then decided that the building should be used to exhibit eight young chimpanzees.[3]

But in 1933 the Gorilla House was regarded as a complete success, and led to Lubetkin and Tecton's most famous commission at London Zoo, and the enduring image of the pioneering phase of the Modern Movement in Britain – the Penguin Pool.

The Penguin Pool

In December 1933 the zoo decided in principle on 'the construction of a new Pond for Penguins in the Gardens at a cost of £1000,[4] and in June 1934 the secretary was given the power 'to proceed with the plans for a new Penguin Pool'. The estimate had now risen to £1500.[5]

The governing body of the zoo was in flux in 1934, with Mitchell planning to retire as secretary in early 1935. He was to be replaced by Sir Julian Huxley, who, like his predecessor, was active in progressive circles. For example, he had been involved since 1931 with an association called Political and Economic Planning, which undertook social and economic research related to public housing, the health service and the location of industry.[6] Once again, Lubetkin was lucky with his client. The pool had been designed in collaboration with Mitchell, so Huxley could have been expected to distance himself from the final work of his predecessor. But not at all. Huxley was a great admirer of Tecton's work and put his full weight behind the completion of the pool as conceived.

As with the Gorilla House, Lubetkin did not seek to simulate the natural habitat of the king penguins for which the pool was intended. Instead, in pursuit of his theory of animal theatre, he wanted to provide a sympathetic setting that responded to their various needs but that, even more importantly, would provide a setting in which they could be closely observed by the public.

This approach, combined with the conviction that this was another opportunity to display before the public the structural and design virtues of Modernism, meant that Lubetkin was tempted to impose upon the design certain ideas that might look attractive and radical but which were not necessarily a response to the real requirements of penguins.

For example, the pool is oval in shape because, explained Lubetkin, of the restricted site. But it is surely no coincidence that oval and streamlined forms were immensely popular among Modernists in the early 1930s, while the double-helix ramps – the dominant feature of the pool – were a standard design in Russian Constructivist architecture of the sort Lubetkin knew well from his youth.[7] This dependence on precedence would not be an issue if Lubetkin had not promoted the pool as a monument to scientific and objective research, and to the belief that a design must be fit for its purpose. In reality, Lubetkin was playing a game of style and aesthetics just as much as the more obviously historicist architects of earlier generations.

The great visual coup and focus of the design – the cantilevered spiral ramps – are extremely dubious as to their functional purpose and their unsupported through space – could be achieved only by the inspired use of this material. Certainly never before in Britain had concrete been used with such verve and in such a daringly sculptural manner. But was this ramp really needed by the penguins? Was it a logical structure in the circumstances, or was it merely a somewhat bombastic display of the glories of modern design and modern materials?

From the day the Penguin Pool opened there were doubters. For example, it was obvious that steel-reinforced concrete was a problematic material to use in this case. The structure would always be wet, and if the thin outer layer of concrete cracked (a possibility if the ramps settled even slightly), then moisture would penetrate and the steel reinforcing bars would rust, expand and blow off the concrete covering. In fact, this is precisely what did eventually happen.

And did the penguins really appreciate the possibilities of their splendid ramp? According to an article published in the *Architects' Journal* on 14 June 1934, when the pool was completed the ramps were intended to have merely a theatrical quality, to provide a suitable stage on which the penguins could waddle up and down to the amusement of the public. This was what Lubetkin meant when he said he would produce a design that would display the creatures' most distinctive characteristics.

But unfortunately for Lubetkin and the zoo, the penguins preferred not to delight the public by waddling up and down the ramps; they refused to disport themselves in the giant fish tank that Lubetkin provided at the top of one of the ramps (thus making at least one of the ramps

means of construction. They are made of steel-reinforced concrete of wafer-like thinness (a very difficult task achieved thanks to the genius of structural engineer Ove Arup) because this was the material of Modernism, and such an elegant and minimal structure – seemingly rising

Above: The Penguin Pool, built in 1934, at London Zoo – the image of pioneering Modernism in Britain.

functionally redundant); and they did not like the very architectural nesting boxes placed on the concrete floor of the pool.

These and other problems led zoo officials to propose demolishing the structure in 1951. As the superintendent at the time observed: '…it has failed dismally… the concrete base is unsuitable for [the penguins] to stand on… in hot weather it is an airless sun-trap… the construction has not proved satisfactory, and extensive repairs have been required.' Demolition did not take place, and, following years of adaptation and repair, the pool still houses penguins, but a much smaller variety than originally intended.

However, these problems, obvious as they may have been, were played down or ignored. The irony of a functionalist building that appeared not to function properly was passed over. The Penguin Pool was more than a mere zoo building: it was an ideological statement, a declaration that rational, streamlined and concrete-built Modernism had arrived in Britain, and, as such, members of the avant-garde fell over themselves to praise it. Typical was the response of leading design pundit Sir Charles Reilly, who wondered in January 1935 'how many citizens of London have brooded over the railings of that pool, envying the penguins as they streak through the blue water or plod up the exquisite incline of the ramp – and have wondered sadly why human beings cannot be provided, like penguins, with an environment so adapted to their needs'.[8] Huxley, in 1937, was even more crusading in his assessment of the Penguin Pool, which, he wrote, 'first dramatically attracted the attention of the world to developments in England [and]

it became evident that England was [now] accepting modern architecture as the logical contemporary way of building'.

Those like Reilly and Huxley, who believed that Lubetkin held the formula for the creation of a successful and distinct twentieth-century architecture, did not have long to wait to see the lessons of housing animals applied to a more demanding and vocal user. Just as the first rave reviews of the Penguin Pool were appearing in mid-1934, Lubetkin was completing the construction of Highpoint One, London's first high-rise, high-class Modernist housing scheme. Now Lubetkin had to apply his scientific and research-based approach to design to build 'collective' housing for humans, and this time any failures or fudges would be severely punished. Gorillas and penguins could not complain, but Lubetkin must have fully appreciated that the articulate occupants of this experimental building would complain long and hard if the vision did not work.

Highpoint One

As with the zoo, the commission to design Highpoint came through Lubetkin's connections. Godfrey Samuel's father, Sir Herbert, was acquainted with the Gestetners, a family of Hungarian origin, and highly successful in the manufacture of modern and rational office furniture. The chairman of the company, Sigmund Gestetner, had been impressed by the way in which Czech industrialists and the Soviet Union provided high-quality housing for their workers, so the idea formed that Lubetkin would design housing for the workforce at Gestetner's north London factory.

The first task was to find a site. While this quest was under way, the nature of the project started to change profoundly. Both Lubetkin and Gestetner were convinced that their scheme should be for collective housing, that is housing with a certain number of facilities and services shared by the community, such as gardens, canteen or laundry. But there was, both seemed to agree, no compelling reason that the collective housing should, in fact, also be workers' housing. At some time during 1934 Gestetner retreated from his ambition to build healthy homes for his work-force and instead opted for an experiment in the marriage of Modernism and speculative housing. Lubetkin seems to have been not greatly, if at all, upset by this fundamental change in the brief. If he had a social programme for the development, he quickly amended it. He persuaded Gestetner that the flats should contain something of a social mix and include some low-rent accommodation (an idea that quickly fizzled out), but his over-riding idea was to demonstrate the advantages of community living within a high-rise, sculptural Modernist building. Whether the occupants were workers or the comfortably-off middle class was not a burning issue with Tecton or Lubetkin. This was a strange oversight on Lubetkin's part. As high-rise housing sprouted in vast numbers in the years after Highpoint One, it soon became very clear that the type of tenants housed, and the extent of management and maintenance, was of prime importance to the social success, or failure, of a scheme – certainly just as important as its architecture or planning.

But back in 1934 Lubetkin could see only that he had the chance to create in London the type of visionary high-rise housing that had been advocated for the last decade by Modernist visionaries such as Le Corbusier, and which was starting tentatively to appear. For example, the Lawn Road Flats in Hampstead, built in 1932 to the designs of Wells Coates, were not pioneering in their techniques of construction, nor did they embody the spirit of Le Corbusier's 'City of Towers', but the development did provide minimalist and functional modern dwellings which were tempting enough to attract both Gropius and Breuer as tenants.

Gestetner gave Lubetkin great freedom in the evolution of the design: the only proviso was that he expected an 8 per cent return on his investment. Clearly aware of estate agents' advice that the three most important things in creating a successful development are location, location and location, Lubetkin started to play his 'Highgate hunch'. In the 1930s Highgate was an elevated and healthy area favoured by London's new European community of cultured and cosmopolitan émigrés and refugees from Germany and Austria. Generally accustomed to living in tall apartment blocks, and progressive and intellectual in their outlook, these émigrés would prove the most sympathetic users for the type of building Lubetkin had in mind. Eventually a site was found on North Hill, a few hundred yards north of the old village centre. Lubetkin later explained that he had popped into a pub and asked the landlord if he knew of any local building sites. 'Yes, right across the road,' was the reply. This anecdote, as Lubetkin was all too aware, gave the development an appealing and popular tone.

Now Lubetkin set himself and his Tecton team, with the addition of engineer Ove Arup, to design this exemplary and ground-breaking project. Highpoint, as the scheme was quickly called because its upper floors would be the highest inhabited point in London, was to be the prototype of rationally planned, high-density modern living that captured something of the spirit of a traditional village community.

As with the buildings at London Zoo, objective research was to be applied to the challenge of the brief and site. This applied to the techniques of construction and to the design of many interior details. Door handles, bathrooms and kitchens were reconsidered from first principles, and reformed to reflect Tecton's research. The structural investigations were particularly far-reaching, for the structural concept and constructional techniques eventually used at Highpoint One were pioneering – at least in British terms. Arup was able to persuade the district surveyor (the local government watchdog) to permit the structure to be formed with monolithic concrete panels, cast *in situ*, and concrete slabs. This concession, permitting a structural technique not covered in the London building regulations, meant that the forest of internal columns that would have resulted from a conventional reinforced-concrete frame-structure were not needed (except where required for artistic reasons, as in the entrance hall). Instead a modern, open and airy interior was achieved. In addition, Arup devised a system of 'climbing shuttering' (reusable timber moulds), which

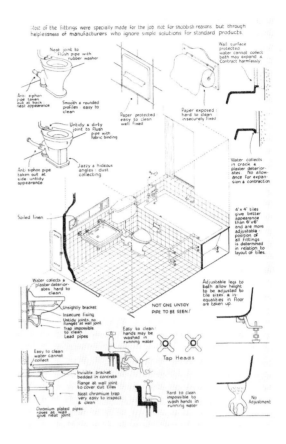

allowed for the quick and economic casting of the concrete panels and slabs. Quite simply, the system started at ground level and was then raised storey by storey to permit the casting of one floor structure after another. This construction technique was already familiar in civil engineering but it was the first time this 'industrial' system had been used in domestic architecture.[9] As well as achieving speed and economy, this climbing shuttering system had profound structural and aesthetic implications. As the external elevations rose, concrete panels were cast directly, one upon

Above: Sheet showing how Tecton reconsidered the design of basic domestic items from first principles.

the other, so that the exterior walls of Highpoint eventually had a very sleek monolithic look. Floor levels were hardly expressed (effectively only by the balconies), and even the joints between panels were often barely noticeable. The surface honestly expressed the material and the construction process, but indicated little about the structure of the building. This was typical of the purist 'white box' aesthetic of the early phase of Modernist architecture.

While the climbing shuttering system robbed the exterior of Highpoint of a certain force of expression, it also – by providing a fully supporting, monolithic concrete carcass for the building – allowed structural elements to be reduced to a minimum thickness. This seemed, at the time, a wonderfully elegant and economic consequence of the pioneering structural system used, but it was a curse in disguise. The thickness of the external concrete walls is only 6 inches (15 centimetres), including 1 inch (2.5 centimetres) of permanent cork shuttering (insulation). This is simply too slight, especially given Lubetkin's Modernist preference not to clutter the elevation

with traditional weathering details that could throw off rainwater. The thin cover of concrete over the steel reinforcing bars meant that water could penetrate through even shallow cracks and visit upon Highpoint the same evils that beset the Penguin Pool, with steel reinforcing rods rusting, expanding and cracking off the concrete cover. This led to a high level of maintenance and restoration, with the entire building being re-coated in 1987–8. John Allan, the definitive and sympathetic biographer of Lubetkin, remains perplexed by this failure. He offers an explanation: 'Such unwarranted faith in the longevity of thin concrete structure seems all the more puzzling in a practice otherwise so conscientious in its investigative approach to technique and detail generally, and is certainly attributable to innocence rather than recklessness. The process of concrete deterioration was not fully under-stood... reinforced concrete was assumed to

Above: Aerial view of Highpoint One soon after completion showing the double cruciform shape of the building.
Opposite: The entrance hall in Highpoint One, showing the pilotis.

last indefinitely'.[10] The best defence that can be mounted of this 'unscientific optimism', even by a champion of Lubetkin, is that of ignorance.

But this failure to base a major and pioneering structural decision on fully developed research should come as no surprise. There are many elements of the building that were not based on objective, site-specific research. The building had a mission and was to carry a message, and the message was written well before design started. To Lubetkin, architecture was social and political philosophy made concrete, and Highpoint was to be the building that blazed the way forward for the philosophy of Modernism. This determination led to a number of key decisions, including the pioneering concrete construction. The building was to be set in a large shared garden, complete with swimming pool and recreation facilities. The building was to be of cruciform plan, to give it sculptural form and to ensure that all its flats enjoyed good natural light and fine views. Sculptural in form and free-standing in parkland, the eight-storey Highpoint was to realize the urban ideal of the 'vertical garden city' promoted by Le Corbusier and other early Modernists. It was to introduce to humdrum and traditional

London the authentic image of the city of tomorrow.

The ground floor of Highpoint One was to be organized for community use, with a generous and startling modern entrance. This Lubetkin intended to be a tour de force of modern space: a statement of intent for all to see. As built, it has a split-level floor, two lines of simple columns (the pilotis so beloved by Le Corbusier) define the space, and light filters through a wall of glass blocks, another Modernist trademark and a technological innovation of the age. The plan of the entrance hall is organized around a pair of axes that radiate from the front door. This is a characteristic piece of Russian Constructivist planning, almost baroque in character. One axis is terminated by a

semicircular alcove in which there were to be tables and chairs, and the other leads to the garden door. This interior, as well as being a showcase of European Modernism and a worked example of Le Corbusier's theory of *plan libre* (free plan), was to provide a hall in which residents could meet and sit. It was also to form a *promenade architecturale* (architectural promenade), again a baroque notion, with residents and their guests parading through the public space of the building to a gardenside tea room (an idea adopted from the traditional Russian dacha). That in turn led to a terrace from which, via diagonal steps and a ramp, the garden is reached.

After this sparkling opening gambit, the interiors of the apartments in Highpoint One are somewhat surprising. There are two main staircases, incorporating lifts, each of which serves one of the two joined cruciform blocks that comprise Highpoint. Typically, at each floor level the staircase/lift serves four flats – two of the larger type and two of the smaller. Being within the centre of each cruciform, the staircases are

Above right: One of the lifts and staircases serving the apartments.
Above: Living room with 'concertina' window.
Opposite left: Entrance hall showing piloti and an original flush door.
Opposite right: An early photograph of a kitchen with original fittings.

dark, receiving only a little borrowed light. The flats are also served by two small service wells incorporating hoists, particularly useful for transporting waste to the communal refuse store at basement level.

The entrance vestibules to the flats are furnished with a couple of Modernist trademarks – a piloti of strangely flattened shape and (in the larger flats) a wall of glazing – but otherwise they are strikingly conventional. There are no split levels, nor are the interiors open plan beyond a double door connecting the living room and dining room in the larger flats. Instead, the flats are divided into a relatively large number of rooms of generally standard form. The large flats have three bedrooms, a bathroom, a small kitchen and – most pleasing – a large, well-lit living room with ingenious folding windows, which open to transform the room virtually into a loggia that can flow into the smaller, adjoining dining room.

These larger flats were even provided with a bedroom that could be used by a maid. (So much for Highpoint being the reflection of a new democratic social order!)

The rooms in the smaller flats are even more conventional, all being of standard rectangular form. In both large and small flats the living rooms are provided with balconies. With their curving concrete fronts and iron side-bars, these balconies make a very striking contribution to the elevations they adorn, on sunny days sending tiers of rippling shadows across the surface of the façade. But, for internal use, they are an odd design indeed. They are too narrow and their walls too low to provide comfortable external seating. They are, in effect, only glorified window boxes. What objective research, one must ask, led Tecton to create such strikingly non-functional balconies? Indeed, the whole basis of the group's use of research comes into question when these

flats are considered. Did it really reveal what Lubetkin and Gestetner must have known from the start? That their target clientele – socially and politically progressive, middle-class intelligentsia of largely middle age – liked the appearance of living in a pioneering Modernist block of collective housing but, within the privacy of their own apartments, wanted traditional and familiar arrangements? Typical of the initial residents were two of Lubetkin's former clients from London Zoo: Sir Peter Chalmers Mitchell and Geoffrey Vevers.

When it came to housing well-connected, cultured and articulate people, who knew how they wanted to live and who had to be attracted to invest in the development, Lubetkin's ideas seem to have been significantly less radical, and certainly more pragmatic, than when he was housing dumb creatures in the zoo.

John Allan's evaluation of Highpoint is revealing: '…it eminently suits those for whom it is eminently suitable… Highpoint demonstrates, perhaps paradoxically, that even a building with such an exemplary reputation has its compromises, such as intrusive overlooking [windows], a maintenance-intensive envelope [exterior], under-sized kitchens, buried heating pipework in a hard-water area, huge opening windows adjacent to almost unusable balconies, and inadequate fire separation of the service lift cores.'[11]

It must also be added that the full implications of the decision to provide private housing rather than workers' accommodation does not appear to have been fully appreciated. This was a fundamental change in the brief, which had many consequences, not least of which was the collapse of the collective ideal. The private, middle-class residents simply did not want to sit around together in the hall or tea room discussing life and politics, and meetings in the garden or by the pool were tolerated rather than relished.

But if Highpoint One represents a compromise of some Modernist ideals of functionalism, fitness-for-purpose, social idealism and research-based design, it is also a triumph. Indeed, it is partly because Highpoint combines new with traditional ideas of living that it has proved such a resounding success with generations of residents. Its simple, white-painted concrete exterior – starkly cruciform and enlivened by the moving shadows of trees or the sundial-like creep of the shadows of the balconies – still has the power to shock. Highpoint remains a daring piece of avant-garde, abstract sculpture, standing stark, still and white in the dark green swirl of its surrounding trees. As Allan concludes: '…the quality of thought underpinning the detailed design of Highpoint One did produce the first significant evidence in England that Modernism was not just a style but a craft.'[12] It could also be said that Highpoint One made it clear that Modernist architecture, when realizing such a complex thing as homes for humans, was not just a science, but an art. And in this sense Highpoint One, with its baroque *promenade architecturale*, has much more in common with traditional, historicist architecture than at first appears. In 1972 Lubetkin himself finally conceded this: 'I quite openly advocated the view that to design a building from a purely technical point of view is impossible… we spared no effort to underline in the "red ink" of imagination the exceptions to the diagram… The virtue of Highpoint One for me is not inherent in the technical exposition, but in the contrast of wilful with schematic logic.'[13]

The Influence of Highpoint

The significance of Highpoint One was recognized immediately. It was accepted, as Lubetkin and Tecton desired, as proof that it was possible to live in cities in a new way. The influential American critic Henry Russell Hitchcock described Highpoint One, in a New York exhibition of 1937 as, 'one of the finest, if not absolutely the finest, middle-class housing projects in the world'.[14] Le Corbusier himself visited the building, at Lubetkin's invitation, and obligingly wrote in 1936 that 'for a long time I have dreamed of executing dwellings in such conditions for the good of humanity. The building is an achievement of the first rate and a milestone that will be useful to everybody.'[15] This was, perhaps, not a surprising compliment since Highpoint greatly resembled two of the cruciform towers of Le Corbusier's own 'contemporary city' design set side by side.

Following its completion, Highpoint One was almost universally regarded as a success. But was it a universally applicable solution to the problem of designing urban housing? Many thought so. All would agree that the model required adaptation to specific circumstances, but it seemed as if Lubetkin and Tecton really had found and applied the formula. Two years later, in 1936, Lubetkin and Tecton themselves tried a variation of the formula with Highpoint Two. This was also to accommodate private residents, but in a subtly and significantly different way. The functionalist machine aesthetic was reduced, with Lubetkin giving more licence to his beaux-arts love for the classical and decorative. The most striking and controversial expression of this is the Greek-style caryatid columns that are used to support the canopy over the entrance. Many saw this as a retreat into whimsy and historicism, or – even worse – a marketing ploy to help attract the progressive yet traditionally minded clients at which the development was aimed. Lubetkin always maintained that the caryatids were not part of the building proper and only somewhat ironical garden ornaments. The development was altogether more upmarket, with lavish apartments containing the Modernist spatial manipulations, such as walls of glass, galleried double-height rooms and open plan, missing in Highpoint One. Reaction to the scheme was mixed: some radical Modernists felt almost a sense of betrayal. One, an architectural student called Anthony Cox, who was to became a major figure in post-war architecture in Britain, wrote in 1938 that the building '…shows a deviation from [the Functionalist] approach [that is] more than a deviation of appearance; it implies a deviation of aim. [It sets] certain formal values above use-values, and marks the re-emergence of the *idea* as the motive force.'[16]

In 1938, the year that Highpoint Two was completed, Tecton received its toughest commission: to demonstrate that the design, constructional and social principles of Highpoint One and Two could be applied to the construction of public housing. Was the formula indeed universally applicable? The client was the

London Borough of Finsbury, which, as the most progressive socialist local authority in London at the time, wanted to house its people in a manner suited to their needs. The charismatic and somewhat enigmatic pro-communist leader of the council, Alderman Harold Riley, had clearly been convinced by Lubetkin and Tecton's claims, and by their work at the zoo and at Highgate. The schemes that laboured into life during the following 20 years (delayed by war, shortage of money, and changing local government leadership and aspirations) show the strengths as well as the fatal flaws of Tecton's approach, and of the influence on urban planning of Modernist social

and architectural theory. In Spa Green, at the head of Rosebery Avenue, and in Holford Square, Pentonville, where work got under way in 1943 and 1946 and was completed in 1950 and 1954 respectively, whole swathes of late Georgian terraces were swept away and replaced by monolithic blocks that were to prove beyond the ability of the local authority to maintain or manage properly.

Lubetkin's attempt to apply some of the principles of Highgate to the Holford Square tower now seem bizarre. The research into the problem undertaken by the architects had led Lubetkin to declare that 'in the light of the economic, social and technical conditions of today, and while the heritage of the past could not be disregarded, it could not, at the same time, be allowed to form a dead weight which might hamper the solution'. Consequently, it was decided to turn the existing Holford Square inside out. Its late Georgian houses were to be demolished and replaced by open space, while the garden in the centre of the old square was to provide a site for the block of flats called Bevin House. Thus Lubetkin attempted to recreate, approximately, the site conditions of Highgate. Similarly, Bevin House is Y-shaped in plan to provide generous amounts of glazing, good natural ventilation and good views; it is built of concrete and is eight storeys high. But here the similarities stop. Unlike the Highpoint flats, there is little attempt to create a sense of communal

Above: The caryatid entrance porch of Highpoint Two.
Opposite: A slab block on the Spa Green estate, Finsbury, designed under the supervision of Lubetkin.

living: the staircase and landings (of spectacular concrete design) are bleakly open to the elements, finishes and details are crimped by cost constraints, and the density is high. All this led, and still leads, to an intensity of occupation that is expressed not only by extreme wear and tear but also through vandalism and what is euphemistically termed antisocial behaviour.

Few in the late 1930s and 1940s seemed to have anticipated the huge difficulties that would arise when high-rise housing accommodated not middle-class private occupants living in tower blocks by choice and willing and able to pay maintenance and management costs, but council tenants, often incarcerated against their will in towers that local authorities had not the will, wit or money to maintain or manage properly. And even less regard was paid to the consequences of tower-block construction in urban locations, particularly historic city centres. The imagination of the 1920s and 1930s was haunted by the image of crowded, often poorly built and cramped

Victorian terraced houses sprawling in airless shade and pollution below viaducts and factory walls. Replacing slums with aspiring towers set in parkland seemed an ideal solution. But as this task was taken in hand by local authorities in post-war Britain, a number of unpleasant realities forced themselves upon the crusading architects, planners and politicians. Apparent slum streets often supported a vibrant community spirit and social infrastructure that was destroyed by redevelopment and did not re-establish itself in the arid atmosphere of public housing, high-rise estates. The traditional grid of streets, with its variety and hierarchy of public and private spaces – courts, mews, squares, alleys and gardens – and its rich mix of uses provided an environment in which communities could easily take root and flourish and in which individuals could find a sense of identity. To sweep all this away and replace it with a swathe of poorly maintained park dotted with residential towers and minimal or non-existent support services such as shops or

pubs, was not just to destroy urban history and memory but also to create misery among tenants who felt demeaned and alienated.

It must be acknowledged that Lubetkin and his colleagues failed to make the Highgate formula work when it came to public housing, and nor could their most talented contemporaries and followers. Denys Lasdun, who had worked for Tecton in the late 1930s, was commissioned in the early 1950s to design public housing in Bethnal Green, an area of east London ravaged by war and riddled with slums. His most striking scheme is the 15-storey tower in Claredale Street, called Keeling House. This is a clear development both of Tecton's work and Le Corbusier's mass housing schemes, but Lasdun also introduced a

slight variation. Taking nature as an inspiration, he conceived the tower as tiers of pods clustering around a stem. The pods are the flats, the stem the service core. The idea behind this 'cluster housing' was, explains Lasdun's biographer William Curtis, to 'turn the previous coherent social unit of the Bethnal Green street up on its end, while also incorporating the high density, services, living conditions, light and air of a modern *Unité d'Habitation'*.[17] Keeling House, completed in 1957, is a memorable piece of architecture, admirable in its ambition, but it

Above: Trellick Tower, designed by Erno Goldfinger.
Opposite: Keeling House, Bethnal Green, completed in 1957 to the designs of Denys Lasdun.

failed as a social experiment. At the time of completion Lasdun, aware that comprehensive urban redevelopment schemes and high-rise public housing were being accused of killing off local communities, claimed that his balconied scheme created 'streets in the air'. It didn't. By the 1990s the local authority had moved its tenants out and declared that the housing block had no future: repair and maintenance costs were so high that demolition was the only solution. In the end, this did not happen. Significantly, given the Highpoint origin of England's high-rise housing, Keeling House was purchased by a developer and now flourishes as a block of well-maintained, well-managed and expensive private apartments favoured by the young and artistic avant-garde. Erno Goldfinger's Trellick Tower of 1966–73 looming over London's Westway, a clear development of Le Corbusier's *Unité* scheme, and the most sculpturally satisfying of all of Britain's post-war high-rise housing blocks, tells a similar story. Salvation came only through improved management and a gradual desire by tenants actually to inhabit the place.

Despite these failures, Highpoint One is one of the most significant buildings ever constructed in Britain because it embodied an idea – an idea far bigger than architecture alone but which all great architecture encompasses. It offered a vision for life itself. Highpoint One spoke of a better world, of social equality, of the humane advances that could be achieved through benign science and technology, of the creative potential of objective and enlightened research and of the vital importance of art – of form and proportion – to man's spiritual and material happiness. This may

all now seem rather naïve, especially since Highpoint One failed to be the universal model that many at the time of its completion believed. But for all its faults and failures, Highpoint One was and remains an inspiration and proof that high-rise urban living can work in reality as well as in the seductive visions of Le Corbusier. And if some of its progeny are regrettable, others are not. It is, in its own terms, an ideal.

Acknowledgements

This book accompanies a television series so, first and foremost, I would like to thank those people from the BBC who made both the programmes and the book possible. Jane Root (Controller of BBC2), Roly Keating (Controller of Arts Commissioning), Franny Moyle (Creative Director of Arts), Basil Comely (Executive Producer of *Britain's Best Buildings*), Julian Birkett, John Bush, Sam Hobkinson, Ben McPherson, Linda Dalling, Nick Barratt, Victoria Page, Matthew Hill and David Vincent.

At BBC Worldwide I want to thank Emma Shackleton, Martin Redfern, Linda Blakemore, Patricia Burgess and Rachel Jordan.

I must also offer special thanks to Sarah Barratt for her research

assistance and for her work on the Holyroodhouse and Blenheim chapters, and to John Parker for the enthusiastic and tireless way in which he worked to produce his excellent photographs. Also thanks to the editor of the *Architects' Journal* for allowing me to use material gathered initially for an article on St Pancras Station.

At Durham Cathedral I would like to thank the Very Reverend Dr John Arnold, Dean of Durham Cathedral, Anne Heywood, Christopher Downes, John McGowan and David Tasker. For their advice and views on the cathedral I must thank Eric Fernie, Keith Critchlow and Eugenia Sartorius. At Windsor, Dr Steven

Brindle of English Heritage for his insights about medieval Windsor and for allowing me access to his draft *History of Windsor Castle*; also to Oliver Everett and Jane Roberts. At Blenheim, Helen Walch and John Foster. At the Midland Grand Hotel, Calum Rollo and London and Continental for information and for access to the hotel when I was conducting my initial research; also to Michael McNamara. At Cardiff Castle, Matthew Williams, curator. At Tower Bridge, Eric Sutherns, the Bridge Master, and his wife Linda; also to Linzi Baltrunas at the Corporation of London. At Highpoint One, Caroline Parmenter and David Rowley.

Notes

Durham Cathedral
1 See *The Coffin of St. Cuthbert*, introduction by E. Kitzinger, drawings by J. McIntyre (University Press, Oxford, 1950).
2 'Simeon of Durham', trans. from the Latin by Joseph Stephenson, in *A History of the Kings of England* (Lampeter, Llanerch Enterprises, 1987). The original MS survives in the cathedral library at Durham.
3 My thanks to Eric Fernie for this observation.
4 Malcolm Thurlby, 'The roles of the patron and master mason in the first design of the Romanesque cathedral of Durham' in D. Rollason (ed.) *Anglo-Norman Durham 1093–1193* (Boydell Press, Woodbridge, 1994), pp. 161–84.
5 This is told in other forms in Matthew 21:44 and Luke 20:17.
6 Based on conversations with Keith Critchlow.
7 Sir Banister Fletcher, *A History of Architecture*, 20th edition (Architectural Press, Oxford, 1996), p. 372.

Windsor Castle
1 Daniel Defoe, *A Tour Through the Whole Island of Great Britain*

(1724–7: Pat Rogers, ed., Penguin, London, 1983), p. 277.
2 *Calendar of Patent Rolls, 1348–50* (HMSO, London, 1891), p. 144.
3 The painting is now in the National Gallery, London.
4 Information from Dr Steven Brindle of English Heritage.
5 Hargrave Jennings, *The Rosicrucians: The rites and mysteries*, fourth edition (Routledge & Sons, London, 1907).
6 Correspondence outlining the plan to take Windsor Castle is in the British Library: Add. MS 18980, f. 25.
7 William Pyne, *The History of Royal Residences* (3 vols, London, 1819), vol. I, p. 176.
8 Charles Knight, *Passages of a Working Life* (Bradbury & Evans, London, 1864), vol. I, pp. 36–8.
9 Christopher Hibbert, *Queen Victoria in Her Letters and Journals* (John Murray, London, 1984), p. 55.
10 Ibid., p. 57.
11 Mark Girouard, *Windsor: The most romantic castle* (Hodder & Stoughton, London, 1993), pp. 80–1.
12 Hibbert, op. cit., pp. 172–3.

Holyroodhouse
1 T. Dickson and Paul J. Balfour (eds), *Accounts of the Lord High Treasurer of*

Scotland (Edinburgh, 1877), vol. II (1500–4), pp. lxxxi–lxxxii.
2 Ibid., vol. II, p. 273.
3 Ibid., vol. II, p. 227.
4 For example, ibid., vol. II, p. 214.
5 Ibid., vol. III (1506–7), p. 275.
6 Ibid., vol. IV (1507–13), p. 445.
7 H.M. Paton, J. Imrie and J.G. Dunbar (eds), *Accounts of the Master of Works for Building and Repairing Royal Castles and Palaces* (Edinburgh, 1957), vol. I, p. 45.
8 Ibid., vol. IV, p. 257.
9 J.S. Brewer, J. Gairdner and R.H. Brodie (eds), *Letters and Papers, Foreign and Domestic, of the Reign of Henry VIII* (22 vols, London, 1862–1932), vol. XIX, p. 199.
10 Ibid., vol. XIX, p. 332.
11 *Holinshed's Chronicles of England, Scotland and Ireland* (1577: 6 vols, J. Johnson, London, 1807), vol. III, p. 837.
12 *Accounts of the Lord High Treasurer*, op. cit., vol. III (1506–7), pp. 299–304.
13 David Laing (ed.), *The Works of John Knox* (6 vols, Edinburgh, 1846–64), vol. II, p. 514.
14 J.H. Burton (ed.) *The Register of the Privy Council of Scotland* (Edinburgh, 1877), vol. VI, p. 501.

15 Ibid., vol. XII, p. 63.
16 Ibid., vol. X, pp. 593–4.
17 Donald Crawford (ed.), *Journals of Sir John Lauder, Lord Fountainhall, with His Observations on Public Affairs and Other Memoranda, 1665–1676* (University Press, Edinburgh, 1900), p. 327.
18 *The Works of Rev. John Wesley A.M.*, third edition (14 vols, London, 1829–31), vol. III, p. 323.
19 Ibid., vol. IV, p. 181.
20 *Edinburgh Courant*, 20 Sept 1832.

Blenheim Palace
1 W.C. Coxe, *Memoirs of John Duke of Marlborough* (3 vols, Longman, Hurst, Rees, Orme and Browne, London, 1818), vol. I, p. 214.
2 Ibid., p. 252.
3 Unpublished letter from Sarah to a legal adviser in the Blenheim archives.
4 Geoffrey Webb (ed.), *The Complete Works of Sir John Vanbrugh*, vol. IV: The Letters (Nonesuch Press, London, 1927), p. 179.
5 Stuart Johnson Reid, *John and Sarah, Duke and Duchess of Marlborough, 1660–1744* (John Murray, London, 1914), p. 219.
6 Webb, op. cit., p. 191.
7 Ibid., p. 187.
8 Howard Colvin, *A Biographical Dictionary of British Architects, 1600–1840* (John Murray, London, 1978), pp. 829–35.
9 David Green, *Blenheim Palace* (Country Life, London, 1951), p. 301.
10 'Henry Joynes Letterbook 1708–16', British Library, Add. MS 19607.
11 Bodleian Library, MS Eng. lett.e.1.f. 241.
12 W.E. Buckley (ed.), *Memoirs of Thomas Earl of Ailesbury* (2 vols, Westminster, 1890), vol. II, pp. 585–7.
13 Isaac d'Israeli, *Curiosities of Literature*, ninth edition (6 vols, London, 1824), vol.V, p. 192.
14 Green, op. cit., plate 29; and Bodleian Library, Oxford MS Top. Oxon a.37.
15 Green, op. cit., pp. 105–6.
16 John Macky, *A Journey Through England* (3 vols, J. Pemberton, London, 1732), vol. II, p. 124.
17 Plans of how the grounds would have looked are in the Bodleian Library (attributed to Vanbrugh) and held privately (Wise). A plan was also published in Colen Campbell's *Vitruvius Britannicus*, vol. III (London, 1725).
18 Webb, op. cit., p. 41.

19 Ibid., p. 44.
20 'Henry Joynes Letterbook', British Library, Add. MS 19609.
21 Green, op. cit., p. 132.
22 Public Record Office, E134/8GeoI/Hil8.

Cardiff Castle
1 *Athenaeum*, 7 July 1860.
2 William Paley, *Natural Theology, or Evidence of the Existence and Attributes of the Deity* (Joseph Graham, Alnwick, 1839).
3 John Ruskin to Henry Acland, 24 May 1851. See E.T. Cook and Alexander Wedderburn (eds), *The Works of John Ruskin* (39 vols, London, 1903–12), vol. 36, p. 115. Quoted in Tim Hilton, *John Ruskin, the Early Years, 1819–1859* (Yale University Press, New Haven and London, 1985), p. 185.
4 *Bridgewater Treatises on the Power, Wisdom and Goodness of God as Manifested in the Creation.* 'Treatise VI: Geology and mineralogy considered with reference to natural theology' by William Buckland, Dean of Westminster (2 vols, William Pickering, London, 1836), vol. I, pp. 484–7.
5 Sir Thomas Browne, *Religio Medici, cum annotationibus* (trans. John Merryweather), Argentorati: sumptibus Friderici Spoor, 1652.
6 J.M. Crook (ed.) with contributions by Mary Axon and Virginia Glenn, *The Strange Genius of William Burges, Art-Architect, 1827–1881* (National Museum of Wales, 1981), p. 11.
7 Alfred, Lord Tennyson, 'In Memoriam' (Edward Moxon, London, 1850).
8 Quoted in Crook, op. cit., p. 10.
9 See J.M. Crook, *William Burges and the High Victorian Dream* (John Murray, London, 1981), pp. 260–1.
10 Ibid., pp. 261–2.
11 Ibid., p. 262.

Midland Grand Hotel, St Pancras
1 Drawings are held in the Drawings Collection of the RIBA in the V&A Museum, and by the Public Record Office and Railtrack. A list of all known drawings of the station and hotel is filed at the RIBA. Contemporary photographs are held by several organizations, including the National Monuments Record and the Science Museum.
2 *Railway Times*: 31 (1869), p. 52.
3 Southern Construction Committee,

Midland Railway Company minutes 1/279–82, min. 101 (1865).
4 Jack Simmons, *St Pancras Station* (George Allen & Unwin, London, 1968), illustrations 5, 6.
5 Ibid., p. 21.
6 Southern Construction Committee, op. cit., minutes 1/19, min. 6912 (1865).
7 Midland Railway Company Board Meeting, min. 7157 (1866).
8 *Building News*: 26 (1874), pp. 554, 558–9.
9 *The Engineer*: 23 (1867), p. 538.
10 Southern Construction Committee, op. cit., minutes 1/279, min. 504 and 1/280, min. 1299 (1870).
11 M.D. Conway, *Travels in South Kensington* (New York, 1882).
12 *Railway News*: 19 (1873), p. 661.
13 Midland Railway Company, op. cit., min. 1/9 for 68th board meeting (19 Feb 1878).

Tower Bridge
1 Public Record Office, WO 94/64/1.

Highpoint One
1 John Allan, *Berthold Lubetkin: Architecture and the tradition of progress* (RIBA Publications, London, 1992), pp. 129–30.
2 Ibid., p. 247.
3 Minutes of the Garden Committee, Zoological Society Library (11 July 1939).
4 Minutes of the Council, Zoological Society Library (20 Dec 1933).
5 Ibid. (17 June 1934).
6 Allan, op. cit., p. 314.
7 Ibid., p. 209.
8 *Architects' Journal* (10 Jan 1935), pp. 69–76.
9 Allan, op. cit. pp. 270–1.
10 Ibid., p. 271.
11 Ibid., p. 277.
12 Ibid, p 277.
13 Ibid., p. 279.
14 *Modern Architecture in England*, p. 25. Entry in catalogue to exhibition held at the Museum of Modern Art, New York (1937).
15 Le Corbusier, 'The Vertical Garden City', *Architectural Review*, vol. 79 (1936), pp. 9–10.
16 Anthony Cox, 'Highgate Two, North Hill, Highgate', *Focus (on Modern Architecture)*: II (1938), pp. 76–9. Magazine published between summer 1938 and summer 1939.
17 William Curtis, *Denys Lasdun: Architecture, city, landscape* (Phaidon Press, Oxford, 1994), p. 51.

Glossary

Abacus A slab that forms the top member of a column capital, from which a vault or arch springs or on which an entablature is supported.

Abutment A masonry wall that resists the outward thrust of an arch, or a structure that restrains the outward thrust of a bridge's arch.

Aisle Passage running parallel with a wider and higher nave in a basilica plan building.

Apse The circular or multi-angular termination of a church choir sanctuary. Derived from the Roman basilica.

Arcade A row of arches supported by piers or columns.

Architrave see *Entablature*

Arris The sharp corner formed by the right angular meeting of two planes.

Ashlar Masonry cut in squares or rectangles and laid in regular horizontal courses with tight joints between blocks.

Aureole In medieval art, the oval or circular shape framing the image of Christ, the Virgin Mary or certain saints. See *Vesica piscis*

Barrel vault A continuous vault of semicircular section. Used particularly in Roman and Romanesque architecture.

Basilica A hall with a central nave flanked by lower aisles, which are divided from the nave by colonnades. The nave is usually top-lit by means of clerestorey windows. In Roman architecture, it served as a court of justice, market and temple. In Christian architecture it provided the form for churches.

Buttress Masonry pier built against a wall to resist the outward thrust usually of an arch or vault. A flying buttress is formed by a detached pier topped by an arch – usually of quadrant form – which withstands the thrust of a vault.

Cabling Continuous moulding of semicircular section placed inside the fluting of a column.

Cantilever A beam or bracket projecting from a wall and fixed at one end. A structural arrangement in which the projecting end of a beam or bracket is balanced by a counter-weight at its other end.

Chancel The most sacred east portion of a church, reserved for the clergy and choir. Usually divided from the main body of the church by a screen or rail. Also called the choir.

Choir see *Chancel*

Clerestorey The upper storey in a building – often not served by a floor – which rises above the roof level of adjoining structures and helps to top-light the space it serves. Usually found in churches of basilica type.

Corbel A block, often carved or moulded, projecting from a wall and supporting the beams of a roof or floor or the rib of a vault.

Cornice see *Entablature*

Curtain wall An external wall that serves no load-bearing function, but which is suspended off the structural frame of a building like a curtain. Part of the design and structural vocabulary of twentieth-century Modernism. Also, in medieval architecture, a defensive wall linking towers and gatehouses.

Entablature In classical architecture, the horizontal feature – on top of a wall or supported by columns – which forms the main horizontal accent in a composition. It forms the top of a building, from which the roof rises, or forms the top of the wall of a room, from which a dome or vault rises or on which a flat ceiling rests. The entablature comprises three elements: (from the bottom) the architrave; the frieze; and the cornice. It is embellished and proportioned in different ways according to the five orders of classical architecture.

Flying buttress see *Buttress*

Frieze see *Entablature*

Golden Section The proportion derived from the division of a straight line into two parts so that the ratio of the whole to the larger part is the same as the ratio of the larger part to the smaller part. A proportion observed in nature and held to be divine, and in use since at least Euclid's time in *c.* 300 BC.

Gothic A system of architecture that utilizes the pointed arch and employs a skeletal approach to structure, incorporating ribs, tracery and flying buttresses. It emerged in the first half of the twelfth century in Europe and continued into the sixteenth and, in some regions, into the early seventeenth centuries. In the early nineteenth century, historians surveying British Gothic divided it into three types according to its structural characteristics and details: Early English (from the end of the twelfth century to the end of the thirteenth century); Decorated or the Middle Pointed style (until the mid- and late fourteenth century); and Perpendicular.

Historicist architecture Usually applied to nineteenth-century architecture when buildings – often incorporating pioneering technology and realizing new building types – were given artistic and cultural validity by being clad in a decorative veneer that evoked past historical styles of architecture.

Impost A masonry block, sometimes moulded, from which an arch rises.

Keystone The central stone, often ornamented, in a curved or flat arch.

Lunette A semicircular or semielliptical window. Often used in classical architecture. Derived from semicircular windows, placed at the top of barrel or groin vaults, that lit the interiors of Roman baths. Consequently also called Thermal windows or Diocletian windows after the Baths of Diocletian in Rome.

Massing The disposition or composition of the main parts of a building in relationship to each other and to their setting. Also called ordonnance.

Motte An earth mound, surrounded by a ditch, on which a wooden or stone-walled keep was placed. Often adjoined by a walled enclosure called a bailey.

Newel The post around which the winders of a timber staircase turn. A stone spiral staircase. The post, often ornamented as a column, that terminates the flight of a staircase.

Orders of architecture The fundamental system of classical architecture which evolved in Greece and developed in Rome and in later epochs and civilizations. The Greeks evolved three orders of architecture: the Doric; the Ionic; and the Corinthian. The Romans added two more – the Tuscan, which is a more robust and simple form of Doric, and the Composite, which combines characteristics of the Ionic and Corinthian to form an order that is more elongated than the Greek Corinthian. An order comprises three main elements, each with three parts: (from the bottom) a pedestal with base or plinth, dado and cap; a column with base, shaft and capital; and an entablature with architrave, frieze and cornice. The proportions and details of the main elements vary from order to order and each order

was deemed to have innate qualities making it appropriate for different types of building.

Peristyle A range of columns surrounding a court or temple.

Pier In classical architecture, a masonry structure, square in plan, which is equivalent to a column but with a very simple capital. Also, in engineering, a strong abutment, especially in bridge construction. In Gothic architecture, the name that can be given to a column made up of a cluster of shafts. See *Shafted pier*

Pilaster In classical architecture, a pier that projects from a wall and has a capital and other details to match those on freestanding columns it adjoins.

Pile A cylinder of timber or concrete, driven into the ground to serve as a foundation for a structure.

Piloti Plain cylindrical columns, usually made of steel-reinforced concrete, which were exposed and made a key feature in a composition. Used in twentieth-century Modern architecture.

Podium A continuous pedestal forming a base, and the enclosing platform of the arena in an amphi-theatre.

Rib A projecting band on a ceiling or vault.

Ribbed arch An arch in a vault in which the arrises are emphasized by ribs. Vaults with ribs appear in Britain in late Romanesque architecture.

Romanesque An international style of architecture based on observations of the remains of Roman architecture. It flourished in Europe with many regional variations from the fall of Rome until the late twelfth century.

Semicircular groin vault Formed when two barrel vaults intersect at right angles.

Shafted pier A masonry column in Romanesque and Gothic architecture which is formed by a cluster of attenuated column shafts. Called a compound shafted pier when many shafts of differing heights are united, for example when supporting the higher and lower vaults of the nave and aisles.

Shell keep The main defensive tower or donjon of a castle formed by a tall, thick, strong wall which often enclosed a space that was partly open or occupied by lower buildings.

Springing The point from which an arch or vault rises from a wall. It can rise from a vertical feature such as a column or shaft or from a horizontal feature such as a cornice or entablature.

Tracery Ornamental stonework in a Gothic window. The design of tracery evolved as Gothic architecture moved through its three different phases. Also, applied to work of the same character in timber panelling. See *Gothic*

Transept The part of a cruciform church that projects at right angles to the nave and chancel.

Transverse arch An arch, or rib, that extends at right angles to a main wall.

Triforium A passage or gallery above the aisles of a Romanesque or Gothic church but below the clerestorey, and opening onto the nave.

Undercroft In medieval architecture, a vaulted room upon which principal rooms, such as the Great Hall, are placed.

Vault boss A stone, usually ornamented with a carving or mouldings, at the junction of ribs in a vault.

Vesica piscis A pointed oval formed by the overlap of two circles of the same size with their circumferences passing through each other's centres.

Bibliography

Allan, John, *Berthold Lubetkin: Architecture and the tradition of progress* (RIBA Publications, London, 1992).

Anderson, William, *The Rise of the Gothic* (Hutchinson, London, 1985).

Ashe, Geoffrey, *The Virgin* (Routledge & Kegan Paul, London, 1976).

Ashmole, Elias, *Institutions, Laws and Ceremonies of the Order of the Garter* (London, 1672).

Bakhtiar, Laleh, *Sufi: Expressions of the mystic quest* (Thames & Hudson, London, 1976).

Barnett, Correlli, *Marlborough* (Eyre Methuen, London, 1974).

Barrett, Francis, *The Magus: A complete system of occult philosophy* (London, 1801).

Begent, Peter J. and Chesshyre, Hubert, *The Most Noble Order of the Garter – 650 Years* (Spink, London, 1999).

Beltz, G.H., *Memorials of the Most Noble Order of the Garter* (William Pickering, London, 1841).

Biddle, Martin (ed.), *King Arthur's Round Table* (Boydell Press, Woodbridge, Suffolk, 2000).

Billings, R.W., *Architectural Illustrations and Description of the Cathedral Church at Durham* (T. & W. Boone, London, 1843).

Boyd, Anne, *Life in a Medieval Monastery* (Cambridge University Press, 1987).

Brindle, Steven and Kerr, Brian, *Windsor Castle Revealed* (English Heritage, London, 1999).

Charpentier, Louis, *The Mysteries of Chartres Cathedral* (Research into Lost Knowledge Organisation, London, 1972).

Clifton Taylor, Alec, *The Cathedrals of England* (Thames & Hudson, London, 1967).

Collins, H., *The Order of the Garter, 1348–1461: Chivalry and politics in late medieval England* (Clarendon Press, Oxford, 2000).

Colvin, Howard, *A Biographical Dictionary of British Architects 1600–1840* (John Murray, London, 1978).

Colvin, Howard (ed.), *History of the King's Works*, vol. III 1485–1963 part I (HMSO, London, 1975); vol. V 1660–1782 (HMSO, London, 1976).

Coxe, W.C., *Memoirs of John Duke of Marlborough* (3 vols, Longman, Hurst, Rees, Orme and Brown, London, 1818).

Crook, J.M., *William Burges and the High Victorian Dream* (John Murray, London, 1981).

Crook, J.M. (ed.), *The Strange Genius of William Burges, Art-Architect, 1827–1881* (National Museum of Wales, 1981).

Curry, Ian, *Aspects of the Anglo-Norman Design of Durham Cathedral* (Society of Antiquaries of Newcastle upon Tyne, 1986).

Defoe, Daniel, *A Tour Through the Whole Island of Great Britain* (3 vols, 1724–26: Pat Rogers, ed., Penguin, London, 1983).

Dobson, R.B., 'Mynisteres of Saynt Cuthbert: the monks of Durham in the fifteenth century', Durham Cathedral Lecture (1972).

Downes, Kerry, *English Baroque Architecture* (Zwemmer, London, 1966).

Fernie, Eric, *The Architecture of Norman England* (Oxford University Press, 2000).

Fitchen, John, *The Construction of Gothic Cathedrals: a study of medieval vault erection* (University of Chicago Press, 1961).

Gimbutas, Marija, *The Language of the Goddess* (Thames & Hudson, London, 1989).

Girouard, Mark, *Life in the English Country House* (Yale University Press, London, 1978).

Girouard, Mark, *Windsor: The most romantic castle* (Hodder & Stoughton, London, 1993).

Godfrey, Honor, *Tower Bridge* (John Murray, London, 1988).

Gonzalez-Wippler, Migene, *A Kabbalah for the Modern World* (Llewellyn Publications, St Paul's, USA, 1990).

Green, David, *Blenheim Palace* (Country Life, London, 1951).

Hall, Manly P., *An Encyclopedic Outline of Masonic, Hermetic, Qabalistic and Rosicrucian Symbolical Philosophy* (H.S. Crocker Co., San Francisco, 1928).

Hibbert, Christopher, *George III: A personal history* (Penguin, London, 1998).

Hibbert, Christopher, *Queen Victoria in Her Letters and Journals* (John Murray, London, 1984).

Hibbert, Christopher, *Queen Victoria: A personal history* (HarperCollins, London, 2000).

Hibbert, Christopher, *The Court at Windsor: A domestic history* (Allen Lane, London, 1977).

Hope, St John, W.H., *Windsor Castle: An architectural history* (3 vols, Country Life, London, 1913).

Hunter, Christopher (ed.) 'Durham Cathedral as it was before the Dissolution of the Monastery, containing accounts of the rites etc.' (Durham, 1733).

Jackson, Michael (ed.) *Engineering a Cathedral* (Thomas Telford, London, 1993).

Jennings, Hargrave, *The Rosicrucians: The rites and mysteries*, fourth edition (George Routledge & Sons, London, 1907).

Kidson, Peter, 'The Architecture of St. George's Chapel' in Maurice Bond (ed.) *St. George's Chapel Quincentenary Handbook* (Gerrard's Cross, Smythe for the Dean and Canons of St. George's Chapel, Windsor, 1975).

Kidson, Peter, 'Systems of Measurement and Proportion in Early Medieval Architecture' (University of London thesis, 1956).

Lawlor, Robert, *Sacred Geometry: Philosophy and practice* (Thames & Hudson, London, 1982).

Le Corbusier, *The City of Tomorrow and its Planning*, English edition (Architectural Press, London, 1929).

Leedy, Walter, C., *Fan Vaulting; A study of form, technology and meaning* (Scholar Press, London, 1980).

Lesser, George, *Gothic Cathedrals and Sacred Geometry* (3 vols, Tiranti, London, 1957).

McIntosh, Christopher, *The Rosy Cross Unveiled* (Aquarian Press, Wellingborough, 1980).

Parkin, Gloria, *Grotesques from Durham Cathedral* (Gilesgate Studio, Durham, 1989).

Pennick, Nigel, *Sacred Geometry* (Capall Bann Publishing, Chieveley, Berkshire, 1994).

Phillips, Geoffrey, *Thames Crossings: Bridges, tunnels and ferries* (David & Charles, London, 1981).

Prowse, W.A., *Vision and Practice: Building the high vault* (Dean and Chapter of Durham Cathedral, 1977).

Pyne, W.H., *The History of the Royal Residences* (3 vols, London, 1819).

Reid, Stuart Johnson, *John and Sarah, Duke and Duchess of Marlborough, 1660–1744* (John Murray, London, 1914).

Richmond, Colin and Scarff, Eileen (eds), *St. George's Chapel, Windsor, in the Late Middle Ages* (Manley Publishing, Leeds, 2001).

Roberts, Hugh, *For the King's Pleasure: The furnishing and decoration of George IV's apartments at Windsor Castle* (Thames & Hudson, London, 2002).

Roberts, Jane, *Royal Landscape. The Garden and Parks of Windsor* (Yale University Press, New Haven, 1997).

Roberts, Jane (ed.), *Views of Windsor; Watercolours by Thomas and Paul Sandby* (Merrell Holberton, London, 1995).

Robinson, John Martin, *Royal Palaces: Windsor Castle* (Michael Joseph, London, 1996).

Shimon Halevi, Z'ev ben, *The Kabbalah: Traditional and hidden meaning* (Thames & Hudson, London, 1979).

Simmons, Jack, *St Pancras Station* (George Allen & Unwin, London, 1968).

South, Raymond, *Royal Castle, Rebel Town: Puritan Windsor in Civil War and Commonwealth* (Barracuda Books, Buckingham, 1981).

Stranks, C.J., *This Sumptuous Church: The story of Durham Cathedral* (SPCK, London, 1992).

Thomson, Katherine, *Memoirs of Sarah, Duchess of Marlborough and of the court of Queen Anne* (2 vols, London, 1839).

Victoria History of the Counties of England, vol. III (City of Durham and cathedral) ed. William Page (St

Catherine's Street Press, London, 1928).

Webb, Geoffrey and Bonamy Dobree (eds), *The Complete Works of Sir John Vanbrugh* (4 vols, Nonesuch Press, London, 1927–8), vol. IV (ed. G. Webb): The Letters.

Welch, Charles, *History of The Tower Bridge* (Smith, Elder & Co, London, 1894).

Wilson, Christopher, *The Gothic Cathedral: The architecture of the great church 1130–1530* (Thames & Hudson, London, 1990).

Yates, Francis, *The Rosicrucian Enlightenment* (Routledge & Kegan Paul, London, 1972).

Index